ROMMEL

A Narrative & Pictorial History

Richard D. Law
&
Craig W. H. Luther

1st Edition

ISBN No.0-912138-20-3

Designed
by
Roger James Bender

Type Set
by
Clyborne Typographics

R. JAMES BENDER PUBLISHING
P.O. Box 23456, San Jose, Calif. 95153 (408) 225-5777

**Foreword
by
V.Adm. a.D. Friedrich
Ruge**

For human development the knowledge of history is indispensable. Although it can never provide infallible precepts, such knowledge offers us a wealth of examples and experiences which challenge us to think about them and to evaluate them. No human being will ever be completely similar to another, therefore history can never be completely objective. A good historian, however, will be reliable in his facts and careful in his deductions. It is to be regretted that nowadays there are so many self-styled historians who write with preconceived ideas and do everything to prove them. In recent years that has been repeatedly the case with events of World War II. It is, therefore, to be warmly welcomed that in this book the authors have laid the greatest stress on describing the events connected with Field Marshal Rommel and his campaigns from 1940 to 1944 as accurately as possible.

During the Second World War, Rommel was Germany's best-known military commander. From November 1943 to August 1944, I served as his naval expert. In October 1944 I stayed overnight in his house just two days before Hitler forced him to commit suicide, by threat to his wife and son. This was among the worst of the "Führer's" many crimes. After the war Rommel would have been invaluable in reconciling Germany with the free nations around the North Atlantic. He had fully

3

recognized the dangers from Soviet despotism; he thought in terms of a united Europe closely cooperating with the USA.

Rommel was not only a first-class general with an excellent technical knowledge of warfare. He also had an active interest in state politics (as opposed to party politics). Personally, he was a man of integrity; first and foremost, he respected his soldiers and his other fellow men as human beings, regardless of their position in life.

If there are great men at all, Rommel certainly was one. In any case, he is among the particularly instructive examples history has given us. The study of his personality will always be rewarding.

F. Ruge
Tübingen
28 March 1980

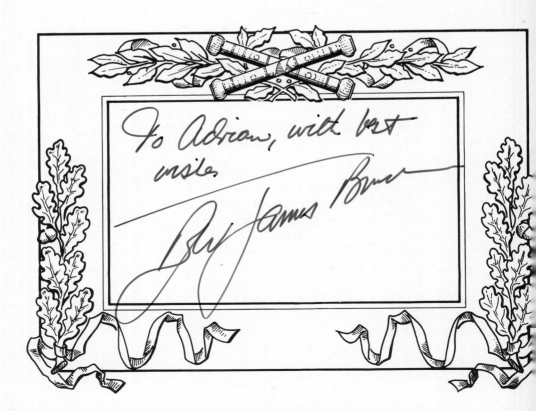

Acknowledgements

The authors and publisher wish to thank the many individuals and institutions who have given of their valued time and effort to assist in the development of this book. Without them, this work would surely not have achieved its high degree of scholarliness and professionalism. Special thanks must be given to Robert Wolfe, George Wagner and John Taylor of the Modern Military Branch of the Military Archives, U.S. National Archives, for their unceasing assistance and patience shown during the prolonged research of this book. A special note of thanks must be extended to Dr. Haupt of the Bundesarchiv in Koblenz and his fine staff of personnel who were such a joy to work with, plus Herr Meyer and staff at the Bundesarchiv Militärarchiv and Herr Horkisch and staff at the Militärgeschichtliches Forschungsamt in Freiburg.

Vizeadmiral Friedrich Ruge and Mr. W.M. James have been of immense importance, contributing several significant documents plus some of the most interesting photos of Rommel and his staff during the Normandy inspection tours.

We owe a debt of gratitude to Dr. Charles Burdick for his moral support when the spirit flagged and his critical proofing of the manuscript. Clayton Trost should also be thanked for his tireless and meticulous arrangement of footnotes and the bibliography. His scholarly acumen has added an extra dimension of quality to the book.

Without the precise translations by Heidi Hack, many of the documents, orders and letters found in this book would have been omitted. The authors owe Mrs. Hack a special note of thanks.

The following individuals and institutions have also been especially helpful in the preparation of this book, and we thank them for their assistance.

J. R. Angolia	Belgium Army Museum, Brussels
Leon Chacona	E. C. P. Armies, Paris
Dick & Joan Clyborne	Luftwaffe Museum, Uetersen
Robert S. Eddy III	The National Archives, Washington D. C.
Clint Hackney	N. Z. War History Collection
Russ Hamilton	Stadt. Sammlung Wiener-Neustadt
Jim Jones	
Thomas Johnson	
Al Kropff	
Richard Mundhenk	
George Petersen	
Proctor Reid	
Richard Shaw	
Jerry Weiblen	

FOR BONNIE:
POUR LES MERVEILLEUX JOURS PASSES AVEC L'ESPOIR DE LENDEMAINS SEMBLABLES DANS L'AVENIR. (Richard D. Law)

TO SARAL, MY FRIEND. (Craig W. Luther)

The following publishers have gratiously consented to allow the reprint of excerpts from their books:

E. P. Dutton - "The Trail of the Fox" by David Irving

Harcourt Brace Jovanovich, Inc. - "The Rommel Papers" edited by B.H. Liddell Hart

Harper & Row, Publishers Inc. - "Rommel: The Desert Fox" by Desmond Young

The MIT Press - "The History of the German Resistance" by Peter Hoffmann

Oxford University Press Southern Africa - "Sidi Rezeg Battles 1941" by Turner and Agar-Hamilton

The Viking Press Inc. - "Hitler's War" by David Irving

6

The Advent of Erwin Rommel, 1918-1939

In November 1918, after four exhausting years of war, Imperial Germany appealed for an armistice. The twin pillars of Wilhelmian security, the Army and the Hohenzollern Monarchy, had collapsed. The bodies of more than two million German soldiers dotted the cratered European continent from Verdun to the Bosphorus.[1] The lofty edifice of teutonic *"Weltmacht"* had crumbled into nothing.

Revolution abruptly swept the shattered Reich. The Weimar Republic, that bastard-child of German militarism and expansionist dreams, made its brave but ill-fated appearance upon the stage of history. Hunger, disease and deprivation ravaged the population, the "dirge of defeat" deepened by lines of hearses bearing their victims to cemeteries.[2]

Against this backdrop of defeat and despair, Erwin Johannes Eugen Rommel could consider himself a fortunate man. He was a captain *(Hauptmann)* with a remarkable and distinguished service record, having fought in the Argonne, Italy and Rumania. He had won the Iron Cross First Class; and, for his brilliant capture of Monte Matajur in the 12th Battle of the Isonzo, he had received the Reich's highest military honor, the Pour le Mérite.[3] Thus he had proven himself a gifted soldier with precocious instincts and command potential. The *Reichswehr*, Germany's restricted 100,000 man army, accordingly elected Rommel to serve as one of the 4,000 officers that Article 160 of the Versailles *"Diktat"* permitted the German armed forces. Rommel accepted the opportunity. War, he had discovered, was his métier. He resolved to make the army a career.

Rommel rejoined his old 124 Württemberg Infantry Regiment, the first regiment he had served with upon entering the army in July 1910. After reporting for duty in Weingarten, Rommel arranged for a short leave to Danzig, a picturesque Hanseatic port. In happier times he had

[1]*Deutschland im Ersten Weltkrieg* (Berlin: Akademie-Verlag, 1970).
[2]Joseph Carter, *1918: Year of Crisis, Year of Change* (Englewood Cliffs, New Jersey: Prentice-Hall, 1968) pg. 19.
[3]For an in-depth treatment of Rommel's World War I exploits, see Heinz von Lichem, *Rommel 1917: Der "Wüstenfuchs" als Gebirgssoldat* (München: Hornung Verlag, 1975).

also gone on leave to Danzig, and there he had met Lucie Mollin, a slender, fair-skinned beauty. They had fallen deeply in love and had married on 27 November 1916.

The trip from Weingarten to Danzig took Rommel through the new "revolutionary" Germany. Traveling in uniform and proudly displaying his Pour le Mérite, he "was questioned, mildly insulted, . . . and once nearly arrested."[4]

In the summer of 1919 Rommel received new orders. He reported to Friedrichshafen (near Lake Constance) and took command of Internal Security Company 32. The company's insubordinate "red" naval personnel did not take easily to Rommel's attempts to impose discipline and soldierly values. They booed and jeered the unassuming, unsophisticated Swabian and eyed his Pour le Mérite with contempt. Rommel, however, reacted with remarkable restraint; soon he succeeded in hammering his men into a respectable military unit. When some of his men subsequently transferred to the police, they asked Rommel to transfer with them, hoping to remain under his command. Rommel's personal file shows that in the spring of 1920 he operated against insurgents in Münsterland and Westphalia. In one rather amusing episode the 28-year old captain "used fire hoses like machine guns against revolutionaries storming the town hall of Gmünd, dampening their violent ardor."[5]

In October 1920 Rommel went to Stuttgart to command a company in Infantry Regiment 13. Here Rommel would remain for nine uneventful years - drilling his men and expanding the breadth of his military knowledge. He even resumed his somewhat maladroit attempt to learn the violin. He discovered, however, that his hands moved with considerably greater dexterity and assuredness when firing and dismantling a heavy machine gun, at which he became quite proficient. Rommel, a great physical fitness buff, found opportunities in Stuttgart for recreational activities of many kinds. He and Lucie canoed, rode horseback, partook of some "light" mountaineering and often skied. On 24 December 1928, Lucie gave birth to the Rommels' only child, Manfred.

Rommel's professional skill had attracted the attention of his battalion commander. He wrote that Rommel was a "gifted" officer who exhibited outstanding qualities as a leader and was good instructor material for one of the *Kriegsschule* (Military Academies). The *Reichswehr's* personnel department agreed with the assessment of the young captain's talents and posted Rommel as a junior instructor to Dresden's School of Infantry. Here he concentrated on shaping his

[4]Desmond Young, Rommel the Desert Fox (New York: Harper and Brothers, 1950), pg. 28. Hereafter cited as Desert Fox.
    [5]David Irving, The Trail of the Fox (New York: E. P. Dutton & Co., 1977), pg. 22. Hereafter cited as The Trail.

young cadets into officers who would save lives, not squander them, as had happened on the battlefronts of the Great War. During his stay at Dresden, Rommel's long-awaited promotion to Major came through (1 April 1932).

In October 1933 Rommel received a battalion command in Goslar in the Hartz Mountains of central Germany - 3 Battalion of 17 Infantry Regiment. This unit was a crack *Jäger* (mountain) regiment with a distinguished service record. The battalion officers decided to put their new major to a test. All highly conditioned athletes and good skiers, they invited Rommel to accompany them for a morning of skiing. The outing commenced with an arduous hike up a local mountain. After an all-too-brief respite, Rommel suggested a run down the slope, which was made at a swift pace. When, after three sorties up and down the mountain, Rommel suggested a fourth ascent, the men gracefully declined. While at Goslar, the army promoted Rommel to Lieutenant Colonel *(Oberstleutnant),* effective 1 March 1935.

Meanwhile, momentous events had rocked Germany. In January 1933 the German people had elected an ex-Bavarian corporal, Adolf Hitler, chancellor. Hitler worked quickly to undermine the Weimar Republic and destroy the last vestiges of constitutional government. On 2 August 1934 the day of President Hindenburg's death and barely a year and a half after the national socialist *"Machtergreifung,"* Hitler demanded a personal oath of loyalty from his armed forces:

> "I swear by Almighty God this sacred oath: I will render unconditional obedience to the Führer of the German Reich and people, Adolf Hitler, Supreme Commander of the *Wehrmacht,* and as a brave soldier, I will be ready at any time to stake my life for this oath."[6]

For Rommel, and every member of the *Wehrmacht,* "loyalty to the constitution of the country no longer existed; there was only loyalty to the Führer. Henceforth, the only valid order or channel of command was that approved by the Führer; this was now the law."[7] This oath would have tragic consequences in the future.

The paths of Rommel and Hitler first crossed on 30 September 1934 at Goslar. Hitler had arrived to attend a thanksgiving ceremony at which Rommel's battalion would parade. When Rommel discovered that a file of SS *(Schutzstaffel:* Hitler's elite guard) men would be placed in front of his unit to serve as Hitler's bodyguard, he refused to turn his men out. To avoid embarrassment Himmler and Goebbles invited him to meet them in a local hotel. Rommel explained to the Nazi dignitaries

---

[6]Peter Hoffmann, *The History of the German Resistance, 1933-1945* (Cambridge, Mass., The MIT Press, 1977), pg. 27.
[7]*Ibid.*

Hitler is greeted by commander of the Goslar Jäger Battalion, Major Rommel.

Rommel's troops are reviewed at Goslar by the Führer.

that the battalion's honor was at stake; he could hardly allow his men to be insulted. The determined major carried the day. The orders were rescinded and Rommel, sporting a steel infantry helmet, accompanied Hitler and the reviewing party.

In 1935 Rommel was posted to the *Kriegsschule* at Potsdam as a full instructor. Here he was selected as the War Ministry's special liaison officer to Baldur von Schirach's Hitler Youth Organization. Rommel and von Schirach, the 29-year old leader of 5,400,000 boys, soon clashed violently. Von Schirach, "handsome and westernized," was "astounded to hear [Rommel] talk in the Swabian tongue when they first met in April in the Youth leader's lakeside home."[8] More fundamentally, he rejected Rommel's emphasis on para-military training for German youth. Von Schirach eventually succeeded in severing Rommel's ties with the Hitler Youth.

This rebuff, however, had no serious repercussions on Rommel's career. On the contrary, his star was rising rapidly. While at Potsdam,

[8]*Irving, The Trail, pp. 30-31.*

Rommel had dramatically rewritten his lecture notes and submitted a concise, exciting manuscript to the Ludwig Voggenreiter publishing house in Potsdam. The result was a brilliant manual on infantry tactics entitled *Infanterie Greift An* (Infantry Attacks). Hitler undoubtedly read the book and was favorably impressed. Rommel, the *"daraufgängerisch"* (dare-devilish) hero of the Great War, was fast becoming one of the Führer's favorites. Like Hitler, Rommel was a "self-made" man of modest origins, a fact which, no doubt, appealed to the Führer.

Rommel's "Infanterie greift an."

In September 1938 Europe tottered on the brink of war. The issue was the Sudeten border territory of Czechoslovakia. The Nazi propaganda machine thundered about the persecution of the Sudetenland's German minority; Hitler demanded the immediate cession of the disputed territory to the Reich. At the eleventh hour, "Il Duce" (Mussolini) intervened and proposed a four-power conference to solve the dispute peacefully. The result was a monument to the bankruptcy of Western diplomacy - the Munich Agreement of 30 September 1938. Czechoslovakia was abandoned; the contested strip of land ceded to Germany.

After this brilliant example of the *"Blumenkreig"* (the "flower war"), the Führer decided to visit his newly-won territory. To act as temporary commandant of his headquarters *(Führerbegleitbatallion,"* Hitler's Escort Battalion), Hitler selected Erwin Rommel. This appointment was a considerable coup for the ambitious officer, for "it catapulted him into the very highest company overnight."[9]

In November 1938 Rommel received yet another posting - Commandant of the officer cadet school at Wiener-Neustadt, near Vienna. His family lived in a comfortable ville in the *Akademiepark*, the former Zoological Garden of the Imperial Castle. The Rommels' stay in Wiener-Neustadt was one of the happiest periods of their lives. Rommel devoted himself to the training of young officers, hampered by little interference from above. He enjoyed his new hobby, photography, for which he exhibited not only a great technical competency, but a "talent for selection and composition."[10]

Stadt. Sammlungen Wiener-Neustadt

The Rommel villa in the Militärakademie-Park. This home was destroyed in an air raid in 1945.

Rommel in his study at Wiener-Neustadt.

---

[9]*Ibid.*, pp. 32-33.
[10]Young, <u>Desert Fox</u>, pg. 43.

National Archives

Rommel's son, Manfred (left) and a friend on the Maria Theresienplatz in the Wiener-Neustadt Akademiepark. In the background is the Military Academy.

In March 1939 Hitler again called upon his "favorite" to command his mobile headquarters. Rommel and the escort battalion accompanied the Führer during the occupation of Prague and yet again when Hitler sailed to the Baltic port of Memel (23 March 1939). Then in August Rommel received a typhus vaccination, which confirmed his expectations: he would command the *Führerbegleitbatallion* during the impending Polish campaign.

After reporting to the Reich Chancellery for his new assignment on the 25th, Rommel discovered, much to his surprise, that Hitler had promoted him to Major General *(Generalmajor)*. The promotion was back-dated to June 1, a sign of Hitler's favoritism. The Führer's escort unit had only recently been expanded and now included 16 officers, 93 NCO's and 274 rank-and-file. It also boasted four 37mm antitank guns, twelve 20mm antiaircraft (flak) guns and the normal issue of small arms.

Hitler had again drummed up the dark clouds of war. This time the pretext was Danzig and the corridor; the enemy - Poland. As early as 3 April, Hitler had ordered his general staff to prepare a plan of campaign against Poland; by late August the men and machines of two German army groups were poised along the frontier ready to strike. **13**

As the crisis reached a fever-pitch, a politically-naive Rommel wrote to his wife:

> How will the situation develop. I still believe that we shall be able to avoid complications of a grave nature.... The Führer knows exactly what is good for us. Up to now he has always been able to solve the most serious problems for us and he will this time, too.[11]

Events moved swiftly. On 30 August Warsaw ordered a general mobilization. Two days later Hitler unleashed his *Wehrmacht*, providing the first awesome display of a new tactical concept - the *Blitzkrieg* - that would frighten and cow his enemies for several years. Buzzing with excitement Rommel again wrote Lucie:

> Polzin, 1 Sept 39
> It happened. I am curious to find out how the operations against Poland will turn out. We expect the honored guest [Hitler] this evening.[12]
> Polzin, 2 September 39
> We have been at war with Poland one day. On this front we did well beyond expectations. The morale of the troops is accordingly high. I am curious to find out whether Britain and France will come to the assistance of this sinking vessel. If they do we can't help it. I am quite convinced that we shall succeed, nevertheless. We are still without the master here. Of course, there is much to be done in Berlin.[13]

Late in the evening of 3 September 1939, the "master" "exchanged the elegant marbled halls of the Chancellery for the special train, "Amerika" *[Sonderzug Amerika]*, parked in a dusty Pomeranian railroad station surrounded by parched and scented pine trees and wooden barrack huts baked dry by the central European sun."[14] "Amerika" was a sight to behold. A long steel caterpillar of 12 or 15 coaches, it required two locomotives to pull it; flak wagons, mounting 20mm guns and manned by Luftwaffe crews (a coup for Göring) immediately followed the powerful prime movers. Next came Hitler's private coach, festooned with a drawing room, bath and four compartments for his adjutants and manservants. The nerve center of the train was the command coach: a long conference room and a communications center, in constant contact with Berlin and OKW

---

[11]*Miscellaneous German Records Collection: The Rommel Collection*, Microcopy T-84, Roll 274, frame #000007. *Hereafter cited as Rommel Collection, T-84, roll no., frame no.*
[12]*Ibid.*
[13]*Ibid.*
[14]David Irving, *Hitler's War* (New York: The Viking Press, 1977), pg. 3.

14

(*Oberkommando der Wehrmacht* or Supreme Armed Forces High Command) via teleprinter and radio-telephone. Bringing up the rear were the dining cars and quarters for the military escort, flak crews, medical personnel and members of the press. There were even accommodations for some private detectives. The train was dominated by brown-shirted Nazi dignitaries; even Rommel was not permitted quarters on "Amerika."

At 0156 hours on the next day (4 September), Hitler's train rolled into Bad Polzin, a modest railroad town in Pomerania. Heinrich Himmler followed in his own special train, "Heinrich." Hitler surprised Rommel and his military advisors by remaining nearly three weeks at the front.

To protect the Führer and the other members of the entourage, Rommel created three security groups. The first group was detailed to guard "Amerika" and its outer perimeter; the second group was the reserve, and the third ("Front Group") was organized to accompany the Führer and the Reich ministers on visits to the front.[15]

The Führer motored to the front almost daily in an open Mercedes (a six-wheeled Mercedes-Benz 770G4W31) in glossy beige with black mud-guards, but with license plates and other insignia covered.[16] Normally Hitler's convoys were divided into two groups: "in the first group there were Hitler's car, two Führer-Begleit-Kommando cars, a car for the aides, and a car for the Chief of OKW and additional aides. The second convoy consisted of two 'minister cars' with von Ribbentrop and Lammers and their aides, one car for Himmler and his aides and bodyguard, one for Reich Press Chief Dr. Dietrich, one for other persons invited to accompany the Führer, a reserve car, a luggage car, a field-kitchen car and a petrol tanker."[17]

Hitler's personal bodyguard was responsible for the immediate security of the Führer, but the convoy protection as a whole was the responsibility of Rommel as the commander of the *Frontgruppe der FHQu. Truppen.*

One of his visits to the scene of operations near Gdingen produced a rather ugly incident. Rommel, thrust into the role of traffic controller, had to direct a long "caravan" of 20 to 30 vehicles through a narrow street down to the water's edge. Hitler's six-wheeled Mercedes occupied the point; the other vehicles, crammed with Nazi officials, jockeyed for positions close to the Führer. Rommel attempted to solve the protocol requirements by arranging for the cars to follow Hitler two abreast. But as the procession drove through the narrow bottleneck the two-abreast formation was no longer possible; Rommel halted most of the vehicles at a barrier and permitted only Hitler's car and an escort car

---

[15]Peter Hoffmann, Hitler's Personal Security (London: The Macmillan Press Ltd., 1979), pg. 197.
[16]Ibid., pg. 135.
[17]Ibid.

to drive on. He stepped onto the road to ensure that his order was obeyed. A third car then came forward and stopped. Inside was the Chief of the Party Chancellery, Martin Bormann. Bormann "made a fearful scene and cursed Rommel in outrageous language because of the supposed slight inflicted on him."[18] But the General coolly snapped back, "This is not a kindergarten outing and you will do as I say."[19] Bormann would not forget the incident.

As the *Wehrmacht's* tanks and planes sliced through the ill-prepared Polish defenses, Rommel was everywhere - watching, absorbing, learning the techniques of the new style of warfare. He carefully noted the value of close cooperation between the ground and air forces, the successes of the German Panzer units and the varied applications of artillery and motorized infantry within the *Blitzkrieg* framework.

Hitler inspects the Westerplatte battle area.

On 2 October, four days before the conclusion of the campaign, Rommel and Rudolf Schmundt (Hitler's Chief Adjutant) traveled to Warsaw to compile a situation report for the Führer. German bombing had reduced the proud Polish capital to a heap of smoldering ruins. Rommel wrote to Lucie describing the suffering of the civilian population and the dreadful destruction of the city.

With Poland defeated, Rommel's duties at Hitler's headquarters settled down to an uninspiring routine. Preparations were in the wing for

[18]Walter Warlimont, <u>Inside Hitler's Headquarters, 1939-45</u> (New York: Frederick A. Praeger, 1964), pg. 37.
[19]Irving, <u>The Trail</u>, pg. 37.

Rommel (far right) at a briefing outside of Warsaw.

Hitler viewing the destruction of Warsaw from a church steeple, six kilometers from the besieged city.

Bundesarchiv

Rommel sleeping on Hitler's private train. At this time he was commandant of the "Führerhauptquartier."

a major offensive against the Western Powers and Rommel was anxious to prove his mettle in a field unit. Exploiting his close personal ties with the Führer, the General (late January 1940) asked for a fighting command. He wanted a Panzer division. On 6 February Hitler granted Rommel's request. Rommel would assume command of 7 Panzer Division which was earmarked for a significant role in the forthcoming western offensive. The Army High Command was horrified. Rommel had no experience with armored troops, they protested; at best, he should be given a mountain unit and preferably one far removed from the future theatre of operations in France. But Hitler impatiently brushed these objections aside; his favorite would get a Panzer division. Rommel caught a train to Bad Godesberg to begin this new and exciting challenge.

Blitzkrieg in the West: France 1940

At mid-morning on 10 February 1940, the officers of 7 Panzer assembled to meet their new commanding officer. Rommel greeted them in a manner most uncharacteristic for a German officer early in the war - with an enthusiastic "Heil Hitler." He ordered the division to prepare for an inspection to take place the following day.

7 Panzer Division had been reorganized since the Polish campaign, where it had served as a "light" division. Unlike most German armored divisions, it had only one reinforced tank regiment, instead of the usual two. The Panzer regiment's three battalions had a compliment of 218 tanks, which included a sprinkling of the excellent Panzer III's and IV's. More than half of the division's tanks, however, were lightly armored Czech 38T models.[1] The Panzer regiment's commander, Colonel Karl Rothenburg, was one of the *Wehrmacht's* foremost tank experts; like Rommel, he also sported the coveted Pour le Mérite.[2]

Rommel's initial impression of his new command's personnel was anything but encouraging. Some of the men were "downright flabby"; most officers, he observed with displeasure, were noticeably lacking in National Socialist spirit. He reasoned that new arrivals would quickly put things right: Lieutenant Karl Hanke, a high-ranking official in Goebbel's Propaganda Ministry; and Corporal Karl Holz, who recently had served as chief editor of the violently anti-Semitic *"Der Stürmer."*

Rommel began an immediate, comprehensive training program to whip his men into shape. Gunnery practice for all units received top

---

[1]B. H. Liddell Hart, ed., *The Rommel Papers* (New York: Harcourt, Brace and Co., 1953), pg. 4.

[2]Hart's *Rommel Papers*, pg. 4, provides this organizational table for 7 Panzer:
Armor: 25 Panzer Regiment (3 battalions)
        37 Panzer Reconnaissance Battalion
Motorized Infantry: 6 Rifle Regiment
        7 Rifle Regiment
        7 Motorcycle Battalion
Engineers: 58 Pioneer Battalion
Artillery: 78 Field Artillery Regiment
        42 Antitank Artillery Battalion
See also Hasso von Manteuffel, *Die 7 Panzer-Division im Zweiten Weltkrieg: Einsatz und Kampf der "Gespenster Division" 1939-1945* (Kameradenhilfe e. V. Kolin, 1965), pg. 49.

priority, but cross-country maneuvers and communications between Rommel and his operations staff were also emphasized. The Major General observed intently as his tanks clattered up and down the training fields at Wahn. He knew that the Western Powers enjoyed a large numerical superiority in tanks and planes, but Rommel was confident that the *Wehrmacht's* superior tactical doctrine and training would decide the coming battle.

7 Panzer officers soon discovered that they had acquired a tough task master. Rommel dealt swiftly with subordinates who failed to please him. By 27 February he had cashiered at least one unfortunate battalion commander - "on his way within ninety minutes."[3]

While the *Wehrmacht* continued its training exercises, Hitler's military staff bustled with activity. The desire for a final reckoning *("endgültige Abrechnung")* with the Allies had gripped Hitler since the days of the Polish campaign. In late September 1939 he had ordered the startled representatives of his armed forces to begin immediate preparations for a campaign in the West.[4] Only reluctantly had OKH *(Oberkommando des Heeres* or Supreme Command of the Army) undertaken this new assignment that threatened to involve Germany in a world war for the second time in thirty years - a war, they well knew, for which Germany was ill-prepared.

The original draft of *"Fall Gelb"* ("Case Yellow," code name for Western offensive) provided for a powerful thrust on the right wing to be executed by Colonel General Fedor von Bock's Army Group B.[5] In effect, this was little more than a repetition of the Schlieffen Plan of 1914, and a move certainly expected by the Western Powers. The Allies planned to counter such an invasion by pushing the bulk of their forces into Belgium to reinforce the Dyle Line, thus shattering the impetus of the German attack.[6]

Then in February 1940 a new plan radically altered the *"Schwerpunkt"* (point of main effort) of the coming German offensive. This was the work of a brilliant staff officer, Erich von Manstein, who would later become one of Germany's greatest Panzer leaders. His famous *"Sichelschnitt"* plan advocated that the main effort be switched farther south - through the Ardennes forest. Since the French considered the Ardennes impenetrable for tank forces, a German thrust through the forest would encounter only light resistance.

---

[3]*Irving, The Trail, pg. 42.
[4]Hans-Adolf Jacobsen, *Dünkirchen: Ein Beitrag zur Geschichte des Westfeldzuges 1940, Die Wehrmacht im Kampf, Bd. XIX* (Neckargemünd: Scharnhorst Buchkameradschaft, 1958), pg. 11. Hereafter cited as *Dünkirchen*.
[5]Gen. St. d. H. Op. Abt. Geheime Kommandosache, "Aufmarschanweisung Gelb," in *Dokumente zur Vorgeschichte des Westfeldzuges 1939-1940*, ed. by Hans-Adolf Jacobsen (Berlin: Musterschmidt-Verlag, 1956), pg. 41. Hereafter cited as "Aufmarschanweisung Gelb," in *Dokumente*.
[6]Vincent S. Esposito, *A Concise History of World War II* (New York: Frederick A. Praeger, 1964), pg. 54. Hereafter cited as *History of WWII*.

Erich
von Manstein

Von Manstein's arguments were persuasive; the final OKH operations draft (24 February 1940) shifted the German *Schwerpunkt* to the southern flank, through Belgium and Luxembourg.[7] Colonel General Gerd von Rundstedt's Army Group A (45 divisions, including 7 of the 10 Panzer Division) would administer the hammer blow.

In detail, *Sichelschnitt* envisioned a dash to the Meuse led by General Edwald von Kleist's Panzer Group (of Army Group A). Von Kleist would have two armored spearheads, 19 Corps (General Heinz Guderian) and 41 Corps (General Hans Reinhardt). Guderian's armor would thrust for Sedan, while Reinhardt aimed for the Meuse around Montherme. Farther north, General Hermann Hoth's 15 (later 39) Corps would drive across the hilly and wooded country of the northern Ardennes, providing Kleist with flank cover and aiming for the Meuse crossings between Givet and Namur. This secondary effort also comprised two spearheads, albeit on a smaller scale - 5 and 7 Panzer Divisions. Hoth's Panzer Corps was tactically subordinate to General Hans Günther von Kluge's 4 Army.[8] If all went according to plan, von Bock's Army Group B would pin the bulk of the Allied forces in the north, while von Rundstedt's armor sliced through to the Channel, bagging the main enemy force north and west of Sedan.

Rommel and Rothenburg were at the firing ranges at Wahn when, on 9 May 1940, OKW flashed the codeword *"Dortmund"* to all units: the assault in the West was about to begin.

---

[7]Jacobsen, *Dünkirchen*, pg. 12. See also text of "Aufmarschanweisung Gelb," *vom 24.2.40 in Jacobsen's Dokumente*, pg. 64.

[8]Esposito, *History of WWII*, pg. 60. See also Hart, *Rommel Papers*, pg. 4.

Rommel is photographed inside his command vehicle by one of his aides during a field training exercise in Germany (early 1940).

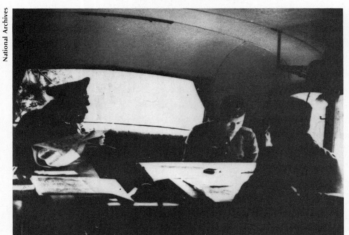

Rommel and his staff during the same exercise.

The efficient crossing of his equipment over swollen rivers was heavily stressed by Rommel during his division's training.

This Pz.Kpfw. II became bogged down in a ditch during field exercises

(above) Rommel on leave shortly before the campaign in the West.
(right) Lucie Rommel.

Dearest Lu,

We're packing up at last. Let's hope not in vain. You'll get all the news for the next few days from the papers. Don't worry yourself. Everything will go all right.[9]

At 0532 hours, three minutes ahead of schedule on 10 May, 7 Panzer motored across the frontier and entered Belgium some 30 miles south of Liége.[10] The tiny Belgian frontier force immediately withdrew, offering little resistance. Rommel's troops at once removed the numerous obstacles and barricades that blocked the roads and forest tracks. Many of the roadblocks were simply by-passed, Rommel's vehicles moving cross-country or over side roads. 7 Panzer brushed aside a French mechanized unit, and following on the heels of the retreating 1 and 4 French cavalry divisions, reached the Meuse on the afternoon of 12 May.

Rommel hoped to seize the bridges at Dinant and Houx in a "coup-de-main" and establish a firm bridgehead on the west bank. French engineers, however, blew the bridges just as the first German tanks attempted to cross. Rommel ordered an immediate crossing by infantry in rubber boats - an exercise he had stressed in training.

At 0400 hours, 13 May, he and Captain Schraepler drove to Dinant. Shells were crashing into the town and burnt-out tanks lined the streets. Proceeding on foot, they scrambled down the steep bank of the Meuse to the valley bottom where 6 Rifle Regiment was poised to cross to the west bank. What they found was discouraging. French infantry, concealed among the rocks, peppered the assault parties with a withering small arms fire; heavy French artillery lobbed well-aimed rounds into the river. One boat after another was destroyed and the crossing was at a standstill.

Rommel acted quickly to get the assault moving again. He knew that a well-laid smoke screen would shield his men from the discomfitting enemy fire. But his division lacked a chemical smoke unit. "I now gave orders," he writes in his Papers, "for a number of houses in the valley to be set alight in order to supply the smoke we lacked."[11]

Farther south, 7 Rifle Regiment had pushed a company across the river, but intense defensive fire had shot their bridging equipment to pieces and delayed an expansion of the small bridgehead. There clearly

[9]Hart, _Rommel Papers_, pg. 6.

[10]For an official account of 7 Panzer campaign in France, see _Records of the German Field Commands_, Divisions, Ia, Geschichte der 7 Panzer Division, Kurzer Abriss über den Einsatz im Westen, 9 Mai-19 Juni, 1940, Microcopy T-315, Roll 401. Hereafter cited as _Divisions_, Panzer unit number, T-315, roll no., frame no. See also _Records of the German Field Commands, Armies_, Ia, Armeeoberkommando 4, Der Ablauf der Kämpfe der 4. Armee in Mai und Juni 1940, Microcopy T-312, Roll 114. Hereafter cited as _Armies_, T-312, 114, Frame no.

[11]Hart, _Rommel Papers_, pg. 8.

Hermann Hoth

Günther von Kluge

was "no hope of getting any more men across at this point without powerful artillery and tank support." Rommel drove back to divisional headquarters where, after a conference with von Kluge and Hoth, the necessary arrangements were made.

A whirlwind of activity, he raced to Leffé (a small village on the outskirts of Dinant) where the crossing had also stalled. He positioned his tanks and heavy weapons on the eastern bank for fire support and took direct command of II./7 Rifle Regiment. Soon the crossing was moving again; Rommel himself forded the river in the second assault wave. Thereafter, he unceasingly supervised the operation, barking orders and urging on his engineers as they laboriously erected their eight and 16-ton pontoon bridges. On this day 7 Panzer's vigorous commander had his first of many scrapes with death. His tank was fired upon and Schraepler wounded by a splinter; later, it was accidentally bombed by the Luftwaffe.

Rommel's personal intervention had had a decisive effect. By 0900 the next day, Rothenburg's Panzer regiment had some 30 tanks across the river, expanding the tiny bridgehead into a major breakthrough. Rommel again had a narrow escape. Driving in a Panzer III, he had just reached the southern rim of Onhaye wood when "suddenly we came under heavy artillery and antitank gunfire from the west. Shells landed all around us and my tank received two hits, one after the other . . ."[12] His driver barreled straight into the nearest bushes, but the tank slid down a steep embankment coming to rest on its side only 500 yards from a French battery. Wounded by a splinter, Rommel bailed out of the tank and "clambered up through the sandy pit, shells crashing and splintering all around. Close in front of us trundled Rothenburg's tank with flames pouring out of the rear."

---

[12]*Ibid.*, pg. 12.

7 Panzer, having burst from its Meuse bridgehead, headed west. Rommel intended to push his armor through the gap without regard for his flanks, which he secured with artillery fire. Kicking up enormous clouds of dust and bolting forward at speeds up to 40 miles an hour, Panzer Regiment 25 quickly scattered weak French elements and, advancing via Philippeville, reached the hills west of Cerfontaine.

Already, less than a week into the campaign, Rommel's command techniques were proving highly unorthodox. He commanded from the spearhead of the advance, usually from a specially-adapted Panzer III, risking life and limb while men dropped dead all around him. His courage and stamina were astounding. To maintain wireless security he devised a simple but effective concept knows as a *"Stosslinie"* (line of thrust). This was nothing more than a line drawn between two prearranged points on a map; "any point could be described by giving its distance along and from this line."[13]

But Rommel's methods, however extraordinary, brought results; by 15 May, 7 Panzer had torn a menacing hole in General Corap's 9 French Army. Farther south, von Kleist's Panzer Group had also met with dazzling success. Guderian's 2 Panzer Division, plunging westward, had seized two bridges intact across the Ardennes Canal; advance elements of Reinhardt's 41 Corps were 35 miles beyond the Meuse. A 50-mile gap yawned between the French 2 and 9 Armies. The breakthrough to the Channel had begun.[14]

The next morning Rommel received orders to "thrust via Sivry through the Maginot Line and on that night to the hills around Avesnes."[15] This was not the Maginot Line proper, but a westward extension where the fortifications were weaker. Rothenburg's tanks crossed the French border at Sivry encountering little resistance. Skirting mined areas, 25 Panzer Regiment rolled westward, slowed only by the orchards and tall hedges. Soon the angular outlines of the French bunkers became visible. The rearward French positions, bristling with artillery and antitank guns protected by concrete bunkers, were smothered with artificial fog and artillery fire. Under this covering fire infantry and engineers of 37 Armored Reconnaissance Battalion filtered into the fortified belt. Rommel administered the knock-out blow that evening. With assault troops of 7 Motorcycle Battalion in the lead, Rothenburg's armor "clanked and clattered" through the fortified zone, quickly effecting a breech of some 3,000 yards in depth.[16]

7 Panzer's lead elements raced through the gap and advanced across sleepy French hamlets crammed with refugees and demoralized French soldiers. Unbelievable chaos wrenched the moonlit night. "Civilians and French troops," Rommel writes, "their faces distorted with terror,

[13]Irving, *The Trail*, pg. 44.
[14]Esposito, *History of WWII*, pp. 61-62.
[15]Hart, *Rommel Papers*, pg. 17.
[16]Young, *Desert Fox*, pp. 49-50. See also Jacobsen, *Dünkirchen*, pg. 42.

During the swift German advance across France, Rommel stops in a small French village to check his maps.

Rommel and officers of his Panzer regiment on May 18, 1940.

27

lay huddled in the ditches, alongside hedges and in every hollow beside the road. We passed refugee columns, the carts abandoned by their owners, who had fled in panic into the fields."[17] Finally, the tanks burst through Avesnes, belching fire as they moved past French batteries on their flanks. West of the town Rommel finally stopped to wait for the rest of 7 Panzer to catch up. That evening he had covered 35 miles, leaving his better-equipped neighbor (5 Panzer Division) far behind. But the lightning advance had disrupted his communications; his infantry brigade was unaware of the breakthrough. Rommel's repeated wireless calls went unanswered. He nevertheless resolved to continue the attack at dawn.

Early on 17 May the 7 Panzer spearheads raced on, seizing intact the bridge over the Sambre at Landrecies. The division was, by now, badly strung out,[18] and French armor nipped repeatedly at 25 Panzer Regiment. Undaunted, 7 Panzer crashed into Cambrai (18 May), raising such immense clouds of dust that the French defenders were unaware that the majority of the attacking vehicles were soft-skinned. The town fell with little resistance. Rommel duly recorded in his diary the value of dust as a deceptive tactic.[19] By 20 May Rommel's thin, finger-like thrust had propelled him across the Canal du Nord at Marcoing to a position south of Arras.[20]

He had taken "enormous risks," for strong French armored forces still hovered menacingly on his flanks. His tactics horrified the more orthodox German General Staff and aroused considerable anxiety in Hitler. But then again the overwhelming success of the entire campaign had shaken Hitler and his military advisors. As early as 16 May, Colonel General Franz-Halder, Chief of Staff OKH, had noted that the breakthrough was developing in a classical form.[21] By 20 May Guderian's Panzer's had reached Abbeville, just short of the Channel, severing the communications of Viscount Gort's British Expeditionary Force. In 11 days the *Wehrmacht* had smashed its way 240 miles, from

---

[17]Hart, Rommel Papers, pg. 19.
    [18]Records of the German Field Commands, Army Corps, 1a Kriegstagebuch (hereafter KTB), XXXIX Armee Korps, Microcopy T-314, Roll 921, frame #000056. Hereafter cited as Army Corps, name of Corps, T-314, roll no., frame no.
    The Germany Army, like all others, kept unit records - daily reports, which in the Wehrmacht were called Kriegstagebücher or KTBs. Even so, from 10 May on, Rommel began to keep his own personal diary, assigning one of his aides the duty of keeping a record of each day's events. He also gave instructions to his staff to keep all his orders, reports and maps with their overlays. Rommel had not done this during World War I and it had proven a disadvantage in writing his first book. As he told his friend, Kurt Hesse, he was planning a sequel to Infanterie Greift An. Rommel also began to photograph his operations. He became an enthusiastic photographer and by the end of the campaign had taken hundreds of photographs.
    [19]Hart, Rommel Papers, pg. 27.
    [20]Army Corps, Ia, KTB, XXXIX Korps, T-314, 921, #000066. See also Lagekarte 20.5.40 17 Uhr. #000122.
    [21]Franz Halder, Kriegstagebuch, ed. by Hans-Adolf Jacobsen (3 vols.; Stuttgart: W. Kohlhammer Verlag, 1962), I, 297.

The campaign situation map for 18 May 1940.

the eastern frontier of Luxembourg to the coast. Hitler, remembering the bloody stalemate of 1914-1918; the endless snaking lines of trenches gourged with barbed-wire and machine guns, could hardly believe his victory. "The Führer," recorded Halder on the 17th, "is extremely nervous. He is afraid of his own success. He would prefer to risk nothing and to stop the advance. Pretext is concern for the left flank."[22] Within the astounding mosaic of events which pointed to a rapid conclusion of the campaign in the West, however, Rommel's accomplishments were brilliant. He was awarded the Knight's Cross (*Ritterkreuz*) - the first divisional commander so honored.

National Archives

This rare photo of Rommel wearing his overseas cap is one of the earliest showing him with his Knight's Cross to the Iron Cross.

Rommel's orders for 21 May called for an advance around Arras to the northwest. Supported by SS Totenkopf Division, 7 Panzer was to gain the Scarpe River line at Acq and Aubigny-Savy. At the same time 5 Panzer was to advance east of Arras, but as this attack was late getting started, 7 Panzer would advance with its right flank completely exposed to the strong Allied forces gathering in the city.[23]

[22]*Ibid.*, I, 302.
[23]Jacobsen, <u>Dünkirchen</u>, pg. 56.

To break the net rapidly closing around the armies in Flanders, the Allied commanders planned a stinging counterpunch. The British 5 and 50 Divisions (with 1 Army Tank Brigade), supported by four French divisions, were to strike south from Arras. When the French support failed to materialize, however, the English commander resolved to put in the attack on his own. Though it was uncoordinated[24] and poorly supported by infantry, it badly shook Hitler and his staff, causing a crisis with far-reaching consequences.

At 1530 hours Rommel's lead elements were already east of Beaumont, advancing northwards, when British tanks (1700 hours) hit the eastern flank of the division.[25] For the first time Rommel was up against the British, and the ensuing desperate hours show him at his best - the born field commander, mastering a crisis with cool-headed resolve and inspiring his troops through personal example.

In Wailly (southwest of Arras) the British counterpunch stunned elements of 6 Rifle Regiment causing chaos and confusion; the regiment's vehicles jammed the roads and yards instead of going into action against the enemy tanks. Here Rommel encountered a new tank, the slow-moving but thick-skinned Matilda (Mark II). As these 26-ton steel behemoths rumbled forward, it was found that the standard German 37mm antitank weapon was useless against them. To avert a major crisis, Rommel brought every available gun into action, including the 88mm antiaircraft guns. He personally directed the fire, running from gun to gun and overruling objections that the range was too great. The lead tanks were soon hit, gushing smoke and fire. The others stopped or turned away.

All at once another group of tanks attacked, debouching from Bac-du-Nord. Again it was only the high-velocity 88 which packed sufficient punch to penetrate the Matilda's three-inch armor plating. No sooner was this second attack mastered when, suddenly, Rommel remembers, "[Lieutenant] Most sank to the ground behind a 20mm antiaircraft gun close beside me. He was mortally wounded and blood gushed from his mouth."[26]

Meanwhile, the British 1 Army Tank Brigade had engaged elements of 7 Panzer in the Achicourt-Agny sector. I./6 Rifle Regiment sustained heavy losses; 42 Antitank Battalion was virtually overrun, its guns and crews destroyed.[27] But fire from the divisional artillery and 88mm batteries succeeded in halting the enemy armor south of the line Beaurains-Agny.[28] Thirty-six brewed-up British tanks littered the battlefield.

---

[24]Army Corps, 1a KTB, XXXIX Korps, T-314, 921, #000076.

[25]Ibid., #000073. See also Lage am 21.5.40 17-18 Uhr. #000125.

[26]Hart, Rommel Papers, pg. 32.

[27]For German reports on the inefficacy of their 3.7cm PAK guns against the British Matildas, see von Manteuffel, 7 Panzer-Division, pp. 76-78.

[28]Hart, Rommel Papers, pg. 33.

While this bitter fighting still hung in the balance, Rommel had ordered Rothenburg's tanks (which had already reached the Scarpe southwest of Acq) to thrust southeastwards to take the advancing enemy armor in the flank and rear. The ensuing fire-fight, tank against tank, cost 7 Panzer three Panzer IV's, six Panzer III's and a number of lighter tanks.[29] Finally, numerous Stuka divebomber attacks brought noticeable relief to Rommel's beleagured force.[30] 7 Panzer losses this day (21 May) were the heaviest of the campaign: 89 killed, 116 wounded and 173 missing.

The situation restored, Rommel continued his advance, steering 7 Panzer south of Arras. On 23 May he reached the village of La Bassée on the Aa Canal. Under pressure of this outflanking movement, the Allied forces in Arras retired to the canal line, running westward from La Bassée to the coast at Gravelines south to Dunkirk.

Suddenly on 24 May the German *Blitzkrieg* ground to a halt. Von Rundstedt, badly shaken by the events of 21 May (as were his subordinates von Kleist and von Kluge), conferred with Hitler. He propsed a temporary suspension of the armored thrust until the greatly-outdistanced infantry could catch up. Hitler, riddled with anxiety for the safety of his exposed armored spearheads, concurred with von Rundstedt's proposal and issued his famous halt order.[31]

Hitler rescinded the halt order two days later, on the 26th. Rommel immediately threw elements of 7 Rifle Regiment across the canal, which was blocked by "immense numbers of sunken barges," and established a small bridgehead. When a machine gun battalion attempted to cross, however, it was beaten back by deadly sniper fire. Again, Rommel was present at the crisis point. Standing atop a railroad embankment and completely exposed to the heavy sniper fire, he personally selected the targets and directed the fire of the antitank crews. "One after another their leading gunners and gun commanders were shot dead, clean through the head, but the general [sic] himself seemed totally immune to the enemy sniping."[32] By midday, 27 May, 7 Panzer had established two bridgeheads; Rommel's tanks crossed the canal on a hastily erected pontoon bridge that wriggled from left to right to avoid the many sunken barges.

---

[29]*Ibid.*
[30]Jacobsen, *Dünkirchen*, pg. 57.
[31]Helmuth Greiner and Percy Schramm, eds., *Kriegstagebuch des Oberkommandos der Wehrmacht, 1940-1945* (4 vols.: Frankfurt am Main: Bernard und Graefe Verlag für Wehrwesen, 1961-1965), I, 179-180E. Hereafter cited as *KTB des OKW*. See also Jacobsen, *Dünkirchen*. The sycophantic Göring had also influenced Hitler's decision, boasting that his air force alone could prevent the evacuation of the trapped BEF in Flanders. The German soldier, however, in high spirits after the intoxicating victories of the preceding two weeks, hardly comprehended the halt order. Army Corps, 1a KTB, XXXIX Korps, T-314, 921, #000088.
[32]Irving, *The Trail*, pg. 51.

Hoth now ordered 7 Panzer to strike for Lille, one of France's largest industrial centers. To support the advance, Hoth placed Lieutenant General von Hartlieb's 5 Panzer under Rommel's command. Rommel immediately ordered a conference with both divisions' tank commanders. When Colonel Johannes Streich (commander of 5 Panzer's 15 Panzer Regiment) pointed out to Rommel that he was reading the maps improperly, a violent altercation resulted - the first of many misunderstandings between the two men.

Rommel's Panzers burst from their bridgeheads and motored northeast; by dusk they had reached a point some ten miles southwest of Lille. Anxious to seal off the city from the west, Rommel ordered his Panzer regiment to continue its advance through the dark. So Rothenburg's tanks lumbered on, their path "marked by the glare of burning vehicles shot up by his force." A wireless signal from Rothenburg at 0140 hours the next morning indicated that he had reached his objective near Lomme.[33]

With this advance 7 Panzer had moved far in front of the main German forces. This could and did create confusion. Unaware of Rommel's swift forward progress, German artillery lobbed 150mm shells on 25 Panzer Regiment's command post, which was also serving as Rommel's headquarters. Seeking cover, Rommel dashed for his signals vehicle, with Major Erdmann (commander of the reconnaissance battalion) running just a few steps in front. Suddenly a heavy shell impacted close to the vehicle. "When the smoke cleared," Rommel writes in his Papers, "Major Erdmann . . . lay face to the ground, dead, with his back shattered. He was bleeding from the head and from an enormous wound in his back. His left hand was still grasping his leather gloves. I had escaped unscathed."[34]

In blocking the roads issuing west from Lille, Rommel had helped to trap half the French 1 Army;[35] on 31 May the battered French divisions surrendered. Meanwhile, the bulk of the BEF and scattered French forces had begun Operation Dynamo - the evacuation from Dunkirk to England. A motley fleet of 848 British, Dutch, Belgian and French vessels plowed repeatedly through the rough Channel waters and, though constantly harassed by the *Luftwaffe* and German coastal batteries, delivered some 338,226 men safely across to England.[36] The first phase of the campaign had come to a close; the surviving French divisions were shepherded back across the Somme for a final stand in the hastily erected "Weygand Line." Rommel's tired division was pulled from the line for a few days' rest and re-equipping.

During this brief hiatus, Rommel prepared a most extraordinary interim report. His division had taken 6,849 prisoners, captured 48 light

[33]Hart, *Rommel Papers*, pg. 40.
[34]*Ibid.*, pg. 41.
[35]*Army Corps, 1a KTB*, XXXIX Korps, T-314, 921. Lage am 29.5.40 12 Uhr #000135.
[36]Esposito, *History of WWII*, pg. 65.

The campaign situation map of May 29/30, 1940.

tanks and destroyed 18 heavy and 295 light tanks. "Not bad for Thuringians," he proudly wrote his wife. The report was dispatched posthaste to Hitler and his adjutant Schmundt. The result was that Rommel, alone of all the divisional commanders, received an invitation to meet with the Führer at Charleville on 2 June. At the conference Hitler greeted his celebrated Panzer leader, exclaiming, "Rommel, we were all very worried for your safety during those days you were on the attack."[37]

On 5 June Rommel was back in action. His division was now attached to von Bock's Army Group B and situated on its extreme right wing between Amiens and Abbeville. Rommel's first objective was to gain a bridgehead across the Somme. Under cover of a violent artillery

[37]Irving, <u>The Trail</u>, pg. 52.

barrage which plastered the French positions on the slopes south of the river, German pioneer troops fanned out across flat, marshy ground and stormed the Somme bridges, which the French had neglected to demolish. The bridges were quickly secured, intact; soon a steady stream of vehicles poured across the river, Rommel's signals van in the lead. But traffic across the railway bridge abruptly ceased when a Panzer IV shed its right track and blocked the entire passage. Some time was lost while other tanks "pulled and pushed" the Panzer IV across the bridge. Soon all was in order and 7 Panzer began its lightning advance to the Seine.

As the 7 Panzer Division started to cross the Somme River bridges, its tanks came under heavy British artillery fire.

After a nasty fight in Hangest, Rommel ordered Rothenburg to advance through 6 Rifle Regiment on Le Quesnoy. At 1600 hours the tanks rattled forward, opposed by black colonial troops. Firing round after round 25 Panger Regiment enveloped the city and swept on past it, entering a "wide and coverless plain to its south. On they went through fields of high-grown corn. Any enemy troops who were sighted were either wiped out or forced to withdraw. Large numbers of prisoners were brought in, many of them hopelessly drunk."[38]

---

[38]Hart, _Rommel Papers_, pg. 49.

As the leading vehicles of this German tank column started to cross a Somme River bridge, a Pz.Kpfw. IV broke down at the bridge's approach, stalling this segment of the advance (see pp. 46-47 of <u>The Rommel Papers</u>).

    The next day, 6 June, Rommel placed his division in extended-order - its front stretched some 2,000 yards and was 12 miles deep. 7 Panzer advanced as if on parade, spitting fire and crushing anything in its path. On it went "up hill and down dale, over highways and byways straight across country."[39] On 7 June Rommel leaped 30 miles, thrusting like a dagger into the heart of the French 10 Army. Late the next evening he reached the Siene at Sotteville.

    Corps Headquarters (Hoth) now ordered Rommel to make a right-angled turn and dash for Le Harve. Such a move, Corps calculated, would trap several French and British infantry divisions retiring rapidly to the coast, hoping to stage a mini-Dunkirk. With Rommel in the van, the attack got underway at 0730 hours the next morning. At speeds approaching 40 miles an hour, 7 Panzer crashed through to the coast at Les Petites Dalles, smashing the enemy motorized columns in its path. Rothenburg's tank plowed through the seawall and drove right up to the water.

    But the real prize, St. Valéry, lay farther up the coast. In this port city huddled thousands of British and French troops awaiting evacuation. Rommel moved quickly; on the morning of 11 June, 25 Panzer Regiment seized the high ground west of the port.[40] Rommel called on St. Valéry to surrender, but the British gamely refused. "They built

[39]<u>Ibid.</u>, pg. 50.

[40]<u>Divisions</u>, 1a, 7 Panzer Division (Vorstoss auf St. Valéry), T-315, 400.

Oberst Karl Rothenburg, commander of Pz.Rgt. 25, was awarded his Knight's Cross on 3 June 1940.

When Rommel's division reached the English Channel on 10 June, his tank commander, Rothenburg, drove his tank onto the beach and stopped it at the water's edge.

Rommel walked up the beach to take this photograph of Rothenburg's tank at the edge of the English Channel.

barricades with their bare hands and fought like wildcats."[41] The fighting that day witnessed a confrontation between a British auxiliary cruiser and a German 88. This unusual fire-fight was only decided by the timely arrival of a German 100mm battery, which scored a direct hit on the cruiser and disabled it.

Only late the next evening did the valiant defenders capitulate, and not until blasted by heavy artillery and Stuka attacks. A dozen Allied generals shuffled into captivity, among them General Fortune (51 British Division), General Ihler (French 9 Corps commander), and the commanders of the French 1, 2, 5, 40 Infantry Divisions and 31 Mountain Division.[42] 12,727 prisoners were taken.

Rommel and French General Ihler in the town square at St. Valéry. Note Rommel's ever-present camera.

General Fortune, 51st Highland Division commander, talks with Rommel at St. Valéry prior to the official surrender of the British forces there.

While 7 Panzer took several well-earned days for rest and reorganization, another celebrated Panzer leader dealt France the knock-out blow. On 12 June Heinz Guderian penetrated the French line at Châlons-sur-Marne; exploiting a gap between the French 4 and 2 Armies, his armor advanced southeast and reached the Swiss border on 17 June, trapping 500,000 Frenchmen in the Maginot line. The fate of France was sealed. She appealed for an armistice.

Hitler, however, wanted his armies to occupy the entire French Atlantic coastline down to the Spanish frontier. Rommel's unit was now switched to south of the Seine. On 17 June the "Ghost Division," as the French had come to call it, was on the move again; its objective, France's most important deep-water port - Cherbourg. 7 Panzer hurtled towards the coast at speeds exceeding 30 miles an hour. One day's advance, over 200 miles, surpassed the greatest distance ever covered in a single day in warfare. Resistance was feeble; the villages crammed with French sailors and refugees.[43]

On 18 June Rommel reached Cherbourg and attacked immediately. The port's powerful fortress guns, supported by the fire of British warships, kept up a tremendous barrage on the advancing German

---

[41]Irving, <u>The Trail</u>, pg. 54.

[42]Halder, <u>Kriegstagebuch</u>, I, 352. See also Divisions, 1a, 7 Panzer Division (Kapituation bei St. Valéry), T-315, 409.

[43]<u>Divisions</u>, 1a, 7 Panzer Division (Cherbourg: 17 June, battle reports), T-315, 401.

20 June 1940: Rommel accepts the surrender of the Cherbourg Fortress.

columns. The next day Stukas swooped from the sky, raining bombs on the Cherbourg forts; heavy artillery fire transformed the dock area into a sea of flames - the cacaphony of battle punctuated by the rumble of exploding munitions arsenals. That settled the issue. French naval officers appeared in Rédoute des Couplets to negotiate a surrender. Thirty thousand men laid down their arms, bullied by a single German Panzer division.

On 21 June, in the sleepy French forest of Compiegne, German and French delegations concluded an armistice. The *Blitzkrieg* through France had come to an end. Rommel's Ghost Division could boast impressive figures. Since 10 May it had captured 97,648 men along with 277 field guns, 64 antitank guns, 458 tanks and armored cars and over 4,000 lorries. Losses were light: 682 killed, 1,646 wounded and 296 missing. Only 42 tanks were destroyed.

The German delegation seated inside the railway car at Compiegne.

Despite their impressive results, Rommel's combat techniques elicited substantial criticism. Reports filtered in to OKH which charged that Rommel had "falsified" the divisional war diary, expropriated bridging equipment belonging to another division and "filched" some tanks from Streich's Panzer regiment. Much of the criticism was justified, but many generals were simply envious of and embittered by Rommel's great successes.

With hostilities ended Rommel returned to Wiener-Neustadt for a short leave. He and Manfred could often be found relaxing in the *Kriegsschule's* olympic-size pool.

While Rommel relaxed, Hitler negotiated. The Führer's attempts to reach a peaceful settlement with England were genuine, if one-sided. When it was clear, however, that his peace offensive had floundered on the rock of Churchillian intransigence, preparations for a cross-Channel invasion got swiftly underway (July 1940). Operation Sealion (code name for the attack on England) consumed the energies of Rommel and his 7 Panzer through the closing weeks and months of 1940.

The German delegation standing before the historic railway carriage in which the Armistice of World War I was signed. Front row from left to right: von Ribbentrop, Raeder, Hitler, Göring, Jodl and Hess. Bruckner and Keitel are behind Hitler.

The training was monotonous - loading and re-loading the converted river barges that were to ferry the division across the Channel.

During welcomed breaks from the numbing routine, Rommel found time to write a detailed history of his operations in France. Upon advice from his friend, Schmundt, Rommel tooled his history into a peppery, continuous narrative, garnished with numerous detailed maps. Rommel presented a copy to Hitler that December.

Rommel after the victory parade in Paris, June 1940.

The following pages of priviate photographs were taken with Rommel's camera during his leave at Wiener-Neustadt, after the French campaign.

Rommel and his son, Manfred, swimming in the olympic-size pool at Wiener-Neustadt.

Lucie and Rommel, shown here wearing his white summer uniform and newly-won Knight's Cross

Manfred looks admiringly at his famous father.

Unternehmen Sonnenblume: Its Antecedents and Execution. June 1940 - April 1941

In June 1940 Adolf Hitler stood at the pinnacle of his military success. In a series of lightning campaigns, he had vanquished his enemies and driven them from the European Continent; he had become the greatest conqueror of the twentieth century. To the outside observer, the *Wehrmacht* seemed the perfect instrument of teutonic *"Grossmacht"* - an indominable monolith comprised of tanks and guns and planes.

The fall of France, however, had brought about a fundamental change in the character of the war. "The continental had become international, the simple more complex;" strategy had replaced the tactics.[1] The *Wehrmacht*, designed for rapid victories over isolated European enemies, was ill-prepared to meet the exigencies of a conflict waged in three dimensions on an international scale.[2]

The "fissures" in Hitler's military machine first became apparent during the Battle for Britain (July-October 1940). The *Luftwaffe* had proven inefficient in terms of numbers, range and quality; the navy unbalanced (too few capital ships) and too small to influence the course of events. By mid-October Hitler had dropped the concept of a cross-Channel attack.

But neither Hitler nor his military advisors had ever evinced much faith in Sealion. Surely, they reasoned, the defiant island-dwellers could be effectively challenged by the application of pressure upon critical links in their sprawling colonial empire. Thus, as early as 30 June, Major General Alfred Jodl (chief of the OKW operations staff) submitted a memorandum to Hitler in which he raised the question of German support for Italy in the African theater.[3] With such support, he calculated, Italy could banish England from the Mediterranean, which

---

[1] Charles B. Burdick, Germany's Strategy and Spain in World War Two (New York: Syracuse University Press, 1968), pg. 2. Hereafter cited as Germany's Strategy.

[2] For a thoughtful discussion of this theme, see Alan S. Milward, "Hitler's Konzept des Blitzkrieges," in Probleme des Zweiten Welkrieges, ed. by Andreas Hillgruber (Berlin: Kiepenheuer and Witsch Verlag, 1967).

[3] Charles B. Burdick, Unternehmen Sonnenblume: Der Entschluss zum Afrika-Feldzug, Wehrmacht im Kampf Series, Bd. XLVIII (Neckargemünd: Kurt Vowinckel Verlag, 1972), pg. 16.. Hereafter cited as Sonnenblume.

Field Marshal Walther von Brauchitsch

would then become an Italian "Mare Nostrum." One month later (July 30, 1940) Field Marshal Walther von Brauchitsch (commander-in-chief, OKH) proposed a five-point plan which included: a) tank support for Italy in Africa, and b) a direct attack on the Suez Canal.[4]

Hitler listened with interest to the strategic views of his General Staff but could decide no course of action. "An amateur with an insufficient comprehension of the totality of strategy,"[5] the Führer was unable to provide his *Wehrmacht* with firm guidance in the form of clear goals and policy directives. Instead, he toyed with a possible eastern venture (Barbarossa) and a surprise occupation of Gibraltar (Felix).

Six weeks later (11 September), Colonel Walter Warlimont (chief of the National Defense Branch of OKW) dispatched a plan to his chief Jodl that envisioned the employment of either a Panzer corps or a Panzer brigade in Africa. Warlimont, a linguistically talented and highly capable staff officer, recommended that units of General Ritter von Thoma's 3 Panzer Division be prepared for transport to Libya; and that Hitler write directly to Mussolini to offer him this support.[6]

---

[4]*Ibid.*, pg. 19.
[5]Burdick, Germany's Strategy, pg. 3.
[6]Greiner, KTB des OKW, I, 73. See also Burdick, Sonnenblume. The Panzer support was to be buttressed by reconnaissance, close-support and flak units of the Luftwaffe.

Before Jodl could respond, however, Hitler's vacillation had yielded to a firmer posture. At a staff conference on 14 September, his intentions were clear: a Panzer corps would be prepared for transport to Africa, provided, of course, that the Italians were receptive to the idea.[7] Influencing the Führer's decision was his fear that England could easily establish air bases in North Africa, from which she could bomb the Italian mainland.[8]

Meanwhile, events in Africa were soon to overtake the leisurely pace of German planning. Libya, an Italian colony since 1912 and only 250 miles (400 kilometers) from Sicily, occupied a position of great strategic significance in Italy's colonial nexus;[9] it provided a natural springboard for a thrust into Egypt towards the Suez Canal and the rich oil fields of the Middle East. The colony's western and eastern provinces (Tripolitania and Marmarica) were thoroughly uninhabitable desert wastes. In the central province (Cyrenaica), however, with its thin, fertile coastal strip, the Italians had constructed modern cities and established numerous settlements; linked together by a highway - the Via Balbia - which stretched 1200 miles from Tunisia to the Egyptian border.[10] Defending Libya were some 200,000 Italian soldiers under Marshal Rodolfo Graziani.

Since Italy's declaration of war on June 10, 1940, Mussolini had prodded the cautious Graziani to undertake offensive action against Egypt - weakly screened by 30,000 troops of General Sir Archibald Wavell's Western Desert Force. On 13 September the long-awaited offensive began. Graziani crossed the Egyptian border. Three days later his army occupied Sidi Barrani, having registered an advance of 60 miles. Wavell's tiny force, vastly outnumbered, withdrew skillfully and in good order to a position farther east. Marshal Badoglio (the chief of the Italian general staff), his self-confidence inflated by press reports heralding a great Italian victory, informed his German allies that Italy would need no Panzer support in Africa.[11]

Then, inexplicably, Graziani halted his advance. His badly dispersed army dug in to await the arrival of reinforcements and supplies. "The cautious, timid nature of the entire advance had had something dreamy about it; it was far removed from the realities of war."[12]

Hitler and his staff were rightly distressed. As early as 10 September, General Enno von Rintelen, the German military attaché in Rome, had

---

[7]Burdick, *Sonnenblume*, pg. 28. See also Halder, *Kriegstagebuch*, II, 100.
[8]Halder, *Kriegstagebuch*, II, 100.
[9]In 1940 Italy's African empire included Eritrea, Italian Somaliland, Ethiopia and Libya.
[10]Hanns-Gert von Esebeck, *Afrikanische Schicksalsjahre: Das Deutsche Afrika-Korps unter Feldmarschall Rommel* (Rastatt in Baden: Erich Pabel Verlag, 1960). Hereafter cited as *Afrikanische Schicksalsjahre*.
[11]Burdick, *Sonnenblume*, pg. 30.
[12]Ibid.

General Sir Claude Auckinleck and Field Marshal Archibald Wavell.

lodged a disturbing report on the Italian army in Libya. Mussolini's forces, he wrote, (twelve infantry and three and one-half cavalry divisions) were poorly equipped. They lacked artillery; most of their armored and motorized units were still in Italy. Graziani, von Rintelen concluded, was hardly prepared to conduct a major offensive operation.[13]

To effect closer cooperation between the two Axis powers, Hitler met with Mussolini at the Brenner Pass on 3 October. In a desultory monologue that skirted many areas of mutual concern, Hitler renewed his offer to dispatch troops, tanks and planes to North Africa.[14] Mussolini promised to resume the offensive in Egypt.

"True" to his word, the Duce attacked; only not in Egypt. On 28 October he hurled large forces into Greece. In this manner, Mussolini disrupted German planning by opening an entirely new theatre of operations. The Führer was furious. His precious Romanian oil was endangered; the prestige of the Axis jeopardized. Faced with this suddenly transformed strategic picture, Hitler decided to let the tactless Italian stew in his own juices: there would be no German Panzer corps for Africa. Hitler could not know that he would soon be drawn inexorably into the vortex of Mediterranean affairs.

Weeks passed, but Graziani refused to budge. General Richard O'Connor, the local British commander in Egypt, made good use of this welcomed hiatus to gather tanks and mechanized units from all over the Empire; by December his modest Western Desert Force numbered 31,000 men and 275 tanks - including 35 heavily armored Matildas. On 9

---

[13]*Ibid.*, pp. 26-27.
[14]Halder, *Kriegstagebuch*, II, 136-38.

December he launched a counterstroke, intended only as a raid to keep the Italians off balance.

Disaster struck. The forward Italian positions - Sidi Barrani, Nibeiwa and Buq-Buq - disintegrated before the onslaught of 7 Armored and 4 Indian Divisions. 38,000 startled Italians, including four generals, marched into captivity. The advance rolled forward; Sollum fell without a fight, British mechanized units crashed through the rusted barbed-wire along the Libyian-Egyptian border and streamed westward, encircling Bardia.

The lone German observer of this singular catastrophe was Major Heinz Heggenreiner, who had come to Libya in August as a permanent liaison officer to Graziani's army. His reports were shocking. The entire Italian motor vehicle pool on the eve of O'Connor's attack comprised less than 2,000 vehicles of all types - below the requirements of a single German motorized division. Italian equipment, moreover, with its paucity of modern antitank and flak guns, motorized artillery and armored scout vehicles (essential for the fluid conditions of desert warfare), was wholly unsatisfactory.

In late December, as the magnitude of the debacle telescoped, the Italians registered their first urgent requests for help. On 28 December the Italian military attaché in Germany, General Efusio Marras, conferred with Keitel (Chief of Staff OKW). Marras emphasized the desperate nature of the situation, pointing out that without swift German intervention all of Italian North Africa would be lost.[15]

Even as Marras and Keitel talked, Hitler had taken his first step to shore up Mussolini's crumbling empire. Lieutenant General Hans-Ferdinand Geissler's X *Fliegerkorps* was in transit from Norway to the Mediterranean. Geissler's assignment was a difficult one: to neutralize the important British island base of Malta, harass English naval forces and secure the Italian lines of communication across the Mediterranean.[16]

Meanwhile, Graziani labored futilely to restore his shattered front. O'Connor's advance swept away anything in its path. The lightly armored Italian tanks simply "split apart" when contested by the heavier British models. Bardia fell on 3 January; the first-class Italian fortress of Tobruk, with its 25,000 man garrison, capitulated three weeks later (22 January). Graziani's battered army fled down the Via Balbia - like a terrified elephant chased by a mouse.

But already on January 9, 1941 Hitler had come to his final decision: a blocking force would be rushed to North Africa - code name for the operation, *Unternehmen Sonnenblume* (Operation Sunflower). The loss of North Africa, the Führer calculated, would not weigh heavily

---

[15]Greiner, KTB des OKW, I, 243-44.

[16]The advance elements of Geissler's Fliegerkorps consisted of 100 bombers (Ju 88 and HE 111), 60 (Ju 87) Stukas, 20 (Me.Bf.109) fighters and several miscellaneous types. Burdick, Sonnenblume, pg. 57.

Rommel's first reconnaissance flight aboard a Caproni Ca.309.

The Castle Benito airfield, where Rommel first set foot in North Africa.

parade. He hoped their presence would serve to stiffen the resolve of his Italian allies, which he found noticeably lacking. That evening, when Rommel dined with the Italian generals, his Pour le Mérite caught the attention of one of Gariboldi's officers. When asked where he had won the medal, Rommel unthinkingly replied "Longarone," the scene of one of Italy's most humiliating defeats in World War I. That promptly ended the dinner conversation. Though the incident was soon forgotten, it underscored a fact which would soon become glaringly apparent: Rommel was no Marlborough; he lacked the requisite sophistication to deal smoothly with tempermental allies.

On 14 February the first German combat units, 3 Reconnaissance (Major Baron von Wechmar) and 39 Antitank Battalions (Major Jansa), arrived in Tripoli.[31] With the situation so serious, Rommel "pressed for their rapid disembarkation," which continued that evening by lamplight despite the danger of enemy air activity.[32] By morning the port

---

[30]These included the rest of Rommel's understrength staff, the division's rations unit, Supply Columns 800 and 804, four companies of 572 Field Hospital, Tire Repair Company 13 (motorized) and Reconnaissance Staff 681.

[31]Army Corps, KTB, DAK, T-314, 21, #000809.

[32]Hart, Rommel Papers, Pg. 102.

53

The reviewing party salutes as they pass the newly arrived contingent of German troops. Rommel and Gariboldi are in the foreground.

(Left and above) Rommel and his Ia, Lt. Col. von dem Borne, in conversation with Italian officials before the march past.

The reviewing party during the march past.

Rommel had the workshops three miles south of Tripoli produce large numbers of dummy tanks which were mounted on Volkswagen vehicles.

had broken its tonnage record. To conceal his true strength, which was still quite negligible, he ordered his workshops to produce large numbers of dummy tanks. Mounted on Volkswagens, these "tanks" of blanket material armor and wood cannon were the first of his many stratagems.

Colonel Schmundt had returned to the Berghof (Hitler's Berchtesgaden retreat), where he handed Hitler Rommel's first status report. Hitler, Schmundt wired back on 19 February, was very pleased with Rommel's "initiative"; 15 Panzer Division would soon be on its way to Africa. The Führer had even chosen a name for Rommel's corps - the Africa Corps (*Deutsches Afrikakorps*).[33] The fastidious adjutant also assured Rommel that a "historical distortion of his services would not take place again."[34] (For a list of German officers assigned to the Afrikakorps, see Appendix II.)

Early on 24 February Rommel penned a short missive to his wife: "It's hard to believe its only February. The sun is already so hot that my face

---

[33]On 21 February Rommel's staff was christened "Stab Deutsches Afrikakorps." Army Corps, <u>KTB, DAK</u>, T-314, 21, #000805.

[34]Schmundt was referring to the incident that occurred during Rommel's service in World War I. In October of 1917 his detachment had penetrated the Italian lines at Kolourat and stormed the hill Monte Kuk, capturing 40 Italian officers and 1500 men. Credit for the victory, however, went to Lieutenant Ferdinand Schoerner, whose men had captured Hill 1114. When the Bavarian Schoerner was awarded the Pour le Mérite, Rommel was furious. Later a second "historical distortion" occurred. When General von Below offered the medal to the first soldier to scale the 5400 foot Monte Matajur, Rommel led his men on a grueling climb to the top which culminated in a battle on the very summit of the mountain. But General von Ludendorff (quartermaster general) announced, much to Rommel's dismay, that the Pour le Mérite would go to Lieutenant Walther Schneiber, who, in Rommel's eyes, had captured the wrong mountain. Rommel's services were eventually recognized and he received the coveted award.

has started peeling."[35] That afternoon the war began to heat up as well. A small German force of armored cars and motorcycle troops encountered the King's Dragoon Guards and a contingent of Australian antitank guns near El Agheila. The skirmish ended with the capture of three British soldiers and the destruction of several vehicles with no loss to the German detachment.[36] "A good omen," Rommel observed.[37]

After this initial flare-up, both sides settled down to a period of quiet patrolling. Rommel busied his small force with drills in desert navagation, cross-country marches and proper radio procedures. He agonized over the slowness of his build-up; no tanks had yet arrived. But he had little to fear from Wavell, who had withdrawn much of his Western Desert Force for an ill-fated expedition to Greece, leaving only minimum forces to screen Cyrenaica.

National Archives

The first German operative base in the desert.

Wavell had diluted his forces to an extent far greater than Rommel realized. 7 Armored Division had returned to Egypt, to rest and refit; its replacement, 2 Armored Division, was an inexperienced formation. 9 Australian Division had replaced 6 Australian Division, but only part of its forces were at the front; the rest remained at Tobruk because of maintenance difficulties. These new formations had also released much of their equipment and transport to support the venture in Greece. O'Connor, moreover, had returned to Egypt; Lieutenant General Sir Philip Neame, his replacement, had no experience in mechanized desert warfare.[38]

In a mood of optimism, Rommel wrote his old friend, General Friedrich Paulus (now chief quartermaster at OKH), on 26 February: "Dear Paulus: I can report from here that day by day the situation is becoming more stabilized. The appearance of German troops at the

[35]Rommel Collection, T-84, 274, #000033.
[36]Army Corps, <u>KTB, DAK</u>, T-314, 21, #000815.
[37]Rommel Collection, T-84, 274, #000033.
[38]Hart, <u>Rommel Papers</u>, Pg. 104.

Sirta-front and the first successful strike at El Agheila has impressed the enemy very much... Cooperation with the Italian [Command] has been good."[39]

Two weeks later the tanks of 5 Light Division reached Tripoli, completing their disembarkation on 11 March.[40] Rommel was there to observe the unloading of the Panzer I, II, III and IV models of 5 Panzer Regiment.[41] His tank crews were still in their striking black uniforms. The tanks were then assembled for a parade. Lieutenant Schmidt watched as they "clattered and rattled by." The Italian spectators, not overly awed by this display of German *Macht,* reserved their enthusiasm for the Italian armor which followed. Schmidt was impressed by the large number of tanks; there seemed to be no end to them. Only later, when he noticed a defect in one of their chains that seemed suspiciously familiar "did the penny drop."[42] To give the appearance of great strength, Rommel had ordered his Panzer crews to round the block and parade by several times.

The crew of this Pz.Kpfw. III still wears the black Panzer uniform.

[39]*Rommel Collection, T-84, 276, #000732.*
[40]*Franz Kurowski, Die Geschichte des Panzerregiments 5 (Bochum: Heinrich Pöppinghaus Verlag, 1975), pg. 22.*
[41]*5 Panzer Regiment fielded 25 IB's, 45 II's, 71 III's and 20 Panzer IV models. Adalbert von Taysen, Tobruk 1941: Der Kampf in Nordafrika, Einzelschriften zur militärischen Geschichte des Zweiten Weltkrieges, published by Militärgeschichtliches Forschungsamt (Freiburg: Rombach Verlag, 1976), pg. 349. Hereafter cited as Tobruk 1941.*
[42]*Heinz Werner Schmidt, With Rommel in the Desert (London: George G. Harrap and Co. Ltd., 1951), pg. 16. Hereafter cited as With Rommel.*

11 March 1941:
Pz.Kpfw. I's being
unloaded at Tripoli
(5 Light Division).

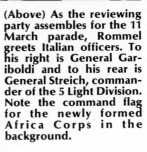

(Above) As the reviewing party assembles for the 11 March parade, Rommel greets Italian officers. To his right is General Gariboldi and to his rear is General Streich, commander of the 5 Light Division. Note the command flag for the newly formed Africa Corps in the background.

Pz.Kpfw I's, II's and IV's in the march-past in downtown Tripoli.

59

The arrival of the Panzer regiment put some real firepower in 5 Light Division and Rommel's excitement was evident in his letter home that evening: "There is much to rejoice over the arrival of the first tanks. The tactical HQ arrived too. Now our machine slowly starts grinding."[43] The "grinding" Rommel had in mind can be gleaned from his own statements. When one of his staff officers - recently driven out of Eritrea by the British - reported pessimistically on the military situation there, Rommel, visibly annoyed, shot back, "What do you know anyway, Herr Lieutenant? We shall reach the Nile, make a right turn and win everything back."[44] As early as 9 March he had boldly declared, "my first objective will be the re-conquest of Cyrenaica; my second, northern Egypt and the Suez Canal." The Canal lay 1,500 miles east of Tripoli, "but Rommel meant every word of what he said."[45]

5 Panzer Regiment rolled through the spacious avenues of Tripoli, lined with palm trees, horse-drawn carriages and bordered by bleach-white buildings. The tanks headed eastward, towards El Agheila and the front. Rommel too was off; on 19 March he flew to Hitler's "Wolfsschanze"(Wolf's Lair) Headquarters, cradled in a marshy, deciduous forest outside Rastenburg, East Prussia. Hitler had a diminutive black box waiting for his Afrikakorps commander; it contained the Oakleaves to the Knight's Cross. But pleasantries ceased when Rommel proffered his plan of operation. He could, he said, conquer the whole of Cyrenaica if given the go-ahead. But OKH was adamant. It had no intention of striking a decisive blow in Africa in the near future; and presently Rommel could expect no reinforcements. Von Brauchitsch conceded that after the arrival of 15 Panzer Division (late May) Rommel could take Agedabia and, perhaps, Benghazi.

Rommel returned to Tripoli deeply disappointed. The General Staff had given him the cold shoulder. What he could not know was that Hitler would soon need every available man and machine for his Barbarossa gamble. To the German Leader, with his continental mentality, Africa was a secondary theatre of war - it could never be more than that.

Once back in Libya Rommel discovered that El Agheila had just fallen to 3 Reconnaissance Battalion (24 March).[46] The British, evidently, were withdrawing on Mersa el Brega, "an Arab village straddling sand hills near the coast." It was a "tactical bottleneck and relatively easy to defend."[47] Rommel had a dilemma. His instructions from both OKH and the Italian High Command, to which he was theoretically subordinate, expressedly forbade even an attack on Mersa el Brega until the arrival of 15 Panzer Division. But the British were fortifying their position and plugging the gaps with reinforcements; by May the prospect of a suc-

[43]*Rommel Collection*, T-84, 274, #000052.
[44]Schmidt, *With Rommel*, pg. 11.
[45]Irving, *The Trail*, pg. 70.
[46]*Army Corps*, *KTB, DAK*, T-314, 21, #000830.
[47]Irving, *The Trail*, pg. 72. *See also Army Corps, KTB, DAK, T-314, 21, #000830.*

(above) Hitler presents Rommel with the Oakleaves to the Knight's Cross.
(right) Colonel Warlimont helps Rommel attach his newly-awarded Oakleaves to his Knight's Cross.

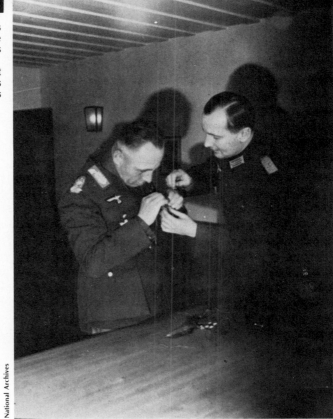

Rommel is driven from the Wolfsschanze to a waiting aircraft. Note he proudly wears his Oakleaves.

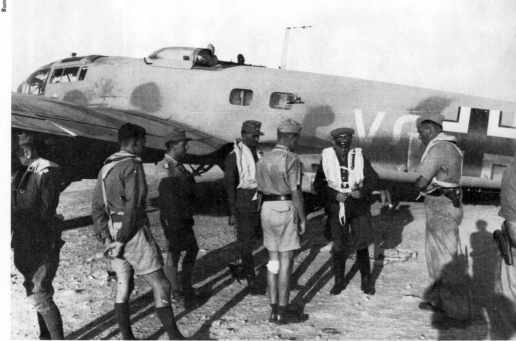

Rommel returns to Africa to carry on the struggle without OKH support.

cessful assault would be greatly diminished. Rommel saw his opportunity slipping away; he resolved to make the most of it in spite of his orders.

On 31 March elements of 5 Light Division stormed Mersa el Brega.[48] The first attempt was beaten back; but that evening 8 Machine Gun Battalion put in a "dashing" attack and lifted the British from their positions. General Streich kept on the heels of his startled foe and overran Agedabia on 3 April.

Rommel's aggressiveness flabbergasted the English High Command. Sometime before, Wavell had confidently assured Neame that a German attack before the end of May was "highly improbable."[49] And if anyone should have known, it was Wavell. The British theatre commander was one of a handful of men privy to the greatest secret of the war - a secret so unbelievable, so vital, it was kept under lock and key until 1974. The British had cracked the German Enigma code machine. All of Rommel's secret wireless traffic was encoded by the "Enigma Machine, rather like a small, wooden-boxed electric typewriter. The Nazi code experts had pronounced this machine absolutely safe from enemy code breakers. The messages were radioed in this code to Rome, and transmitted by wire to Hitler's headquarters. Deep in the English countryside, however, the enemy had constructed a far superior machine, as big as a house, capable of decoding the secret Enigma signals. Radio listening posts fed the German signals to the machine, a large multiservice organization translated and interpreted the fantastic results and they were transmitted back, marked 'Ultra Secret,' to the enemy commanders facing Rommel."[50]

Ultra intercepts fed Wavell a steady diet of invaluable intelligence data. He knew about *Unternehmen Sonnenblume* before the first German transport had reached Tripoli; he knew the exact units which would comprise the Afrikakorps; he also knew that Rommel had explicit instructions to stand fast.[51] But he did not know Rommel. Wavell expected his opponent to follow his instructions; when he didn't the British were caught flat-footed. This explains the suddenness of the subsequent British collapse in Cyrenaica.

Rommel had already devised a bold stroke, determined to swallow Cyrenaica in one gulp. Three columns would sweep eastward and converge on El Mechili, an important British outpost south and slightly west of Derna. The southernmost column, commanded by Count Gerhard von Schwerin and consisting of elements of 5 Light and Italian Ariete Divisions, would move directly through the desert interior along an

---

[48]Army Corps, KTB, DAK, T-314, 21, #000834.
[49]D. W. Braddock, The Campaign in Egypt and Libya, 1940-1942 (Aldershot: Gale Ploden Ltd., 1964), pg. 29.
[50]Irving, The Trail, pg. 81.
[51]Ronald Lewin, Ultra Goes to War (New York: McGraw-Hill, 1978) pp. 159-60. Hereafter cited as Ultra. The signals traffic of Geissler's X Fliegerkorps was a particularly fruitful source of Ultra information.

ancient caravan trail, the Trigh el Abd. This trail ran via Ben Gania, Bir Tengeder, Bir Hacheim and Bir el Gubi to the Egyptian frontier. Still a fourth column (Italian Brescia Division) was to thrust north and then east along the Via Balbia as far as Derna.

On 3 April Rommel's machine began to grind. He advanced elements of Ariete towards Ben Gania and ordered Streich to put 3 Reconnaissance Battalion on the road to Benghazi.[52] General Streich protested, claiming his division needed a good four days to bring up petrol before it could resume its forward movement. Rommel overruled his subordinate and ordered him to offload his supply trucks and send them back to the dumps to rush up supplies. Again Streich balked. Such a move, he warned, would immobilize his division for at least a day. Rommel grew impatient. The risk would have to be run, he said, for the British were falling back and they must not slip from his grasp.

Rommel's sudden advance not only perplexed his adversary, it sent ripples of alarm through the German and Italian High Commands as

well. He had exceeded his orders. Gariboldi and Keitel independently signaled their impetuous subordinate, admonishing him to go no further.

That evening Rommel motored up the Via Balbia to check on the progress of his reconnaissance battalion. Von Wechmar (its commander) had yet to make contact with the British; Rommel ordered him to push on to Benghazi. Rommel then returned to Agedabia, where an enraged Gariboldi was waiting for him. In the ensuing altercation the two men worked themselves into such a state that they almost came to blows. "At that very moment," Rommel writes in his Papers, "a signal arrived 'deus ex machina' from the German High Command."[53] This was Keitel's memorandum and its meaning was clear - Rommel was to stop. But the stubborn Rommel used the message as a tour-de-force to cow his red-faced Italian superior. He had just received, he confidently exclaimed, a signal giving him "complete freedom of action." The slow-witted Gariboldi didn't spot the bluff. He acquiesced.

The advance continued. The columns plunged eastward across a monotonous lunar landscape broken only by stunted pines and small thorny shrubs. The temperature soared to 120°F and more; in the evenings they dropped just as rapidly to a bitter cold. A terrible thirst clawed at the back of one's throat and swarms of voracious insects added to the

[52]Army Corps, _KTB, DAK_, T-314, 21, #000838-000839.
[53]Hart, _Rommel Papers_, pg. 111.

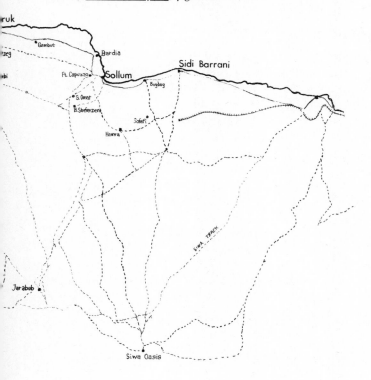

Improvised protection from the violent desert storms.

miseries of the men. Violent sandstorms, known as "Ghibli's" (also the name of an Italian aircraft) could appear at a minute's notice, swirling tons of sand and dust through the air. Rommel describes his first encounter with one of these primeval wonders:

> Now we realized what little idea we had had of the tremendous force of such a storm. Immense clouds of reddish dust obscured all visibility and forced the car's speed down to a crawl. Often the wind was so strong that it was impossible to drive along the Via Balbia. Sand streamed down the windscreen like water. We gasped in breath painfully through handkerchiefs held over our faces, and sweat poured off our bodies in the unbearable heat. So this was the Ghibli.[54]

On 5 April Rommel's "Kampfstaffel" was moving down the Trigh el Abd. Rommel himself followed in his Storch, a small reconnaissance aircraft.[55] Luftwaffe reports and wireless intercepts (his English-speaking wireless intercept company was now in Africa) confirmed that Neame

---

[54]Ibid, pg. 105.
[55]The Kampfstaffel, a small unit formed to protect Corps or Army Headquarters, should not be confused with Rommel's Gefechtsstaffel.

was still pulling back. Olbrich's Panzer regiment now received instructions to advance on Msus, destroy the enemy there and then push on to Mechili.[56] Rommel then flew to Ben Gania, where he learned that Mechili appeared to be undefended. He urgently signalled von Schwerin, the commander of his southernmost spearhead: "Mechili clear of enemy. Make for it. Drive fast."[57] But bad news swiftly followed. The British had shot down the Heinkel 111 carrying Captain Baudissin, Rommel's Ic (chief intelligence officer), who was captured; and they were now positioning themselves in force around Mechili.

This "Storch" reconnaissance aircraft was put at the disposal of Rommel.

Despite the unexpected strength of the Mechili position, heavy British vehicular traffic was observed fleeing eastward. Swift action was essential. Rommel ordered elements of 5 Light Division to fan out in an attempt to block the thoroughfares leading east from the town. But the assault on Mechili was postponed, for his columns were now scattered over the desert and many immobilized due to lack of fuel. The vehicles of 5 Panzer Regiment, choked with dust and sand, had broken down or overheated.[58]

The next day, 7 April, Rommel sped westward with his "Gefechtsstaffel" and its petrol reserves; he would locate and supply

---

[56]Army Corps, KTB, DAK, T-314, 21, #000843.
[57]Hart, Rommel Papers, pg. 113.
[58]German planning for Sonnenblume was marred by numerous errors. The German tanks, for example, were equipped with regular gas-burning engines when, as was quickly discovered, diesel engines were much more appropriate for conditions in the desert. See Burdick's detailed study Sonnenblume, pp. 118-26. See also Oskar Munzel, Die deutschen gepanzerten Truppen bis 1945 (Herford: Maximilian Verlag, 1965), pg. 244.

the stranded columns himself.[59] He quickly located von Schwerin's force and personally positioned it around Mechili, helping to place the artillery pieces. Through his field glasses he could see the town, and the small, crumbling stone fort that was its most prominent feature. Rommel attempted to negotiate a surrender, but the British were obdurate; Mechili would only be taken by storm.

But most of the Afrikakorps had yet to reach the fort. Rommel climbed into his Storch and flew off to find his missing columns. Swooping low over some unidentified vehicles he was nearly shot down - British! Soon he spotted some black dots in the sand - more vehicles. Rommel could discern the bright red, white and black swastika flags draped over the hoods of the trucks. He had found his reconnaissance battalion. He issued speedy instructions and was off again. As the sun sank below the horizon, Rommel detected a wall of dust in the distance; it turned out to be Olbrich's missing tanks. Rommel raged at his tardy tank commander and ordered him to move up at once.

Rommel in his "Storch."

---

[59]"*This small command staff, which included the chief of staff and a number of messenger officers, was mounted on one or two command cars and five or six Volkswagens for the messenger officers. It was followed by 14-15 motorized radio stations, which maintained communications with the command post, the Africa Corps, the assigned Italian Corps and some of the divisions. For his own protection (Rommel) took along only two armored reconnaissance cars. This small staff was always on the move and it was from here that Rommel conducted operations. Personal orders from Rommel were transmitted with a special radio signal call and took preference over all other messages.*" Alfred Gause, "Command Techniques Employed by Field Marshal Rommel in Africa," Armor Magazine, July-August, 1958, pp. 23-24.

The vast seas of sand which comprised the theatre of operations, and which lacked reference points of almost any kind, produced a strange disorientation. Rommel wrote his wife that he had lost all idea of time and space. "Today will be another decisive day," he continued. "Our main force is on its way up after a 220-mile march over the sand and rock of the desert. ... It's going to be a 'Cannae,' modern style."[60]

The long-delayed attack on Mechili got underway on the morning of 8 April. Rommel was up early in his Storch, viewing the battle from overhead. Olbrich's tanks were still not in position so Rommel again flew after them. Olbrich was nowhere to be found. Spying an 88 gun and its crew, he attempted to land; and succeeded in taxiing into a sandhill and ripping up the plane's undercarriage. He purloined a lorry and raced back to Corps headquarters - just escaping from a cloud of dust kicked up by an approaching British column. Rommel, as yet uninformed about the progress of the attack, set out for Mechili, but a raging Ghibli soon forced him to halt. In the meantime the fort had fallen; British attempts to break out to the east were crushed by the German and Italian artillery fire.[61] Farther north Ponath's 8 Machine Gun Battalion was astride the Via Balbia at Derna. The indominable machine gunners had taken over 800 prisoners and captured four generals, including Neame and O'Connor, who were scooped up traveling virtually unescorted.

Ponath reported that his men were exhausted and down to their last rounds of ammunition. But Rommel, having hurled the British from Cyrenaica, had no intention of suspending the pursuit. He wanted Tobruk; then, in a final lunge, he would force the Suez Canal. Unknown to him was the fact that strong Australian forces, withdrawing eastward from Cyrenaica, had already manned Tobruk's extensive perimeter of Italian-built fortifications; Churchill had ordered that they fight to the death.

The first elements of 15 Panzer Division reached the front on 9 April. Rommel and Captain Hermann Aldinger (his ADC) conferred with General Heinrich von Prittwitz, 15 Panzer commander. A mixed battlegroup comprised of 3 Reconnaissance, 8 Machine Gun and 605 Antitank Battalions was placed under his command, with orders to continue the pursuit to Tobruk. Rommel, still unaware of the great strength and depth of the perimeter defenses, hoped to capture the fortress in a quick strike. His unwarranted confidence is evident in his instructions for 10 April:

> I am convinced that the enemy is giving way before us. We must pursue him with all our forces. Our objective, which is to be made known to all troops is, the Suez Canal. In order to prevent the enemy breaking

---

[60]Hart, *Rommel Papers*, pg. 116.
[61]At Mechili, 5 Light Division captured an English general, 60 officers and some 1700 men. Army Corps, *KTB, DAK*, T-314, 21, #000849.

out from Tobruk, encirclement is to go forward with all available means.[62]

That day von Prittwitz launched his attack on Tobruk from a point near Kilometer Stone 18, astride the Via Balbia. The fortress artillery immediately pounded the attacking German columns, which struggled forward some 2,000 yards towards the perimeter defenses, only to meet a wall of artillery and machine gun fire. The attack broke down. Von Prittwitz jumped into his staff car and sped towards the enemy lines, hoping to get it moving again. As he stood erect, encouraging his men, a well-aimed antitank shell slammed into the car killing him instantly.

Disturbing reports were beginning to filter in on the Tobruk defenses mentioning "invisible" strongpoints. Rommel drove forward for a closer look, and climbed atop his "Mammoth," an imposing armored command vehicle he had captured from the British at El Agheila. Even from this vantage point he could discern nothing of the brilliantly camouflaged bunkers and firing points; he had no knowledge of the covered antitank ditches.[63]

The envelopment of Tobruk was completed on the morning of 11 April and Rommel called for Stuka attacks shortly thereafter. El Adem had fallen the day before and its captors, 3 Reconnaissance Battalion, made for Bardia. By 12 April the investing forces were sufficiently strong for Rommel to order a renewed assault on Tobruk.

Brescia Division went forward that afternoon, followed by 5 Light Division at 1630 hours. Swirling dust and sand concealed the advancing troops and tanks from the defender's fire. But when the tanks reached the break-in point, heavy artillery fire began to fall among them. They groped forward, only to stall before an unexpected antitank ditch which curled out of sight on either side.[64]

Faced by unexpected and determined resistance, Rommel called off the assault. He would await the arrival of his artillery and the Italian armored division Ariete to strengthen his investing forces. Rommel's African *Blitzkrieg* had abruptly ended before the antitank ditches of Tobruk.[65]

---

[62]*Ibid.*, #000851.

[63]Aldinger states that "although the Italians possessed the complete defense plans, which they themselves prepared, they denied having them and did not hand them over." Young, Desert Fox, pg. 76.

[64]5 Panzer Regiment was, by now, greatly reduced in strength. Many of its tanks had broken down and lay scattered across the desert. On 13 April it reported 37 tanks ready for action out of an establishment of 161. Taysen, Tobruk 1941, pg. 106.

[65]"The Italian defenses [at Tobruk] consisted of a semicircle of concreted underground posts behind barbed wire entanglements five feet high. Outside this was an uncompleted antitank ditch. The posts were two deep, each inner post being midway between the two outer posts, and each outer post protected by its own antitank ditch and wire. The outer posts were generally 600-800 yards apart and the inner line 500 yards behind the outer." Gavin Long, To Benghazi (Canberra: Australian War Memorial, 1966), pg. 240. Originally the antitank ditch had been covered by a layer of thin boards and sand, so that it could not be detected even at a short distance.

**Rommel's
desert office.**

As time passed, and Tobruk witnessed more and more fighting, this covering disappeared almost completely.
Tobruk had a 30 mile defensive perimeter with 128 numbered outposts, beginning with "S43" on the extreme west overlooking the Mediterranean and ending with "Z-84" at the extreme eastern end of the perimeter.

71

From Tobruk through Battleaxe, April - August 1941.

Fortress Tobruk blocked a twenty-two mile stretch of the Via Balbia, effectively rerouting and menacing the Afrikakorps lines of communication and supply to the Egyptian frontier. A successful sortie by the Tobruk garrison against these vital arteries would disrupt the flow of men, machines and fuel that sustained Rommel in the field. The Tobruk harbor, moreover, was the best in Cyrenaica. Tobruk had to be conquered.

Far into April Rommel nurtured the delusion that his enemy was evacuating the fortress - a' la Dunkirk. But Wavell had no such intention; on 10 April Churchill had cabled him impatiently, "...nothing but a raid dare go past Tobruk.... We are convinced you should fight it out [there]."[1] The fortress garrison, commanded by Major General Leslie Morshead, was determined to do just that. Hidden among the perimeter's numerous sunken strongpoints and heavily concreted bunkers were the stolid warriors of 9 Australian Division and 18 Brigade of 7 Australian Division - ready to inflict a brutal and unexpected setback upon a Rommel bent on their destruction.

Rommel scheduled a "reconnaissance raid" against Tobruk for the afternoon of 13 April. Machine Gun Battalion 8 (von Ponath), would advance to the antitank ditch while the Italian Brescia Division demonstrated outside the perimeter, kicking up dust to simulate a large-scale attack in its sector. Von Ponath would then seize a bridgehead and blow in the antitank ditch, clearing a corridor for the armor that would put in the main assault the following morning.

The raid commenced at 1800 hours.[2] German and Italian artillery and the flak units of Major Hecht blanketed the perimeter strong points with support fire. Reports on the fighting filtered back slowly. Rommel learned only that von Ponath's machine gunners had breeched the defenses and seized a bridgehead.

The main assault of 5 Light Division opened early the next day.[3] The first progress reports were favorable. By daybreak Rommel had driven

[1]Winston S. Churchill, The Second World War, Vol. III: The Grand Alliance (Boston: Houghton Mifflin Co., 1950), pg. 208.
[2]By 14 April the strength of 8 Machine Gun Battalion had sunk from 1400 to 300 officers and men. Army Corps, KTB, DAK, T-314, 21, #000856.
[3]Ibid.

to the front, stopping about 100 yards from the perimeter wire; but artillery fire from the fortress compelled him to pull back. At 0900 Rommel was at DAK headquarters.

Shortly thereafter he learned that the attack had broken down; the bridgehead was too narrow. Tobruk's artillery and the heavy Matilda tanks had turned the tide. General Streich and Colonel Olbrich (commander, 5 Panzer Regiment) spelled out the bitter news. The infantry had suffered heavily, they reported, and large numbers of them were still bottled up inside the perimeter and had "probably been lost." This incensed their petulant commander. Rommel demanded that both men return to the front, to deliver another assault and relieve the trapped men.

Rommel motored to Ariete headquarters. The division, he ordered, was to move to a point south of Ras el Medauuar and support the attack of 5 Light Division. But the joint effort failed when Ariete was hit by light artillery fire. It "broke up in complete disorder, turned tail and streamed back in several directions to the south and southwest."[4] Surrender leaflets, dropped by Stukas earlier, still littered the smoking battlefield.

> "The German Officer commanding the German forces in Libya hereby requests that the British troops occupying Tobruk surrender their arms. Single soldiers waving white handkerchiefs are not fired on. Strong German forces have already surrounded Tobruk and it is useless to try and escape. Remember Mechili. Our dive-bombers and Stukas are awaiting your ships which are lying in Tobruk."

Another attempt to rescue von Ponath's doomed machine gunners took place on the night of 14-15 April. It also failed; by now, most of 8 Machine Gun Battalion was wiped out - von Ponath also lay dead. But Rommel refused to draw the obvious conclusions from his "bloody tactical biopsies" into the Tobruk defenses. "The enemy is embarking," he wrote, "so we can expect the fortress to be ours shortly." He ordered another assault for the 16th. His commanders were horrified.

15 Panzer was still unloading its vehicles in Tripoli; but Ariete was now back in the line after its disasterous attack on the 14th. Rommel informed General Baldassare, Ariete commander, that he planned to use the division's armored battalion for an evening assault on Ras el Medauuar. From this dominating height the Australians threatened Afrikakorps supply convoys around the fortress perimeter.

Baldassare's armor clattered forward at 1700 hours on 16 April. The "iron coffins," as the Germans sarcastically labeled the lightly armored Italian tanks, drove directly to the highest point of the hill. Then they suddenly stopped. Within minutes a hail of artillery fire was plowing the

---

[4]Hart, _Rommel Papers_, pp. 125-26.

ground around them. The tanks promptly retired at full throttle, stopping in a wadi (dried river bed) "confused and unwilling to resume the attack." The accompanying infantry, 62 Regiment from Trento Division, also fled in disorder. A brisk counterattack by Australian armored scout vehicles rounded up and captured two companies of them.[5] Undaunted, Rommel again hurled Ariete into the fracas the next day. But the division had already lost 90 of its 100 tanks, mostly to mechanical failure.

The few tanks that drove bravely forward soon outdistanced the following infantry and left them unsupported at the perimeter wire - another failure. The bloody losses of the past week had finally opened Rommel's eyes. He suspended operations against the fortress to await the arrival of 15 Panzer.

With a lull in the fighting, Rommel inspected the ground he had captured. He drove to Bardia in his Mammoth on 19 April and decorated von Wechmar with the Knight's Cross. In the city he discovered large quantities of war material in and around the fort, evidently abandoned by the Italians during their headlong retreat in 1940. He ordered his pioneer troops to place some of the Italian artillery pieces in workable order and headed back to Tobruk. Enroute British aircraft twice strafed Rommel's small party, destroyed his radio truck and badly wounded the driver of his Mammoth. Rommel climbed into the driver's seat and, near Tobruk, turned off the coast road and motored south to bypass the

[5]Army Corps, _KTB, DAK_, T-314, 21, #000860.

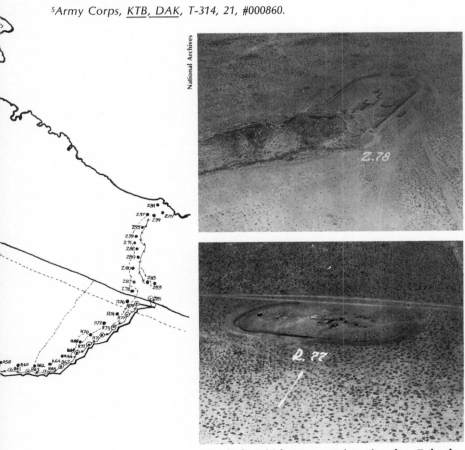

Typical British strongpoints in the Tobruk defenses. Note their position on map at left.

fortress. Navigation by the stars proved impossible on that cloudy night and Rommel had to laager in the open desert.

That same day the Italians had presented Rommel with the plans of the Tobruk defenses. But the intelligence data furnished by the Italians was extremely meager and the Italian maps "so inaccurate and incomplete that they were used only for the lack of something better."[6] It was readily apparent, however, that the Italian-built fortifications were quite formidable, and the British had effected numerous improvements of their own. Rommel faced a protracted and difficult siege.

To tighten the encirclement ring, Rommel reorganized his forces. He requested two static divisions from the Italians to relieve his motorized forces on the investment front, thus freeing them for mobile operations. He also petitioned Commando Supremo (Italian High Command) for authority to locate the Trento Division astride the Egyptian border - in Sollum and Bardia. Brescia Division would be situated east of Tobruk, to free 2 Machine Gun Battalion for mobile use.

Morshead had no intention of conducting a passive defense. He planned to harass his attackers with sudden counterthrusts and night raids. Some 1,000 yards outside the perimeter was Hill 201 (Carrier Hill). Concealed in the "dead ground" directly behind the hill were Italian infantry and artillery. Too close for comfort, Morshead reasoned. At 0640 hours on 22 April, a raiding party slipped from the fortress and moved against the Italian position. Flanking Hill 201 on either side, the Australians took the startled defenders completely by surprise.[7] A spirited charge with fixed bayonets shattered the Italian defense. The Australians rounded up 386 men (including 16 officers), as well as a battery of 20mm antitank guns.

At a conference on 23 April, attended by Gariboldi, General Mario Roatta (the Italian Chief of Staff) and Minister Signor Terruzzi, Rommel received the Italian Medal for Bravery. But the German High Command was not so enamored with their African general. They decided to dispatch General Paulus to Africa on an inspection tour. The heavy losses suffered by DAK before Tobruk had caused consternation at Hitler's headquarters; in Halder's view, Paulus, an old friend of Rommel's, was "the only man with sufficient personal influence to head off this soldier gone stark mad."[8]

---

[6]Alfred Toppe, "German Experiences in World War II: Desert Warfare," MS P-129, pg. 1. Hereafter cited as "Desert Warfare," P-129. To remedy the poor situation regarding maps and intelligence, OKH dispatched a number of map reproduction units (Korps and Division Kartenstelle) and military geographical units (Wehrgeologenstelle) to Africa. "The military geographical units attached to Afrikakorps commenced a systematic assembly of data and methodological reconnoitering immediately after arrival. Each unit included two geologists and ten auxillaries."

[7]Barton Maughan, Tobruk and El Alamein (Canberra: Australian War Memorial, 1966), pg. 175.

[8]Halder, Kriegstagebuch, II, 377-78.

Rommel is awarded the Italian
Medal for Bravery at the April
23 conference.

Paulus arrived at Rommel's headquarters on 27 April. That same day, advanced elements of DAK reached the Sidi Omar Line, which they occupied along with Halfaya (Hellfire) Pass. For several days Paulus inspected the front and found the living conditions of the troops "inhuman and intolerable." He learned from his guide, Captain Schmidt, that provisioning of front line units was possible only at night; by day, the men crouched uncomfortably in their shallow trenches, any movement drawing a hail of gun fire. The heat was unbearable; the rations scarcely palatable - sardines in oil, canned sausage *(Bierwurst)* and diminutive round tins of tough Italian beef which were stamped "A.M." The troops supposed this stood for *"Alter Mann"* (Old Man) or, perhaps, "Asinus Mussolini." Potatoes and at first, bread, were not shipped to North Africa. Bread, the Germans thought, would go moldy in shipment;[9] potatoes would spoil in the intense African heat. Thus, legumes (peas) and *Zwieback* were substituted. It never occurred to the responsible authorities that canning would preserve the potatoes. The Italians supplied some foodstuffs, most noticeably coffee beans, grated cheese, cooking oil and marmalade. Thus Afrikakorps troops received sufficient carbohydrates and some protein, but fresh fruits and vegetables were noticeably lacking.[10] To balance their deficient diet the Germans depended upon captured British stocks.

Planning for a renewed assault on Tobruk progressed feverishly. "Am very busy," Rommel wrote his wife, "since the battle for Tobruk will begin tonight. Paulus will remain here to watch the events. Otherwise everything fine. We have high hopes. The enemy has become remarkably quiet although we have put the heat on him."[11] Paulus had consented to a resumption of the attack, to take place on 30 April, but had warned Rommel "not to weaken the Sollum position which protected his flank toward Egypt, but to leave Group Herff - 115 Rifle Regiment from 15 Panzer - to stiffen the Italians there."[12]

The Stuka squadrons of General Stefan Froelich *(Luftwaffe* Commander Africa) swooped over the fortress at 1830 hours to open the attack.[13] DAK artillery smashed the break-in points with well-aimed fire. The defenders fought back savagely, but the German assault parties quickly penetrated the defenses to a depth of two miles north and south of Ras el Medauuar. Rommel now possessed a three and one-half mile arc of the fortress perimeter, from post S-7 to R-7. At 2130 hours Major

---

[9]By mid-March 1941, however, Bakery Company 531 had begun operations and fresh bread was then available.

[10]Roger James Bender and Richard D. Law, <u>Uniforms, Organization and History of the Afrikakorps</u> (Mountain View, Ca.: R. James Bender Publishing, 1973), pp. 23-24. See also Burdick, <u>Sonnenblume</u>, pp. 121-22.

[11]Rommel Collection, T-84, 274, #000134. It is obvious that Rommel resented the General Staff "looking over his shoulder," even if it was through his friend Paulus.

[12]J.A.I. Agar-Hamilton and L.C.F. Turner, <u>The Sidi Rezeg Battles 1941</u> (Capetown: Oxford University Press, 1957), pg. 30. Hereafter cited as <u>Sidi Rezeg Battles</u>.

[13]Army Corps, <u>KTB, DAK</u>, T-314, 21, #000877.

Voigtsberger's 2 Machine Gun Battalion stormed and captured Ras el Medauuar from the rear.[14] Rommel ordered Ariete up to its jump-off position, from where it would advance to exploit the breech. He drove to Lieutenant General Heinrich Kircheim's headquarters. Dissatisfied with Streich, Rommel had placed Kircheim, a tropical warfare specialist, in command of the assault.

Heinrich Kircheim

Rommel soon discovered that Ariete had been slow in moving forward. And when artillery fire dropped among the division, the distressed Italians crept under their vehicles and refused to go forward. Without support from Ariete Rommel had to settle for the modest gains made by Kircheim's group. Australian counterattacks on 2 and 3 May were easily repulsed. Rommel's frustration is evident in a letter to his wife dated 3 May: "Bitter fighting is taking place at the moment. I hope our men will hold their positions. It's terrible to be obliged to sit so far back behind the front and not be able to help effectively. I hope to receive reinforcements in the next few days and then I'm sure I can do it.[15]

But in a month of severe combat, Afrikakorps had incurred prohibitive losses; Rommel slowly confronted the fact that the Tobruk

[14]*Ibid.*, #000878.
[15]*Rommel Collection*, T-84, 274, #000134.

battle had entered a new and foreboding phase. "The fighting around Tobruk," he wrote home on 10 May, "has turned into positional warfare of a very tenacious kind. Heavy naval fire at night. Yesterday we repulsed successfully an attempt to relief of the garrison and attacks on Bardia and Sollum. But we have grave supply problems."[16]

Rommel's logistical headaches were severe indeed. From naval and air bases on the island of Malta, the British harried the Italian convoys as they moved through the Mediterranean - laden with thousands of tons of precious war material for the Axis forces. As the sinkings of Italian merchant vessels increased, Rommel smelled a rat; he had a simple explanation for his mounting supply crisis: Italian treachery. Today, the real reason for his problems is clear. Ultra intercepts provided the British with accurate data regarding the routes and schedules of Axis shipping.[17]

---

[16]Ibid., #000149. See also Maughan, Tobruk and El Alamein, pg. 269, for an account of the Axis forces surrounding Tobruk; those forces included:

Brescia Division	Derna Road Sector
16 Italian Artillery Regiment	north of salient
II./104 Infantry Regiment	Salient Sector
I./115 Infantry Regiment	(from right to left)
II./115 Infantry Regiment	
2 Oase Companies	
2 Machine Gun Battalion	
2 German Artillery Battalion	
16 Italian Artillery Regiment (3 batteries)	
3 Pioneer Battalion	
900 Pioneer Battalion	
Ariete Division (to be relieved by Pavia Division	Pilastrino
132 Infantry Regiment	and El Adem Roads -
46 Artillery Regiment	east of Salient
Trento Division	Bardia Road Sector

[17]Charles B. Burdick, "The Ultra Question," San Jose State University, San Jose, Ca. Because of the overriding importance of Ultra, the authors quote Professor Burdick in some detail:

"In Africa the total use of radio was required for communication. Ultra was an avid listener. The British seldom missed a detail. Certainly no leader in WWII had more reason to complain about the tricks fate played on him by Ultra than Erwin Rommel. No other military commander over so prolonged a period was affected so outrageously by the ability of his opponents to look into his cards. His troubles were compounded by his isolation and requirement to communicate at length on situations about which it was not easy to gain understanding in Berlin. He was under constant pressure to employ exceptional frankness, to lay clear his chief anxieties and vulnerabilities, to describe his needs in fulsome detail for his superiors. Many of his detailed reports reached their destination at about the same time they reached his opposing commander's desk.

"Equally as serious as these specific, enduring blows to his position was the systematic strangulation of his supply services. There was really no purpose, for example, whether his tankers sailed from Naples, Taranto or Piraeus. The British knew their schedules and travel routes. They could send a lone submarine or aircraft to a precise

Paulus flew back to Berlin on 6 May, but not before he personally called off the attack on the fortress, leaving strict orders "that for the time being Rommel was to remain on the defensive and at all costs to hold onto Cyrenaica."[18] Earlier, Paulus had signaled his observations back to Berlin: no more troops should be sent to Africa until conditions there improved; Rommel was short of ammunition, fuel, vehicles and food. British listening posts intercepted Paulus' coded message; Ultra deciphered it. By 7 or 8 May the complete text was in Wavell's hands.[19]

Halder, too, had examined Paulus' report. He was not pleased. "The situation in North Africa," he jotted down in his diary, "is unpleasant. Ro [Rommel] by exceeding his orders, has created a situation with which present lines of communication can no longer cope. Ro is not up to that job."[20] Paulus himself professed wonderment over the vast horde of war correspondents and press photographers who seemed to surround Rommel at all times.[21] Thus on 13 May 1941, Halder approached von Brauchitsch with a plan to "manage Rommel through a German Chief of Staff to be posted to Italian headquarters in North Africa."[22] General Gariboldi, "surprised and irritated" by Halder's proposal, required careful persuasion before he would accept this further German encroachment upon his authority.

In the desert so much depends on the armored balance. The opponent with the better tanks, and more of them has a distinct advantage. Churchill, as he brooded over his strategic dilemmas in April of 1941, was fully aware of the dominant role of armor in desert warfare; he was also acutely cognizant, through his precious "Golden Eggs" (as he called the Ultra intercepts), of the Afrikakorps' present difficulties. But the tanks of 15 Panzer would soon be in Africa, adding much needed firepower to Rommel's depleted ranks. Churchill made a brave decision. He would send a convoy of five merchant ships, with 295 tanks,

---

point. There was no wasted searches, no costly expenditures of men, machines or time; no embarrassing failures. Only chance or other occupations allowed the arrival of a few ships.

"Rommel's victories came from his personal initiative, ability to create something out of nothing, willful disregard of orders, purposeful understatement of his resources, and the dissonance in the British command structure. From his arrival until his departure, the British knew virtually every aspect of the Afrikakorps' resources, plans, strengths, etc. Ultra clearly provided the decisive ingredient of British, and subsequently, Allied victory. From this success came the Allied landings in Italy and Sicily, the fall of Mussolini, and much else that counts among the nails in Hitler's coffin."

[18]Walter Goerlitz, Paulus and Stalingrad (New York: The Citadel Press, 1963), pg. 30. Hereafter cited as Paulus.

[19]Lewin, Ultra, pg. 163.

[20]Halder, Kriegstagebuch, II, 407.

[21]Goerlitz, Paulus, pg. 31.

[22]Agar-Hamilton, Sidi Rezeg Battles, pg. 17. Despite the problems with his own High Command, Rommel received another award from the Italians on May 12. Rommel mentioned this to Lucie in his letter the same day: "The awarding of the Italian House Order, the Commander's Cross of the Crown of Savoya turned out to be a very solemn ceremony."

directly through the Mediterranean to Alexandria - eschewing the much safer, and much slower route around the Cape of Good Hope. Wavell, strongly reinforced, could use his crushing armored superiority to sweep Rommel from the desert. A bold plan! The convoy, code named "Tiger," steamed past Gibraltar on 6 May.

But Churchill's "tiger cubs" would not arrive for a week; once in Africa, several weeks would be needed to condition them for desert warfare. Wavell decided to launch a preliminary stroke "to drive the enemy from Sollum and Capuzzo [and to] inflict as much loss as possible and exploit success towards Tobruk."[23]

At dawn, 15 May, the British began Operation Brevity, their first offensive against the Afrikakorps. The 55 tanks of 7 Armored Division and 22 Guards Brigade, commanded by General W.H.E. Gott, moved forward against Rommel's Sollum front. The defenders, under Colonel von Herff, resisted valiantly, but were driven from the Halfaya Pass.[24] "The Halfaya and Sollum Passes," writes Rommel, "were points of great strategic significance for they were the only two places between the coast and Habata where it was possible to cross the escarpment - of anything up to 600 feet in height - which stretched away from Sollum in a southeasterly direction toward Egypt. The Halfaya positions gave an equal command over both possible roads. In any offensive from Egypt, therefore, possession of these passes was bound to be of utmost value to the enemy."[25] Early the next day von Herff struck back; by evening he had recaptured all the lost ground except for the pass.[26]

Maximilian von Herff

[23]C.B. Playfair, _The Mediterranean and Middle East_, Vol. II: The Germans Come to the Aid of Their Ally (London: Her Majesty's Stationery Office, 1956), pg. 159. Hereafter cited as _The Germans Come to the Aid._
[24]Army Corps, _KTB, DAK_, T-314, 21, #000899.
[25]Hart, _Rommel Papers_, pp. 136-37.
[26]Army Corps, _KTB, DAK_, T-314, 21, #000907.

The British, meanwhile, had swept across the frontier wire and overrun Fort Capuzzo; but a spirited counterattack by II./5 Panzer Regiment recaptured the stone fort and part of the Durham Light Infantry. The British now pulled back 7 Armored Brigade, its left flank uncovered by the loss of Capuzzo. "Disconcerted by the fact that the Germans had shown greater strength than had been expected, the British command decided to withdraw the whole force, leaving a garrison at the Halfaya Pass."[27] Thus ended the appropriately named Operation Brevity.

Despite its victorious outcome, the battle had shaken Rommel. During its course he had sent a series of nervous signals at regular intervals to Berlin. On 25 May von Brauchitsch warned the General to show more restraint in his messages, and to avoid reporting too optimistically or pessimistically under the immediate influence of events. Rommel wrote his wife the next day and mentioned a "considerable rocket" from von Brauchitsch; yet he failed to comprehend the reason for it. From now on, however, he would "keep his mouth shut" and forward future reports in the "briefest form."

Wilhelm
"Papa" Bach

On the evening of 26 May, Rommel ordered three assault groups to occupy positions in front of Halfaya Pass. The next morning von Herff, supported by 8 Panzer Regiment, stormed the pass and dislodged the startled defenders.[28] The British fled eastwards, abandoning considerable quantities of equipment. Major Wilhelm "Papa" Bach, a former pastor, took over the defense of the pass. His command, I./104 Infantry Regiment, constructed skillful positions, buttressed by a handful of precious 88mm flak guns sited in firing pits that all but concealed them from view.

---

[27]Hart, _Rommel Papers_, pg. 136.
[28]Army Corps, _KTB, DAK_, T-314, 21, #000919.

At the end of May, Lieutenant General Alfred Gause and his staff arrived in Africa. OKH planned to attach Gause to the Italian High Command as a second Chief of Staff; under no circumstances was he to place himself under Rommel's direct command. But the pliant Gause - the man Halder had picked to pull the reins in on Rommel - did just that. During the Sollum fighting - which would begin on 15 June - Gause "marveled at Rommel's grasp of the battle, decided the Afrikakorps' commander could 'cope' very well and promptly placed his entire and impressive staff at Rommel's disposal."[29]

Dissatisfied with General Streich's performance at Tobruk, Rommel now relieved his outspoken subordinate from his command and packed him off to Germany. Streich, Rommel rather unfairly contended, had withdrawn his forces prematurely from the 14 April attack, leaving the infantry within the perimeter "in the lurch." Streich's successor was Major General Johann von Ravenstein. In early June the tanks of Colonel Walter Neumann-Silkow's 15 Panzer Division reached the front.

Leon Chacona

Johannes von Ravenstein

Walter
Neumann-Silkow

As summer approached temperatures climbed to well over 100⁰ in the African wastes; tank crews complained of temperatures inside their vehicles of 160⁰. But even in this stifling heat the war continued; signs of an imminent British offensive began to appear on the Sollum front. In anticipation of Wavell's thrust, Rommel moved his headquarters to Bardia, settling into a "slightly damaged house just below the village church - a building no doubt known to thousands of South African, Australian and British troops."[30] Here Rommel experienced an assassination attempt undertaken by British raiders. As he, Schmidt and Alfred Berndt (Rommel's diarist) inspected the Bardia defenses, they came under well-aimed fire from isolated snipers. A nervous half-hour followed. A subsequent search turned up nothing. "I must be worth quite a lot to the Englishmen," Rommel joked later.

On 14 June at 2100 hours, Rommel placed the Sollum front on alert; the 5 Light Division in reserve south of Tobruk, was soon moving up to cover the Afrikakorps' right flank. Rommel, tipped off by wireless intercepts, anticipated a major British offensive.

Churchill's Tiger Convoy had docked in Alexandria on 12 May. Only one ship, the *Empire Song,* with 57 tanks and 10 aircraft, had sunk - the victim of a mine; 238 tanks, including 135 Matildas and 82 of the new Mark II Cruisers were unloaded.[31]

On 15 June (0400 hours) Wavell's Tiger cubs smashed forward. Churchill's long-awaited "Operation Battleaxe" had begun. The British, under the local command of General Beresford-Peirse, advanced on four fronts. On the far left the Support Group of 7 Armored Division formed a screen towards Sidi Omar to protect the southern flank. In the center, "7 Armored Divison, 7 Armored Brigade and 'Jaxo' (Jock) Column from the Support Group were to advance by bounds to Hafid Ridge and beyond."[32] 4 Armored Brigade and 22 Guards Brigade were to sweep south of the Halfaya Pass and then wheel to the north on Capuzzo. On the coast - along the escarpment - 4 Indian Division had the task of conquering Halfaya Pass and destroying the enemy in the Sollum-Bardia area. In this manner, with most of his armor sweeping round the southern flank, Wavell hoped to envelop and destroy the Afrikakorps.

4 Indian Division attacked without artillery support, "which had become bogged in sand on the approach march."[33] The division's heavy Matilda's rolled ponderously forward towards the pass. To the German defenders, crouching breathlessly behind their antitank guns, the approaching tanks looked like tiny black boxes, enveloped by swirling sand and dust. The tanks were now almost on top of Bach's men. The

[29]Irving, *The Trail*, pg. 108.
[30]Schmidt, *With Rommel*, pg. 66.
[31]Paul Carell, *Die Wüstenfuchse* (Hamburg: Henri Nannen Verlag, 1958), pg. 38.
[32]Playfair, *The Germans Come to the Aid*, pg. 165.
[33]Maughan, *Tobruk and El Alamein*, pg. 281.

88's answered: 11 of the 12 Matildas exploded in flames. Below the pass, a well-laid minefield claimed four of six tanks that stumbled into it.

British armor moved against Capuzzo at 0900 hours. Rommel ordered 15 Panzer not to commit its tanks - the situation was still unclear. But by late afternoon 22 Guards Brigade had captured the crumbling fort and wheeled towards Sollum.[34] 8 Panzer Regiment (15 Panzer Division) now moved forward and collided with the advancing enemy armor. A violent battle ensued. Pillars of black smoke curled upwards and darkened the sky - each signifying a brewing tank.

On the southern flank, at Hafid Ridge, the British made little progress. The Germans had entrenched behind a series of low ridges; a morning mist helped to conceal their exact location from the advancing enemy armor. 7 Armored Brigade made three assaults, supported by a troop of 25 pounder guns. One attack overran a section of the German lines, but the remainder held tenaciously. A battalion from 5 Panzer Regiment reinforced the defenders and the British suffered accordingly. By nightfall 7 Armored Brigade was reduced to 48 runners.

Afrikakorps' positions had held. Rommel planned a bold counterthrust. He would send 5 Light Division on a wide sweep to the south. Von Ravenstein would then wheel north, push through to Halfaya Pass and cut the British lines of communication.[35] Simultaneously, Neumann-Silkow's 15 Panzer was to race southwards from Fort Capuzzo, cross the frontier line and hit Wavell's exposed southern flank. Of this maneuver Rommel writes, "I planned to concentrate both armored divisions suddenly into one focus and thus deal the enemy an unexpected blow in his most sensitive spot."[36]

Rommel rose early on the 16th; he had been unable to sleep. 15 Panzer lumbered forward and crashed into 4 Armored Brigade which was supported by a regiment of British artillery. The attack made little headway; by 1030 hours Neumann-Silkow had broken off the engagement. He was reduced to 35 runners, having started the day with 80.[37] 5 Light Division was also stalled - by the remaining tanks of 7 Armored Brigade. The two forces had clashed near Hafid Ridge. The ensuing firefight "moved away from the Hafid area and zig-zagged down the frontier towards Sidi Omar."[38]

The battle had reached its critical point. 15 Panzer commander "seriously considered pulling out what was left of [his division] in a fighting withdrawal to bar the road to Tobruk. He decided, however, to keep the struggle open and to rally his mobile troops, including the 88's for a final drive to find and link up with 5 Light Division.[39] According to

---

[34]Army Corps, _KTB, DAK_, T-314, 21, #000937.
[35]Ibid., #000940-000941.
[36]Hart, _Rommel Papers_, pg. 144.
[37]Army Corps, _KTB, DAK_, T-314, 21, #000941.
[38]Playfair, _The Germans Come to the Aid_, pg. 169.
[39]Agar-Hamilton, _Sidi Rezeg Battles_, pg. 13.

Rommel, "this was the turning point of the battle." He immediately ordered 15 Panzer to move forward on the northern flank of 5 Light Division towards Sidi Suleiman, leaving only a light screen to hold the position north of Capuzzo. Advancing on parallel routes, Rommel's armored divisions would then wheel northwards, strike for the coast at Halfaya and bottle up a sizeable portion of Wavell's army.[40]

Von Ravenstein's 5 Light Division moved out of its night laager early on the 17th. By 0600 it had reached Sidi Suleiman after a "headlong advance."[41] Rommel sensed victory within his grasp. Wireless intercepts revealed the confusion and panic that had gripped his adversary. The British were short of fuel and ammunition; they pleaded urgently "for the presence of the commander of the desert force."[42] An ominous turgid ball of dust rolled northwards - 5 Light and 15 Panzer. By 1600, 5 Panzer Regiment had reached Halfaya Pass, lifting the siege on Bach's indominable grenadiers.[43] But in a maneuver that left Rommel exasperated, the two armored divisions then turned and advanced side by side to the north. "This was a very unfortunate move," writes Rommel, "as its result was to squeeze out the pocket instead of closing it and preventing the enemy's escape."[44] He was furious. He was also mistaken, for the main British striking force had already withdrawn to the south, escaping the Afrikakorps' pincers.

But Rommel had won a great triumph. The battle displayed the Afrikakorps' qualitative superiority over its opponent, its superior tactical training. Rommel forced the British to commit their armor prematurely. Wavell's tanks had raced bravely forward, to be smashed by cunningly-laid lines of 88's and antitank guns. Only when the British had exhausted their armor did Rommel commit his own. The three-day battle cost the British 122 dead, 588 wounded and 259 missing. Rommel claimed to have destroyed over 220 enemy tanks; Afrikakorps had lost just 12.[45] Many more had been disabled during the battle, but Rommel's excellent tank recovery and repair units had salvaged them from the battlefield.

After Battleaxe a welcome calm descended over the desert; but, for the thousands of men who fought in the African theatre, the battle with their environment never ceased. In Africa one's thirst and hunger could be conquered, at least momentarily - but the heat! In the frantic staff planning that preceded *Sonnenblume*, it had not proven possible to properly acclimatize the German soldiers destined for Africa to the continent's searing temperatures. The men had all received special medical examinations to determine their fitness for the tropics; they

[40]Army Corps, KTB, DAK, T-314, 21, #000942. See also Hart, Rommel Papers, pg. 144.
[41]Army Corps, KTB, DAK, T-314, 21, #000946.
[42]Agar-Hamilton, Sidi Rezeg Battles, pg. 13.
[43]Army Corps, KTB, DAK, T-314, 21, #000949.
[44]Hart, Rommel Papers, pg. 145.
[45]Army Corps, KTB, DAK, T-314, 21, #000953.

also attended lectures by specialists in tropical medicine. Little was done beyond that. The scanty information the men received, however, "gave the troops wrong impressions of what they were to expect from the effects of heat, sand, insects and diseases instead of orienting them properly."[46]

But yet, how could a northern European prepare himself for the armies of voracious sand fleas? These tiny creatures - so small one could hardly see them - would bore into the skin and suck blood until they were as round as balls. A man with a good antitank gun could humble a steel monster weighing twenty tons - but against a tiny sand flea he was helpless. More than one Afrikakorps soldier was driven to madness by the ubiquitous, blood-sucking creatures.

National Archives

During a lull in the fighting, German gun crews test fire both Allied and Italian weapons.

Rommel spent the latter half of June reorganizing his command and initiating an intensive tactical training program. He knew only too well that substantial reinforcements were now an impossibility, for Hitler had plunged the *Wehrmacht* into Russia on 22 June 1941. Italian engineers, meanwhile, worked frantically to build a 47 mile long bypass road around the Tobruk fortress. The *"Achsenstrasse"* (Axis Road), as it was called, would secure Afrikakorps supply convoys from Tobruk's powerful fortress guns. It was not completed until 8 August.

The Afrikakorps' victorious commander was riding a crest of popularity home in Germany. He had humbled a worthy opponent twice in two months. His reputation was "sky high." Many of Rommel's former officers, however, did not share this sudden infatuation. The OKH file's

[46]Toppe, "_Desert Warfare_," P-129, pp. 6, 9.

bulged with nasty letters from men who had found Rommel a bitter pill; Streich, Kircheim, Olbrich, Rommel's former chief-of-staff von dem Borne, as well as von Schwerin and von Herff - they all had complained about Rommel's command techniques. But no amount of criticism, however well-founded, could dim the glow of Rommel's rising star. On 1 July Hitler, despite vehement protestations from Halder, promoted Rommel to full general. Rommel was only 49. It had been a meteoric climb. Six weeks later (15 August), with the firm backing of General Ugo Cavallero (Chief of Staff, Commando Supremo), Panzergruppe Afrika was formally established - again over Halder's protests. General Gause and his "mission" provided the headquarters staff for the new Panzer group. This arrangement unified the Afrikakorps and Lieutenant General Enea Navarrini's 21 Corps under Rommel's personal command; it institutionalized his growing authority over his Italian allies:

**North Africa Command
(Marshal Ettore Bastico)**

Panzergruppe Afrika
(General of Panzer Troops Rommel)

20 Italian Armored Corps
(General Gambara)
Ariete
Trieste

Afrikakorps
(General Cruwell)
15 Panzer (Neumann-Silkow)
21 Panzer (von Ravenstein)[47]
Afrika Division for Special Services (Sümmermann)[48]
Savona

Italian 21 Corps
(General E. Navarrini)
Trento
Bologna
Brescia
Pavia

---

[47]Reinforced with armor, Rommel had reorganized 5 Light Division into a full Panzer division.

[48]Africa Division for Special Services (zur besonderen Verfügung) was formed from various units already in Africa and from troops dispatched by air transport.

Crusader - The Winter Battle.

Men and supplies were now reaching Rommel in increased numbers. A new division arrived, the Afrika Division for Special Services (the future 90 Light Division) commanded by General Max Sümmermann. But the reinforcements were hardly adequate to meet the Panzergruppe's growing needs. By the end of September it had received only a third of the troops and a seventh of the supplies which were needed.[1] OKW refused to make a major commitment in the African theatre; nothing was done to eliminate the threat to Axis shipping posed by the British island base of Malta. Between July and November 48 Axis ships would be sunk: 200,000 tons of precious war material sent to the bottom of the Mediterranean. On 9 November, in fact, a hastily assembled British surface striking force (Force K - the cruisers *Aurora* and *Penelope* and the destroyers *Lance* and *Lively)* would annihilate the Duisburg convoy (seven merchant vessels of 40,000 tons). Rommel's Panzergruppe hung by a slender logistical thread.

That summer new additions to Rommel's staff reached Africa, "the big names who were to dominate [his] career."[2] The Panzergruppe's new operations officer was a 39 year old Lieutenant Colonel - the brilliant, independent-thinking Siegfried Westphal. In October the Afrikakorps received a new chief-of-staff, Fritz Bayerlein. The 42 year old colonel had served in France and Russia as Guderian's chief operations officer. Major Friedrich Wilhelm von Mellenthin, who had earlier arrived to serve as Rommel's chief intelligence officer, offers an insightful impression of his new commander:

> Rommel was not an easy man to serve; he spared those around him as little as he spared himself. An iron constitution and nerves of steel were needed to work with Rommel, but I must emphasize that although Rommel was sometimes embarrassingly outspoken with senior commanders, yet once he was convinced of the efficiency and loyalty of those in his immediate entourage, he never had a harsh word for them.[3]

---

[1]Fritz Bayerlein's "*The Winter Campaign, 1941-1942,*" in Hart, *Rommel Papers,* pg. 155.

[2]Irving, *The Trail,* pg. 117.

[3]F. W. von Mellenthin, *Panzer Battles*: A Study of the Employment of Armor in the Second World War (New York: Ballantine Books; Oklahoma: University of Oklahoma Press, 1956), pg. 54. Hereafter cited as *Panzer Battles*.

Siegfried
Westphal

J.R. Angolia

Fritz
Bayerlein

As Hitler's other Panzer leaders were smashing eastwards, along the sandy paths of central Russia and the Ukraine, Rommel's attention was riveted on Tobruk. He was preparing a great set-piece battle, to blast the stubborn fortress into submission. But it was now September, and his men had been idle for months. To boost morale and hone their fighting qualities, Rommel planned a limited operation - code name *"Unternehmen Sommernachtstraum"* (Midsummer Night's Dream).

The target of the operation was the British supply dump located at Bir Khireigat some 15 miles beyond the frontier wire. After the successes of the preceding months, Rommel's troops had acquired an appetite for British rations and uniforms;[4] the supply services were increasingly dependent upon captured enemy vehicles. But there was another important reason behind Midsummer Night's Dream: "The operation was undertaken to clarify the situation before the attack on Tobruk and to

---

[4]*The Afrikakorps olive-green tropical uniforms were designed by specialists at the Tropical Institute in Hamburg. They had proven unsatisfactory, however; the British and Italian uniforms afforded much greater comfort.*   **91**

capture British orders which might give information on the enemy's order of battle."[5]

21 Panzer Division (the newly reorganized 5 Light) moved from its assembly areas and headed southeast on 14 September.[6] The division consisted of two *Kampfgruppen* (battlegroups) - Stephan and Schütte. *Kampfgruppe* Schütte was to steal the loot while Stephan fended off any unwelcomed guests. To mask the operation 3 Reconnaissance Battalion raced along the frontier raising clouds of dust and transmitting bogus wireless chatter.

Von Ravenstein's tanks bolted forward with Rommel at the helm. But the sweeping maneuvers of the German columns netted nothing. The British (7 Support Group under Brigadier "Jock" Campbell), possibly forewarned by Ultra intercepts, simply stepped back from the frontier, leaving a frustrated and confounded Rommel in the lurch. The only scrap of encouraging news was that earlier in the day, "the orderly room vehicle of 4 South African Armored Cars broke down and fell into German hands, with important documents and cipher material undestroyed."[7]

The circus-like pursuit came to a sudden halt when 21 Panzer ran out of fuel. To add insult to injury, two squadrons of South Africa Air Force bombers suddenly pounced on the immobilized tank columns.[8] "Two trucks laden with gasoline blew up at once; the Panzer regiment had six men killed and a flak gunner died, too. Rommel's Mammoth was hit, his boot heel was blown off by a bomb blast and his driver badly injured. It was a thoroughly unsettling experience. He ordered the pursuit abandoned, and the whole force beat an undignified retreat back into Libya.... [The captured documents], - together with the emptiness of the desert he had just invaded - led Rommel to a fateful conclusion: that the enemy was not currently planning any offensive against him. There is evidence that the British had arranged to have Rommel capture these documents."[9]

Having survived a "dream" that ended in a nightmare, Rommel turned his thinking back to Tobruk. As his Panzergruppe grew in strength, his interest in the fortress became an obsession. His timetable demanded its fall by late October or November. Rommel's ambitions were "vast and precise." With adequate reinforcements, he calculated, he could "rebuff a British attack during the winter, reach the Canal in the spring, and then drive for Iraq with the objective of seizing Basra and severing the supply route to Russia."[10] But Rommel evoked little sym-

[5]As quoted in Agar-Hamilton, *Sidi Rezegh Battles*, pg. 25.

[6]Army Corps, *KTB, DAK*, T-314, 21, #001038. Kampfgruppe Stephan got underway at 0300. Its start was hindered by darkness and dust.

[7]Agar-Hamilton, *Sidi Rezegh Battles*, pg. 27.

[8]Army Corps, *KTB, DAK*, T-314, 21 #001043.

[9]Irving, *The Trail*, pg. 121.

[10]Ronald Lewin, *Rommel as a Military Commander* (London: B.T. Batsford Ltd., 1968), pg. 50. Hereafter cited as *Rommel*.

pathy from higher circles. Halder hated the man. "Rommel cannot cope," he had written in his diary. And besides, the war in Russia had taken a nasty turn; its limitless demands were proving a bottomless pit, leaving little for Africa. Rommel recognized his dilemma. The African theatre was a "stepchild" - he would have to make do with what he had.

General Sir Claude Auchinleck, the new British theatre commander in the Middle East, had no such problems. North Africa was Churchill's own private obsession; the Cruisers and Matildas that lumbered to and fro across its limitless expanse were the Empire's first line of defense. Thus Auchinleck received an unbroken stream of war material to fill the formations of his Eighth Army - as the Western Desert Force was now known. According to the *British Official History,* by the end of October, 300 cruisers, 300 Stuarts, 170 'I' tanks, 34,000 lorries, 600 field guns, 80 heavy and 160 light A.A. guns, 200 antitank guns and 900 mortars had arrived.[11]

The British were stockpiling for a massive offensive. Eighth Army, now led by the chain-smoking General Sir Alan Cunningham, planned to suck Rommel's armor into a grinding tank battle, destroy it and then smash a corridor through to the Tobruk garrison, which would undertake a synchronized break-out attempt. In detail, 30 Corps, (General Willoughby Norrie, the armored counterpart of Afrikakorps, would thrust across the frontier between Maddalena and Sidi Omar to a position 30 miles west at Gabr Saleh. Here it would stop and wait for the certain German armor challenge. To the right of 30 Corps, General Godwin-Austen's 13 Corps "would outflank and contain the enemy's frontier posts."[12] Only after the destruction of Rommel's armor was the Tobruk garrison, commanded by General Scobie,[13] to make its break-out attempt. The offensive, code named Crusader, would begin on 18 November.

On 26 October Rommel issued orders for the attack on Tobruk, to take place between 15-20 November. This "concentration of his mind on Tobruk temporarily warped Rommel's judgment";[14] he ignored the proliferating mass of evidence that pointed to an imminent British offensive. When *Luftwaffe* photographs revealed the extention of the British railhead westward from Matruh, a certain sign of offensive preparation, Rommel discarded them in disgust.

In early November Rommel and von Ravenstein flew to Rome, to discuss supplies and dispute Jodl's order to "leave Tobruk alone and get ready to meet Auchinleck's attack."[15] After a stormy session with von

---

[11]*Ibid.,* pg. 59.

[12]*Ibid,* pg. 60.

[13]*Upon the urgent requests of the Prime Minister of Australia, Mr. Fadden, 9 Australian Division was relieved from Tobruk by the British 70 Division.*

[14]Lewin, *Rommel,* pg. 57.

[15]Young, *Desert Fox,* pg. 82. "A British soldier in a hospital in Jerusalem told his nursing sister, a German agent, that the British were soon to launch a big attack upon Rommel." The news was signaled to OKW and Hitler.

While in Rome, on 15 November, Rommel is presented with a silver framed portrait of Hitler by General von Rintelen.

At a reception shortly after the presentation of the Hitler portrait.

After the official 14 November conference, Rommel and von Ravenstein stayed over for Rommel's birthday which was the next day. In Rome they were joined by Frau Rommel (above) and Countess von Ravenstein, then they took in the sights.

Rintelen, Rommel telephoned Jodl at OKW to complain: "I hear you wish me to give up the attack on Tobruk. I am completely disgusted." He assured the OKW operations chief that 21 Panzer could contain any British offensive. Jodl relented. On 15 November Frau Rommel met her husband in Rome where, with the von Ravenstein's, they celebrated his fiftieth birthday.

That same evening 21 Panzer moved south of the Trigh Capuzzo, in adherence to Rommel's guarantee to Jodl. 3 and 33 Reconnaissance Battalions, combined into one group under von Wechmar, probed across the Egyptian border to check for possible enemy activity. Along the frontier the hollow thud of exploding mines mingled with the cracking thunder of an approaching storm front - British sappers were blowing corridors through the German minefields.

Crusader was preceded by one of the most extraordinary actions of the war. On the night of 15 November two British submarines (Torbay and Talisman) slipped quietly into a small inlet on the Cyrenaica coast. British commandos of the Long Range Desert Group scrambled from the subs into small rubber boats. It was no easy operation. Choppy seas tossed the men about and repeatedly capsized the boats; at least two men drowned. The rest - some two dozen men - managed to reach the beach and work their way inland.

On the stormy night of 17 November they stood in a sand dune, close to Beda Littoria; two hundred miles behind the battlefront. In front of them lay the two-story Prefettura building, nestled in a cypress grove. There was the headquarters of Rommel's Panzergruppe Afrika; and there Rommel himself slept or worked. Or so they thought.

Shortly past midnight the commandos, led by Major Geoffrey Keyes, stormed the building in an attempt to kill Rommel and eliminate the nerve-center of the German command just hours prior to the start of Crusader. In the ensuing melee several men were killed, including Keyes, but Rommel was nowhere to be found.

Only later did the British discover their error. Several months earlier Rommel had established his headquarters at Beda Littoria, but he had soon left his lush surroundings for more austere quarters closer to the front - at Ain Gazala. The Prefettura building housed only Rommel's Quartermaster's staff. Keyes was awarded the Victoria Cross for his gallantry and buried by Rommel with full military honors. But when Rommel returned from Rome on 18 November he was confronted by difficulties far greater than another bungled assassination attempt - Crusader had begun.

For the sun-baked warriors of the Libyan desert, the morning of 18 November 1941 brought events which would not be soon forgotten. The first, the most obvious, was the rain - "the most spectacular thunderstorm within local memory." Air fields turned to quagmires, wadies were flooded and telephone lines ripped down. The other event, more historically memorable, was that "after seventeen months of war in the desert, the Allied forces were about to carry out their biggest offensive ... but indeed, the greatest to date by the British Commonwealth since the war started."[16]

First contact with the British onslaught came at 1030 hours when von Wechmar reported a reconnaissance in force in his sector. Considerable armored forces, he later reported to DAK headquarters, were moving up from the southwest - some 200 tanks. General Ludwig Crüwell, the Afrikakorps commander, repeatedly warned Panzergruppe that the British movements heralded a "serious attack." He decided to act on von Ravenstein's proposal to send a tank force to Gabr Saleh to check the British "demonstration."

When Rommel met Crüwell at Gambut early in the evening he cancelled his deputy's move. "We must not lose our nerve," he admonished. "The enemy's advance [involves] nothing more than negligable harassing operations."[17] Similarly, the Panzergruppe's chief operations officer signaled DAK - "no reason for anxiety," he assured.[18] Crüwell was not convinced. But Rommel refused to face the facts; he resented this interference with his plans to take Tobruk.

Rommel's failure to act puzzled Eighth Army. The next day General Norrie, the 30 Corps commander, pushed 7 Armored Brigade to Sidi Rezegh and sent 22 Armored Brigade to attack the Ariete Armored Division. He held 4 Armored Brigade at Gabr Saleh to cover his left flank. In this manner he planned to force Rommel to show his hand. But what Norrie had really done was to splinter his armored spearhead into three groups and to fatefully dismember Cunningham's plan to draw Rommel into battle against a concentrated 30 Corps. Eighth Army had begun Crusader with a great tank superiority - 738 tanks to some 400 Axis, of which 146 were the lightly-armored Italian M 13/40's.[19] Norrie's actions on the 19th squandered this advantage.

After a long approach march, 22 Armored Brigade collided with the Ariete at Bir el Gubi. In a violent battle the Italians lost 34 tanks; the British, however, broke off the assault. They, too, had suffered heavily - to mines and to the courage of the Italian antitank gunners - and left some 50 burnt-out tanks on the battlefield.[20]

---

[16]C. Shores and Hans Ring, _Fighters Over the Desert_ (London: Spearman, 1969), pg. 61. Hereafter cited as _Fighters_.

[17]Rainer Kriebel, "North African Campaign," MS T-3, Vol. I, part 2, pg. 56. Hereafter cited as "North African Campaign," Vol. No., part no.

[18]Panzergruppe Afrika, Ia, Battle Report, Appendix 5 for 18 Nov. 1941, New Zealand Translations of Captured Records Pertaining to German Army Units Participating in the North African Campaign from August 1941 to May 1943. Hereafter cited as NZT (New Zealand Translations).

[19]For a detailed breakdown of the opposing forces, see Hermann Büschleb's _Feldherren und Panzer im Wüstenkrieg: Die Herbstschlacht "Crusader" im Vorfeld von Tobruk, 1941, Die Wehrmacht im Kampf_ (Neckargemünd: Kurt Vowinckel Verlag, 1966), Bd. XL. Hereafter cited as _Feldherren und Panzer_. According to Büschleb, the Afrikakorps entered Crusader with some 150 Pz. III G's and Pz. IV's. These were far superior to the tanks of their opponent.

[20]Agar-Hamilton, _Sidi Rezegh Battles_, pg. 139.

At a late morning conference, Rommel once again conferred with General Crüwell. Crüwell emphasized the seriousness of the Afrikakorps' position. Strong British armored forces had driven his reconnaissance units across the Trigh el Abd; the enemy tanks were now moving northwards. The attack, he correctly maintained, was not a reconnaissance but a major Eighth Army offensive operation. This time Rommel accepted Crüwell's proposal to strike southwards. A group of armor under Colonel Stephan (120 tanks of 5 Panzer Regiment with ar-

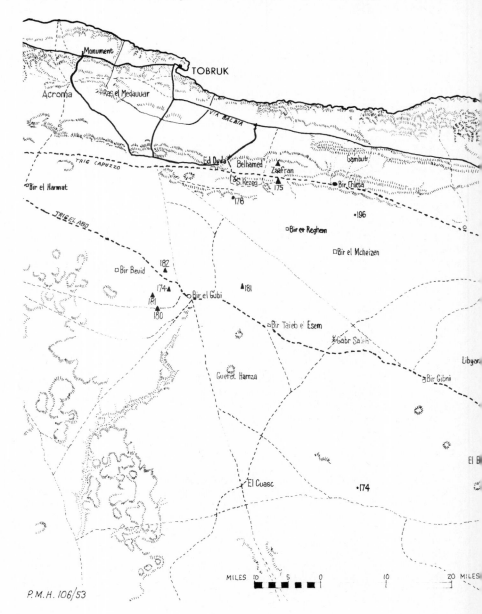

P.M.H. 106/53

tillery and flak support) was to advance towards Gabr Saleh and destroy the enemy threatening 3 Reconnaissance Battalion.

At 1530 hours Stephan's Panzers made contact with 4 Armored Brigade northeast of Gabr Saleh - opening a hail of fire from 1500 yards. The British sent their American-built Stuart ("honey") tanks into action, "weaving, zigzagging, making full use of their forty miles an hour to minimize themselves as targets." The lightly armed and armored Stuarts (1-37mm cannon and 44mm armor plate) collided and intermingled with their attackers - utter confusion followed. The battle's only respite came when the Panzers pulled back to refuel and resupply from their petrol and ammunition column. Although this concentration of stationary tanks, fuel and ammunition vehicles was certainly inviting, the Germans with their heavier guns and "steady" gun platforms kept the British tanks in frustrated "time out." By dusk Stephan had badly bloodied two regiments of 4 Armored Brigade.

That evening the overall situation was still far from clear at Panzergruppe headquarters. During the day enemy tanks and armored cars had seized the Sidi Rezegh airfield from a weak force of startled Italians; *Luftwaffe* reconnaissance had detected "three long motorized

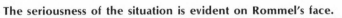

The seriousness of the situation is evident on Rommel's face.

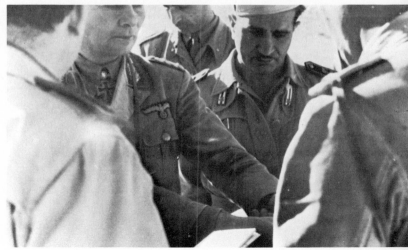

columns with armor - beginning and tail not visible - moving northwards between Girabub and Bir el Gubi."[21] Von Ravenstein proposed that 15 and 21 Panzer Divisions be combined into one force to counter the threat. Crüwell agreed. With a united striking force, he could attack and destroy the scattered Eighth Army columns in succession. As for Rommel, he was slowly beginning to recognize the danger to his Panzergruppe. At 2100 hours his chief of staff, Gause, signaled DAK, giving Crüwell a free hand "to destroy the enemy who had broken into the Bardia-Sidi Omar-Gabr Saleh-Gambut area."[22] Late in the night 15 Panzer reported its battle strength at 135 tanks - 38 Pz. II's, 76 Pz. III's and 21 Pz. IV's.[23]

The next day, however, Crüwell misread the *Schwerpunkt* of the Eighth Army offensive and sent the united Afrikakorps marauding eastwards. On the 19th the King's Dragoon Guards had chased 3 Reconnaissance Battalion across the Trigh Capuzzo towards Sidi Azeiz. Falsely identifying the action as a large-scale enemy maneuver, Crüwell had resolved to deal with it: 21 Panzer rumbled off towards Sidi Omar, after a two-hour delay due to the late arrival of its supply columns; 15 Panzer, straddling the Trigh Capuzzo, moved on Sidi Azeiz. But it was a lunge into empty space, for the British had already disappeared from this sector. Crüwell forfeited most of the day "chasing an imaginary enemy."[24] 5 Panzer Regiment (21 Panzer) was soon stranded, having run out of fuel. It appealed urgently to Panzergruppe headquarters for fuel and ammunition to be flown in by air.[25]

When Crüwell recognized his mistake, he swung 15 Panzer Division in a wide sweep to the southwest. At 1630 hours 8 Panzer Regiment and 15 Rifle Brigade encountered a strong enemy tank force supported by artillery and antitank guns. This was the 4 Armored Brigade, which was still in position around Gabr Saleh. A furious tank battle developed; but "as darkness fell slowly, the firing died down and the [British] pulled back."[26] 15 Panzer reported to DAK headquarters that it had "reached the Trigh el Abd after heavy tank fighting."[27] During the night supply columns replenished von Ravenstein's immobilized division, which had laagered at Bagr Lachem.

While Neumann-Silkow's Panzers were locking horns with the British tanks at Gabr Saleh, 7 Armored Brigade and 7 Support Group had strengthened their grip on the Sidi Rezegh airfield and beaten back the counterattacks of Afrika Division. Aware of the threat this posed to his Tobruk encirclement ring, Rommel decided that the next day he would

---

[21]Kriebel, "North African Campaign," T-3, I, part 2, pg. 69.
[22]Agar-Hamilton, Sidi Rezegh Battles, pg. 154.
[23]KTB, 15 Panzer Division, 19 November 1941, NZT.
[24]Von Mellenthin, Panzer Battles, pg. 76.
[25]KTB, 15 Panzer Division, 20 November 1941, NZT.
[26]Ibid.
[27]Ibid.

attack northwards from Gabr Saleh and destroy the enemy force advancing on Tobruk. He had awakened to the seriousness of British intentions, as is evident in a letter to his wife that day: "The battle is at its height right now. I hope we get through it all right. Our position is not too good."[28]

The German countermoves on the 20th had brought thoroughly unsatisfactory results. "There is no doubt," von Mellenthin asserts, "that we missed a great opportunity on 20 November. Cunningham had been obliging enough to scatter the 7 Armored Division all over the desert, and we had failed to exploit his generosity."[29]

Early on the 21st, 21 Panzer completed its resupply and at 0300 drove southwest to link up with 15 Panzer. An hour later Rommel sent a nervous signal to Crüwell, explaining "the situation in this whole theatre is very critical;"[30] he demanded that the Afrikakorps "get going in good time."

Protected by a screen of 88's and antitank guns, the German tanks broke contact with the British 4 and 22 Armored Brigades at Gabr Saleh and swept northwards. At Sidi Rezegh they crashed into 7 Armored Brigade. Rommel "could see the dust and blaze as the Afrikakorps tanks charged to the airfield perimeter and opened fire at a range of 2,000 yards."[31] By noon the Panzers had reduced the enemy brigade to a heap of twisted, smoking metal. Its "ten surviving tanks, most of them obsolete cruisers and damaged at that, succeeded in slipping through the [DAK] units around Abiar en Nbeidat and attached themselves to the 4 Armored Brigade near Bir el Reghem."[32] 15 Panzer occupied the high ground that overlooked the airfield from the south, but attempts to seize the airfield itself floundered in the face of determined opposition. The division's tanks then retired "behind the inevitable screen of antitank guns," to refuel and to replenish their ammunition.[33]

Rommel had not participated in the Afrikakorps' assault, for on the Tobruk front General Scobie had begun his attempt to break out from the fortress. In support of Scobie's thrust, 7 Support Group (Brigadier Campbell) had smashed northwards in an effort to capture the Sidi Rezegh escarpment and to hammer a corridor through to the besieged garrison.[34] The attacks started almost simultaneously at 0745 hours. Elements of 7 Support Group - 1 King's Royal Rifle Corps and a company from 2 Rifle Brigade - scrambled up the escarpment, capturing 700-800 prisoners from the Axis force opposing them. On the Tobruk perimeter Scobie's 70 British Division and 32 Army Tank Brigade broke through

---

[28]*Rommel Collection*, T-84, 274, #000462.
[29]Von Mellenthin, *Panzer Battles*, pg. 78.
[30]*KTB, DAK*, 21 November 1941, NZT.
[31]Irving, *The Trail*, pg. 131.
[32]Agar-Hamilton, *Sidi Rezegh Battles*, pg. 179.
[33]*KTB, 15 Panzer Division*, 21 November 1941, NZT.
[34]Cunningham had again changed his plan, for the break out was not to go forward until the destruction of Rommel's armor.

units of Afrika and Bologna Divisions. The situation was a desperate one. Afrika Division recorded in its diary that it "was fighting for its very existence."[35] Instinctively, Rommel rushed to the danger point taking personal command of von Wechmar's armored cars and a few 88's. One by one the advancing British tanks went up in flames - victims of the magnificent 88's. Thus Rommel was able to seal off Scobie's breakout attempt.

Meanwhile, "ominous reports came in from the frontier area." 13 Corps,   with the New Zealand Division in advance, had "thrust behind the [Afrikakorps'] frontier fortresses and crossed the Trigh Capuzzo on both sides of Sidi Azeiz. This brought them dangerously close to Panzergruppe headquarters at Gambut, and Rommel ordered [his staff] to move to El Adem during the night."[36] Rommel had no reserves to meet this new threat; the next day he would merely send 3 and 33 Reconnaissance Battalions eastwards to mask the movements of 13 Corps.[37]

Generals Neumann-Silkow (left) and Crüwell (center) discuss the day's operations.

---

[35]KTB, Afrika Division z. b. V., 22 November 1941, NZT.
[36]Von Mellenthin, Panzer Battles, pg. 80.
[37]Büschleb, Feldherren und Panzer, pg. 53.

By the evening of the 21st of November, Crusader had broken down into a confused melee of interlocking actions. The situation was an extraordinary one: "Over the 20 or so miles of country from the front of the Tobruk sortie to the open desert southeast of Sidi Rezegh airfield the forces of both sides were sandwiches like the layers of a Neapolitan ice [sic]. In turn, starting from the north, there were (a) the troops of 70 Division who had broken out, opposed by (b) German and Italian troops facing north and west; (c) a layer of Axis troops facing south, opposing (d) part of the 7 Support Group north of the Sidi Rezegh airfield; the rest of 7 Support Group and 7 Armored Brigade facing south to oppose (e) the bulk of DAK heading north, pursued by (f) the 4 and 22 Armored Brigades. To complete the picture there were troops of the 361 Afrika Regiment on Point 175 to the east of Sidi Rezegh airfield and the whole of the 155 Regiment to the west."[38]

After dark Crüwell - against the protests of Neumann-Silkow - withdrew the Afrikakorps from the battlefield south of the airfield. With his tanks short of fuel he could not afford to risk a mobile battle with strong enemy armored forces.[39] Thus, 15 Panzer regrouped south of Gambut, while 21 Panzer descended the escarpment overlooking the Trigh Capuzzo and assembled in the Belhamed area.[40]

While Afrikakorps refueled, Rommel designed an aggressive plan. At about mid-day, 22 November, he ordered von Ravenstein to send his armor on a wide arc across the Axis bypass road at El Duda to attack Sidi Rezegh airfield from the west. To support the attack 21 Panzer infantry and elements of Sümmermann's Afrika Division would assault the Sidi Rezegh escarpment from the north.[41] Major General Karl Böttcher's heavy artillery would plaster the airfield with shell-fire.

At 1300, 5 Panzer Regiment stormed onto the airfield.[42] Though taken by surprise, the British gunners resisted furiously with their twenty-five pounders. "The photographs show their corpses draped unromantically across the wreckage of their [guns]."[43] 22 Armored Brigade lodged a desperate counterpunch, but, by darkness, 45 of its 79 tanks were out of action.[44] The airfield was back in German hands.

Again operating independently, Crüwell put in his own attack that evening against the eastern flank of 7 Armored Division. At about 1900 hours, I./8 Panzer Regiment (15 Panzer Division) broke into a large concentration of vehicles in night laager. "The battalion commander recognized the vehicles as English tanks at 10 yards. He burst through the enemy laager in his command vehicle and ordered [his companies]

---

[38]British Official History as quoted in Lewin, Rommel, pg. 67.
[39]Büschleb, Feldherren und Panzer, pg. 50.
[40]Von Mellenthin, Panzer Battles, pp. 80-81.
[41]Büschleb, Feldherren und Panzer, pg. 52.
[42]KTB, DAK, 22 November 1941, NZT.
[43]Irving, The Trail, pg. 132.
[44]Büschleb, Feldherren und Panzer, pg. 52.

Night fighting in the desert near the Sidi Rezegh airfield.

to surround the enemy."[45] While the company adjutant shot off flares, the tanks shone their headlights and the commanders jumped out with their machine pistols."[46] The British were dumbfounded. A few tanks tried to escape but were quickly shot up, lighting the sky like daytime. The commander of 4 Armored Brigade, 17 officers and 150 men were captured, along with 35 tanks.[47]

The engagements on the 22nd had ended in two significant successes for the Afrikakorps. 7 Armored Division had lost two-thirds of its original establishment of tanks: 4 Armored Brigade had ceased to exist, 7 and 22 Brigade were greatly reduced in strength. Crusader had swung in Rommel's favor. The next day would bring a greater triumph.

The last Sunday in November is the day Germany traditionally honors her war dead. It is called *Totensonntag* - "the Sunday of the dead." This Sunday, 23 November 1941, would see much dying..

Rommel planned to crush his battered enemy with a two-pronged tank attack. 15 and 21 Panzer would advance southward while Gambara's Ariete thrust north from Bir el Gubi. The enemy - remnants of 7 Armored Division and 1 and 5 South African Brigades - would be encircled and destroyed.

At 0430 Afrikakorps headquarters received Rommel's directive - a long-winded, coded wireless signal with a surfeit of details "absolutely unimportant for the Afrikakorps."[48] Crüwell is reported to have "tossed it aside." He had his own plan. Ignoring his commander's directive, he ordered 15 Panzer, reinforced by 5 Panzer Regiment, to move across

---

[45]*KTB, 15 Panzer Division, 22 November 1941*, NZT.
[46]*Ibid.*
[47]*Army Corps, Panzer Regiment 8 Gefechtsbericht über die Vernichtung der englischen 4./Pz.-Brigade am 22.11.41.*, DAK, T-314, 2, #0000175.
[48]*KTB, DAK, 23 November 1941*, NZT.

the rear of 7 Armored Division and 5 South African Brigade. His tanks would then link up with Ariete and, advancing northwards, drive the British against the infantry and guns of 21 Panzer holding the escarpment south of Sidi Rezegh airfield.[49]

After the thick morning mist had lifted, Crüwell's "long columns of tanks, lorries and guns rumbled off." Earlier that morning Crüwell and his chief of staff, Bayerlein, had just escaped capture when elements of 6 New Zealand Brigade overran and captured DAK headquarters at Bir el Glaser.

At 0815 hours the Afrikakorps' lead elements encountered vast enemy transport columns west of Sidi Muftah. The sight of German armor threw the soft-skinned supply vehicles into great confusion; they stampeded across the desert in an effort to avoid destruction. Crüwell's armored armada sailed southwards; shortly after noon it had forged the link with Ariete. Two hours later the entire force - Ariete, 5 and 8 Panzer Regiments - was "parading abreast in a line near Bir el Gubi, facing north and ready to bully the enemy back towards Sidi Rezegh."[50] Soon the Axis columns reached full speed - tanks, troop carriers, vehicles of all kinds hurtled across the hard, wet ground. Thick sheets of defensive fire slammed into them and many tanks were hit. The infantry also suffered greviously, for Crüwell had ordered it "not to debus until it [came] under heavy infantry fire."[51] The German officers and NCO's standing upright in their vehicles were cut down in droves.

If the tactics were costly, the results were spectacular. 5 South Africa Brigade disintegrated; the tank strength of 7 Armored division was reduced "to a shadow." But Afrikakorps' Panzer regiments and motorized infantry had also suffered heavily.[52] Rommel had spent a nervous day at 21 Panzer's command post. He had intended to join Crüwell that morning, but was "prevented from doing so by the advance of 6 New Zealand Brigade from the east."[53] The New Zealanders had then slammed into 361 Afrika Regiment at Point 175 and Rommel "was drawn into the fray." The actions on *Totensonntag* had further consolidated the Afrikakorps' position. Cunningham's morale had faltered; only Auchinleck's firm resolve kept him from breaking off the battle. Rommel, on the other hand, was jubilant; at midnight he signaled Rome and Berlin: "Intentions for 24 November: (a) to complete destruction of 7 Armored Division, (b) to advance with elements

---

[49]Von Mellenthin, *Panzer Battles*, pg. 85.
[50]Irving, *The Trail*, pg. 134. 8 Panzer Regiment fielded 120 tanks; 5 Panzer Regiment 40. Army Corps, Panzer Regiment 8, Schlacht am Totensonntag am 23.11.1941, DAK, T-314, 2, #0000188.
[51]Panzergruppe Afrika, Ia, Battle Reports, 23 November 1941, NZT. For a graphic account see Army Corps, Schützen Regiment 115, Gefechtsbericht, Die Schlacht am Totensonntag, DAK, T-314, 2, #0000176-0000178.
[52]Büschleb, *Feldherren und Panzer*, pg. 64. 8 Panzer Regiment put its losses for Totensonntag at 45 tanks. Army Corps, Die Schlacht am Totensonntag, DAK, T-314, 2, #0000190.
[53]Von Mellenthin, *Panzer Battles*, pg. 84.

of forces towards Sidi Omar with a view to attacking enemy on Sollum front."[54]

Rommel was about to launch the "most controversial act in the whole of his military career."[55] In a daring thrust to the Egyptian frontier, he planned to cut off the retreat of 30 Corps and to hurl 13 Corps back upon the Sollum minefields - Eighth Army would be finished. Mellenthin and Westphal expressed serious reservations about Rommel's design. It would be unwise, they said, to move the Afrikakorps so far from Tobruk, where the situation was still a dangerous one. Their commander disagreed. The time had come, Rommel instructed a startled Westphal, "to complete the destruction of the remnants of the enemy and cut their lines of withdrawal to Egypt. He would, therefore, put himself at the head of DAK with Panzer Division Ariete under his command and begin the pursuit."[56] He would, he said, be back that evening or the next morning.

But *Totensonntag* "had ended with Afrikakorps in a state of great confusion." Bayerlein writes: "the wide area south of Sidi Rezegh had

[54]Agar-Hamilton, *Sidi Rezegh Battles*, pg. 281.
[55]Lewin, *Rommel*, pg. 73.
[56]Kriebel, "*North African Campaign*," T-3, I, part 2, pg. 139.

become a sea of dust, fire and smoke ... Hundreds of burning vehicles, tanks and guns lit up the battlefield. Not until midnight was it possible to gauge the results of the battle, to organize the formations, to assess losses and gains, and to appreciate the general situation."[57] When the billowing clouds of smoke and fire had cleared, it was evident that Afrikakorps had lost 72 of its last 162 tanks. Panzergruppe Afrika, though victorious, was exhausted; Rommel had overestimated his success.

Ignoring a strong New Zealand force moving from Bardia on Tobruk, Rommel began his "dash for the wire." For the next few days his anxious subordinates would know little of his movements or intentions. By 1030 hours, 24 November, the Afrikakorps' remaining tanks were driving eastwards along the Trigh El Abd, with 21 Panzer and Rommel in the lead. Earlier, RAF fighters had strafed 5 Panzer Regiment and mortally wounded its valiant commander, Fritz Stephan.

Rommel sped "like a maniac" through the desert, "looking neither left nor right as he charged down the very axis of the enemy's [30 Corps]. Like picnickers before an angry swarm of bees, the enemy

[57]Von Mellenthin, *Panzer Battles*, pg. 88.

24 November 1941. Rommel standing in his "Horch" somewhere between Tobruk and Sidi Omar. Gause is at the far right.

began to flee eastward and southeastward as the Afrikakorps made its unannounced and desperate foray."[58] 21 Panzer Division rolled through parks of defenseless transport vehicles and blasted them at will. Cunningham, himself, narrowly escaped capture; his Blenheim bomber was shelled as it took off.

At 1600 hours Rommel reached Gasr el Abid and the frontier wire - a thick barbed-wire entanglement that stretched north and south beyond the horizon. He found himself almost alone, for his wild charge had outdistanced his own communications vehicles and left most of DAK behind. When he met Crüwell an hour later, only his chief of staff (Gause), a tactical headquarters, and a modest signals section were with him. Rommel informed the Afrikakorps commander that he had "directed von Ravenstein [21 Panzer Division, minus its tank regiment] to Halfaya Pass. Afrikakorps' job was to cooperate with the [Italian] Motorized Corps, bottle up and destroy the enemy [east and west] of the Sollum front and at Bardia."[59] The order appalled Crüwell; his two Panzer divisions were now scattered over 60 miles of desert. Rommel's decision, moreover, was based on "an incorrect impression of the situation on the Sollum front." He assumed large enemy forces were located in that sector. He was mistaken. "Only one Indian Brigade, the 7th," writes Mellenthin, "was actually there, and this brigade had just captured Sidi Omar, where it was protected by our own minefields."[60]

At dusk Rommel and Gause drove on into Egypt. Alfred Berndt, Rommel's aide, describes the adventure: "His car's steering column snapped. His escort car had been left behind somewhere, and the last trucks of the Panzer division were vanishing into the distance. His driver had to get out every 100 yards and kick the front wheels into the correct angle."[61] Then the motor died. But at just that moment Crüwell and Bayerlein - on their return trip to Gasr el Abid - "stumbled across Rommel and Gause stranded in the desert."[62] This was a welcome sight to the two Generals, "shivering with cold." They promptly piled into Crüwell's Mammoth, which headed back for the frontier - all the senior officers of Panzergruppe Afrika crowded inside.

The following few hours were extraordinary. At the frontier wire they failed to find a gap to get them back to Libya. Back and forth they drove. The frustrated Rommel even took the wheel himself, but his efforts proved quite useless. He and his staff had no choice but to laager for the night on the enemy side of the wire. It was a night filled with anxiety for the VIP's crouched in their dusty Mammoth. Indian dispatch riders buzzed to and fro, and trucks of all types repeatedly passed within a few yards of them. But the Mammoth, a captured British vehicle, must have looked unassuming, for no one disturbed it. At first light Rommel again

---

[58]Irving, The Trail, pg. 136.
[59]KTB, DAK, 24 November 1941, NZT.
[60]Von Mellenthin, Panzer Battles, pg. 90.
[61]As quoted in Irving, The Trail, pg. 137.
[62]KTB, DAK, 24 November 1941, NZT.

took the wheel; a gap in the wire was quickly discovered. By 0700 he had reached Gasr el Abid.

Since the South Africans had held up Ariete at Taieb el Esem, Rommel now ordered Crüwell to attack on his own. 15 Panzer was to seal off the Sollum front from the west, while 21 Panzer did the same in the east. 5 Panzer Regiment (still detached from von Ravenstein's main force) charged the enemy outposts at Sidi Omar and lost half its remaining tanks. The rest of 21 Panzer floated about, south of Halfaya Pass, without making contact with any Eighth Army forces. In the afternoon 15 Panzer scored a minor success when it obliterated the workshops of 1 Army Tank Brigade. The RAF bombed repeatedly and inflicted heavy casualities on the Afrikakorps; at dusk 5 Panzer Regiment had 12 tanks left; 8 Panzer Regiment had 53.[63] "In short," writes von Mellenthin, "25 November was a thoroughly unsatisfactory day in which we suffered heavy losses for little result."[64]

Shivering in the wooden huts which served as their headquarters at El Adem, Westphal and von Mellenthin "viewed the situation with increasing anxiety."[65] During the day 2 New Zealand Division had arrived in force in the Sidi Rezegh area - putting 90 Light Division in a difficult situation. Westphal dispatched urgent signals and sent off five Storch aircraft in a futile effort to locate Rommel.

The next day, 26 November, the siege of the fortress reached a crisis. The Tobruk garrison smashed through the investment ring. Group Böttcher and a *Bersaglieri* Regiment from Trieste Division suffered heavy losses; the important height at El Duda was lost. The night before, 2 New Zealand Division had stormed and captured Belhamed; a corridor now existed between the garrison and the New Zealanders. Westphal, unable to reach either Rommel or Afrikakorps headquarters, bravely took matters into his own hands. He cancelled all pursuit orders and called 21 Panzer back "into the crisis zone - back to Tobruk."[66]

At 1030 hours that morning, Rommel met Crüwell at the frontier. He ignored the stack of frantic signals from Westphal, though he did admit that the situation at Tobruk was more serious that he had imagined. Nevertheless, he persisted with his attempt to crush the enemy he still believed - erroneously - to be massing at the frontier. He ordered Crüwell to "kick up dust" to deceive the enemy. Rommel then raced northwards to the coast with Neumann-Silkow's Panzer division and reached Bardia in the middle of the afternoon.

That evening von Ravenstein reported to Rommel at Bardia. To his horror Rommel discovered that 21 Panzer Division was now back in

[63]Wolf Heckmann, *Rommel's Krieg in Afrika: Wüstenfuchse gegen Wüstenratten* (Bergisch Gladbach: Gustav Lubbe Verlag, 1976). Hereafter cited as *Rommel's Krieg*.

[64]Von Mellenthin, *Panzer Battles*, pg. 92.

[65]*Ibid*.

[66]Agar-Hamilton, *Sidi Rezegh Battles*, pg. 306.

During the lightning fast movements of late November, Lunch usually consisted of no more than a moment's break and a few bitefulls in his "Horch."

Libya - on orders from Westphal. Beside himself with anger, his first reaction was that Westphal's message was a fake - the British had broken his codes and issued the orders themselves.

Rommel was still boiling when he reached Panzergruppe headquarters at El Adem. He neither greeted nor spoke to anyone. Instead, he stalked silently into his command vehicle and gazed at the situation maps. As he fumed in silence, Gause stood beside him, while other officers gestured to their chief of staff to speak to Rommel and explain Westphal's orders. But before Gause could speak, Rommel turned and "suddenly left the vehicle, remarking that he was going to lie down. To everyone's relief, next morning [he] did not mention the business at all. He was friendly as ever."[67]

Early the next day, 27 November, Rommel ordered 21 Panzer to head for El Adem and Tobruk; 15 Panzer was to clear up Capuzzo and Sidi Azeiz. 8 Panzer Regiment had soon won a "notable success" when it steam-rolled the headquarters of 5 New Zealand Brigade at Sidi Azeiz and captured 800 prisoners, 6 guns and large quantities of material.[68] Satisfied with this victory, "Rommel decided to leave the Sollum front and ordered 15 Panzer to press westwards towards Tobruk."[69] Westphal

---

[67]Agar-Hamilton, _Sidi Rezegh Battles_, pg. 347.
[68]_Ibid_.
[69]Von Mellenthin, _Panzer Battles_, pg. 93.

and Crüwell "had persisted in the view that Tobruk, and the forces attempting its relief, were the critical center of the battle. At last Rommel accepted their diagnosis."[70]

His dramatic dash to the wire has triggered a lively debate among military historians. According to Liddell Hart, Rommel's raid "resulted in more forfeit than gain. When the raid started, he had almost won the battle. When the raid ended, the scales had tilted against him. But the margin was very narrow, ... [for] Rommel's daring stroke came very close to proving decisive."[71] This was because the Afrikakorps' lightning thrust across the 30 Corps' lines of communications had shattered what little morale Cunningham had left. He was inclined to admit defeat; to pull back his army into Egypt. But at this point, Auchinleck intervened decisively in the battle, and "brought victory out of defeat." Determined to continue his offensive, he cashiered his bullied deputy, and replaced him with Major General N.W. Ritchie. Rommel, of course, could never have anticipated that Auchinleck would "change horses in midstream"; or that his unexpected sortie would not have the same effect on Auchinleck as it did on Cunningham. In the final analyses, then, it was Auchinleck's ability to keep a firm grip on himself that tipped the scales of the battle against Rommel.

Had the raid succeeded, Desmond Young asserts, military historians would have judged it a masterpiece. But the fact remains that it failed to achieve Rommel's desired results. Rommel's battle technique during the raid, moreover, was spotty at best. In his thoughtful study of Rommel's command methods, Ronald Lewin observes: "At Sidi Rezegh Rommel had made firm and constructive decisions, but during this period on the frontier his control of the battle - if it can be said to be control - was ill-considered, impetuous and erratic. It is hard not to feel sympathy for Crüwell as he watched the dissipation and destruction of his previous tanks."[72]

Although the overall picture had rapidly deteriorated, Rommel's personal morale was still high. He wrote to his wife: "The battle rages in the desert since the 19th and also at Tobruk and Sollum. The communiques must keep you informed about the main events. I think we are through the worst and the battle will be of major importance for our victory. Personally I am well. I have been in the desert for the last four days without a toilet set leading our counterattack which is coming along splendidly."[73]

Rommel would now renew the fighting around Sidi Rezegh, but "under conditions which were far less propitious than three days before. The New Zealanders had made a firm junction to the Tobruk garrison ... The Afrikakorps ... was only a fraction of the magnificent force which

---

[70]Lewin, _Rommel_, pg. 81.
[71]Hart, _Rommel Papers_, pg. 166.
[72]Lewin, _Rommel_, pg. 75.
[73]_Rommel Collection_, T-84, 274, #000462.

had entered the battle on the 18th. The British armor had been given a respite; many tanks had been salvaged, large tank reserves had been sent up from Egypt, and the 4 and 22 Armored Brigades were again formidable fighting formations. The Royal Air Forces dominated the battlefield, and our unprotected columns were repeatedly hit."[74]

Panzergruppe Afrika's turbulent commander returned to Gambut airfield. He wired DAK that its "General Staff officers [were to] proceed there as soon as possible to be put in the picture."[75] Crüwell and Bayerlein left for the conference at 2100 hours. After a long search in the dark, they spotted a number of lorries, which they approached cautiously. Inside one of them they found Rommel, "unshaven, worn with lack of sleep and caked with dust. In the lorry was a heap of straw as a bed, a can of stale water to drink and a few tins of food,"[76] - modest quarters for a Panzer general.

The danger of a collapse on the Tobruk front was now apparent to Rommel. But in the following few days he recaptured his touch and administered a series of hammer blows that drove General Freyberg's New Zealanders from Sidi Rezegh and resealed the investment ring. In these battles Rommel was again the brilliant Panzer leader; his powers of endurance were phenomenal.

The first blow fell on 29 November; it met with only partial success. Characteristically, Rommel and Crüwell disagreed on its execution. Whereas Crüwell wanted to drive the New Zealanders into the fortress, Rommel planned to cut them off from Tobruk and surround them.[77] As it turned out, Rommel's plan was put into effect. Afrikakorps roared into action. Von Ravenstein's remaining tanks (20 in all) made little progress astride the Trigh Capuzzo. Neumann-Silkow, however, (with 43 tanks) wheeled northward, smashed into the enemy on the *Achsenstrasse* and retook El Duda.[78] But late that evening the British counterattacked with tanks and hurled 15 Panzer back from the heights.[79] Rommel not only lost a hill that day; earlier, a battalion of New Zealand troops had nabbed General von Ravenstein at Point 175, taking him prisoner.

Early the next day Rommel's hammer struck with greater authority and cleaved through the indominable New Zealanders. The battle opened with a five-hour artillery barrage on Sidi Rezegh. In typical fashion, the British failed to concentrate their armor swiftly enough to help Freyberg's beleaguered force. At 1400 hours Rommel was again at

---

[74]Von Mellenthin, *Panzer Battles*, pg. 93. For a discussion of the multiple strains upon the small German air forces in the Mediterranean Theatre, see Büschleb's *Feldherren und Panzer*.

[75]*KTB, DAK*, 27 November 1941, NZT.

[76]Hart, *Rommel Papers*, pg. 168.

[77]Büschleb, *Feldherren und Panzer*, pg. 88.

[78]*Ibid.*, pp. 88-89. Army Corps Panzer Regiment 8, Gefechtsbericht über den Angriff auf El Duda am 29.11.1941, DAK, T-314, 2, #000080.

[79]*KTB, DAK*, 30 November 1941, NZT.

General Neumann-Silkow in his command tank.

The artillery barrage on Sidi Rezegh.

113

DAK headquarters, "to watch the jaws close on the enemy. The large-caliber guns were tearing huge craters in the enemy positions at Sidi Rezegh; the ridge and the airfield were obscured by dust and smoke. The enemy's twenty-five pounders were running out of ammunition."[80] Neumann-Silkow then moved in for the kill; Sidi Rezegh was again in German hands.[81]

On 1 December a final blow settled the matter. The remaining tanks of Kramer's 8 Panzer Regiment overwhelmed 4 New Zealand Brigade at Belhamed and captured "hordes of prisoners and vast quantities of war material."[82] General Freyberg then ordered a breakout to the southeast and managed to extricate a part of his division. Tobruk was again tightly encircled.

Success had followed success, and Rommel now planned "one last battle" to liberate his trapped garrisons on the Sollum front. His troops were bone tired, but Rommel spared neither himself nor his men. Man and machine were to be pushed to the limits of their endurance. To raise morale he issued a stirring proclamation to his troops: "The preliminary battle in Marmarica has reached a victorious conclusion. By 1 December, after continuous hard fighting against an enemy far superior in numbers, 814 tanks and armored cars have been destroyed, 127 aircraft shot down and huge quantities of war material captured. Over 9,000 prisoners have been taken. Soldiers! This great victory is due to your bravery, hardness and endurance. But the fight is not over. Forward once more until the enemy is finally trampled in the dust."

While the bulk of the Afrikakorps remained in the Sidi Rezegh area to reorganize, its non-armored elements formed two battle groups (under Geissler and Knabe) and headed eastward - for the Sollum front garrisons. Crüwell bitterly contested this further dismemberment of his now-skeletal force, but to no avail. Kampfgruppe Geissler charged down the Via Balbia; Knabe down the Trigh Capuzzo. At 1300 hours 28 Maori Battalion massacred Geissler's column, opening fire from "every weapon within reach, including Bofors [a Swedish-designed 40mm antiaircraft gun]... The front was soon strewn with blazing vehicles and Geissler reeled back." He left behind over 200 dead.[83] Knabe then also withdrew. On the Tobruk front an attempt was made to recapture El Duda the next morning (4 December) by 8 Machine Battalion, 200 Pioneer Battalion and Group Mickl, but the attack disintegrated in the heavy fire of the fortress artillery.

---

[80]Irving, the Trail, pg. 144.
[81]See Army Corps, 8 Panzer Regiment's Gefechtsbericht über den Angriff am 30.11.41 auf Sidi Rezegh, DAK, T-314, 2, #000083-000084.
[82]KTB, DAK, 1 December 1941, NZT. The attack cost 8 Panzer Regiment 12 Panzer III's and 7 Panzer II's. Army Corps, Panzer Regiment 8, Gefechtsbericht über den Angriff auf Belhamed am 1.12.41, DAK, T-314, 2, #000049-000050.
[83]W.E. Murphy, The Relief of Tobruk (Wellington: Department of Internal Affairs, 1961), pp. 477-478.
[84]KTB, DAK, 4 December 1941, NZT.

Rommel views the crumbling Axis front in early December 1941.

On 5 December the Chief of Command Supremo's Operations Branch, Lieutenant Colonel Giuseppe Montezemolo arrived at Panzergruppe headquarters with a disconcerting message from Rome: Rommel could expect no further reinforcements before January. Rommel suddenly awakened to the desperateness of his situation. His once-powerful Afrikakorps could still field some 40 tanks. Ritchie's Eighth Army, on the other hand, had rapidly increased in strength and possessed an overwhelming superiority in armored fighting vehicles. Rommel reached the inescapable conclusion: he would have to abandon Cyrenaica and conduct a fighting withdrawal back to the prepared defenses around Gazala. The next day Rommel learned that Neumann-Silkow was dead - killed by a shell-burst.

Montezemolo promptly returned to Italy and reported to Bastico. Rommel had been exceedingly frank with the Colonel. "The Panzergruppe," Rommel had informed him, "is no longer capable of continuing the battle without disengaging from the enemy... The siege of Tobruk had to be given up [for]...the Bologna Division and 90 Light Division had suffered such heavy losses they could no longer resist enemy pressure. The Savona Division and its subordinate units had received orders to retire to Bardia [and to abandon the Sollum Line], as all available ammunition and food supplies ... have been expended."[85] Four thousand Germans and an equal number of Italians had been killed. The Afrikakorps was down to 40 tanks - Ariete, 30.[86]

---

[85]*Air Historical Branch Translations of Captured German Documents: VII/80-81 - High Level Reports and Directives Dealing with the North African Campaign 1941-1942. Hereafter cited as AHBT (Air Historical Branch Translations).*

[86]*For the losses of the Afrikakorps during the Crusader battles, see Army Corps, Gesamtverluste Deutsches Afrikakorps, Zeit 18.11.41-10.12.41, DAK, T-314, 2, #000040. The Panzerarmee officer corps had been especially hard hit: killed were General Major Neumann-Silkow, Lieutenant Colonel Zinke, Major von Grolman and Major Fenski from 15 Panzer Division and Lieutenant Colonel Stephan from 21 Panzer. Numerous other officers were killed or wounded.*

Bastico was badly shaken by this report, which he passed on to his superior in Rome, General Cavallero. A major retreat would be a big blow to Italian prestige, thus Cavallero notified Rommel not to throw away all of Cyrenaica without good reason - Benghazi must be held as long as possible as a supply port.

On 12 December, after a masterful withdrawal protected by well-disciplined rearguards, the troops of the Panzergruppe reached the Gazala Line. Rommel's hopes of holding this position were quickly smashed. On 13 December the British penetrated the positions of the Italian 20 Motorized Corps to a depth of twelve miles. Although a counterthrust later "checked" the breakthrough, Afrikakorps was now enveloped on both flanks. Rommel signaled OKW and stated his estimation of the unpleasant situation and warned of his intentions:

> After four weeks of uninterrupted and costly fighting, the fighting power of the troops - despite superb individual achievements - is showing signs of flagging; all the more so as the supply of arms and ammunition has completely dried up. While the Army intends to maintain its hold on the Gazala area during 16 December, retreat through Mechili-Derna will be unavoidable, at the latest during the night of the 16th, if it is to escape being outflanked and destroyed by a superior enemy.[87]

At 0930 hours on the 16th, Crüwell received instructions to disengage and retire to the Mechili area. 21 Italian Corps was to occupy a delaying position in the intervening area of Timimi.[88]

These instructions shocked the Italian High Command. Cavallero immediately flew from Rome to confront Rommel and question his conduct of the campaign. At the conference that followed, Rommel bluntly stated that only one course of action was still open after the events of the preceding few days - withdrawal across Cyrenaica towards Mechili. The Italian troops, he continued, "had little fight left in them." The latter statement was more than Cavallero could stomach, and he promptly departed. Shortly thereafter, he returned unexpectedly, accompanied by the new German Supreme Commander South, Field Marshal Albert Kesselring, as well as Bastico and Gambara.[89] Bastico demanded that orders to abandon the Gazala Line be rescinded. In this he was strongly supported by Kesselring, who expressed particular concern over the surrender of Derna airfield. But Rommel refused to be budged, stating that his decision was unalterable, for many units were already pulling

---

[87]Hart, *Rommel Papers*, pg. 174.
[88]*Ibid.*, pg. 175.
[89]*Kesselring had no operation authority over Rommel, being responsible only for his supplies and air support. Kesselring had arrived in Rome on 28 November. He experienced very quickly the problems of coalition warfare. See his memoirs, Albert Kesselring, Soldat Bis Zum Letzten Tag (Bonn: Athenaum-Verlag, 1953), pp. 140-41. Hereafter cited as Soldat.*

14 December 1941. Rommel at a forward observation post during the retreat through Cyrenaica.

back. At this Bastico and Gamara became quite heated in their arguments. Rommel then queried Bastico as to how he, the commander-in-chief of the North African Forces, would tackle the situation. Bastico grumbled that operational command was not his business; the delegation beat a hasty retreat.

On 19 December the 4,700-ton merchantman *"Ankara"* docked in Benghazi. It delivered 22 tanks - Rommel's first reinforcements since the early days of the Crusader battle.

"We're pulling out," Rommel candidly informed Lucie. "There was simply nothing else for it. I hope we manage to get back to the line we've chosen. Christmas is going to be completely messed up."[90] He poured out his frustrations to von Rintelen. In a letter received by von Rintelen on the 22nd, Rommel blasted the Italians for their poor performance. Even the good Italian formations, he felt, had let him down. The Italian generals were inefficient and had refused to cooperate with him. He had no choice but to pull back even further, to the positions south of Arco dei Fileni.[91]

The Axis units streamed westwards past Beda Fomm and Antelat to Agedabia. The British had been unable to exploit any of their numerous chances to outflank the Panzergruppe. A final attempt to do so on 27

[90]Hart, Rommel Papers, pg. 175.
[91]AHBT. The Arco Dei Fileni ("Marble Arch") was a "towering white triumphal arch" erected by Mussolini in 1937 at the border between Tripolitania and Cyrenaica.

December led to a stinging defeat for their 22 Armored Brigade. It lost 37 tanks; Crüwell, who engineered the defeat, lost only 7. But Rommel was unimpressed with the possibilities for defense at Agedabia. The city, he contented, could be easily outflanked if his enemy made a "wide hook" through the Cyrenaican desert. Thus Rommel made one final step back - to Mersa el Brega on 2 January 1942. The same day the garrison at Bardia capitulated, though the Axis troops at Halfaya Pass continued to resist until 17 January.

On New Year's Day, Rommel received a greeting from the Führer:

> Together with my thanks for your greetings for the New Year I am sending my warmest wishes to you and your Panzergruppe Afrika; the performances of which fill me with pride and admiration. I know that also during the new year I can rely on my Panzergruppe.
>
> Adolf Hitler[92]

It provided little consolation for six weeks of gruelling combat that had ended in defeat.

A tired Rommel explains his withdrawal to Italian liaison officers attached to the Panzerarmee.

[92]*Rommel Collection*, T-84, 274, #000537.

The Reconquest of Cyrenaica and the Gazala Battles
January-June 1942

In war, as in all human endeavors, timing is an element of decisive importance. By mid-January 1942 several factors had conspired to turn the strategic tables back in Rommel's favor. At the end of 1941 Hitler had transferred some two dozen submarines to the Mediterranean; an entire air force - *Luftflotte II* - had arrived from Russia and had begun to subject Malta, so long a thorn in the Axis' flesh, to a terrific pounding. This rapid shift in forces brought a sudden and unexpected collapse of British naval power in the eastern Mediterranean.

With Malta temporarily neutralized, Panzergruppe Afrika began to grow fangs again. On 5 January a convoy docked at Tripoli - it disgorged 55 tanks, 20 armored cars, various antiaircraft guns and significant stocks of fuel and ammunition. This was "as good as a victory in battle," and Rommel was now cautiously optimistic. "Maybe better times are coming," he wrote to his wife, "in spite of everything."

On "the other side of the hill," Auchinleck's position had palpably deteriorated. In addition to the serious reversals in the Mediterranean, British arms had suffered defeat in another corner of the world: On 7 December Japan launched its desperate gamble for Far Eastern hegemony. Churchill's military commitments were now global in nature and this had an almost immediate effect on Auchinleck. His superiors reduced his forces to shore-up Britain's besieged empire in the Far East.

This quick sketch of the African strategic balance offers insight into Rommel's course of action at the start of 1942, for after a crushing defeat in which he had lost 386 of his 412 tanks, he was again gearing up to take the offensive.

"We drive back and forth across the desert at a hellish tempo,"[1] wrote Rommel's new interpreter, Lieutenant Wilfried Armbruster. Rommel knew far more Italian than he let on, but he still preferred to have an interpreter at his side during important conferences. For several days he toured the front - barking orders and whipping his soldiers into shape for the coming battle. At night he conferred with his staff to finalize his plans.

---

[1] Irving, *The Trail*, pg. 154.

IM NAMEN
DES DEUTSCHEN VOLKES
VERLEIHE ICH
DEM GENERAL DER PANZERTRUPPE
ERWIN ROMMEL
DAS EICHENLAUB MIT SCHWERTERN
ZUM RITTERKREUZ
DES EISERNEN KREUZES

FÜHRERHAUPTQUARTIER
DEN 20. JANUAR 1942

DER FÜHRER
UND OBERSTE BEFEHLSHABER
DER WEHRMACHT

At the first opportunity to leave the battlefields of North Africa, Rommel is presented the award document for his Oakleaves and Swords personally by Hitler on 26 September 1942.

Still suspecting Italian perfidy, Rommel kept his intentions quite secret - informing neither the Commando Supremo nor his own high command of the forthcoming attack. To deceive his enemy he even "leaked" word of further withdrawals; soon this was common knowledge in both the Axis and Allied camps.

Through wireless intercepts Rommel learned of Auchinleck's acute logistical difficulties.[2] He was determined to exploit this advantage. Early on 21 January, just two hours before he attacked, Rommel wrote his wife: "After carefully weighing the pros and cons, I've decided to take the risk. I have complete faith that God is keeping a protective hand over us and that He will grant us victory."[3] The day before, Hitler had awarded him the Oakleaves and Swords to the Knight's Cross of the Iron Cross for his skillful withdrawal from Cyrenaica.

Rommel's award document for his Oakleaves and Swords to the Knight's Cross of the Iron Cross. This photo was taken shortly after its construction was completed and before Hitler had signed it.

---

[2]*Rommel, too, it seems, benefitted from code-breaking. In September 1941 Italian agents had burglarized the American embassy in Rome and photographed the important "Black Code" cipher system. In Cairo the Americans had, since 1941, a military attaché named Colonel Fellers. Fellers, a keen observer of military affairs, signalled to his superiors at the Pentagon detailed appraisals of Eighth Army's equipment, supplies and future plans - all of course, via the Black Code. The Axis intercepted a number of these signals, "Little fellers" as Rommel dubbed them; the information gleaned from them was often of great value. Fellers was recalled to Washington in July 1942, and the source dried up.*

[3]*Hart, Rommel Papers, pg. 180.*

Preparations for the offensive were completed during the night. To simulate a new withdrawal, the Germans burned petrol drums and started fires in the town and harbor of Mersa el Brega. All wheeled traffic towards the front was prohibited.[4]

At 0830 hours Panzerarmee Africa,[5] supported by German and Italian artillery, launched its attack - Rommel's second Cyrenaican offensive.[6] An hour later Rommel issued a stirring proclamation to his troops:

> The Führer has invested me with the Oakleaves and Swords to the Knight's Cross of the Iron Cross in recognition of the defensive victory gained, up to the present against superior enemy forces, by the heroic German-Italian troops. I am proud of this award in which we all share. Let it, henceforth, spur us on to inflict final defeat upon the enemy.
>
> (signed) Rommel

The attackers traversed the enemy minefields without loss, thanks to the excellent work of the German sappers. The first word the Commando Supremo received of this new push came *after* zero hour, when Rommel's orders were posted in all the Cantonieras (Road Maintenance Depots). This was a surprise the Italians could have done without. They fumed.

Ritchie, Eighth Army commander, was equally confounded. Ultra had provided no advance warning, for Rommel had sent no radio signals mapping his intentions. The British were hardly prepared to resist a concerted thrust. They had withdrawn 7 Armored Division, badly bloodied during the Crusader battles, to the area south of Tobruk to refit. In its place, near Agedabia, stood the inexperienced and incomplete 1 Armored Division. Farther back was 4 Indian Division, but its brigades were widely dispersed - at Benghazi, Barce and Tobruk.

Rommel's plan was to trap 1 Armored Division. For this purpose DAK was to advance north of the Wadi el Faregh while Group Marcks (mobile elements of 90 Light Division with some tanks of 21 Panzer), moving along the Via Balbia, pinned the enemy frontally. Rommel's first attempt failed when Afrikakorps tanks experienced "extremely bad going on bad terrain."[7] The enemy slipped from the pocket.

The next day Rommel put himself at the head of Group Marcks and advanced swiftly on Agedabia. It fell at 1100 hours; Antelat six hours later. But again, the Afrikakorps encountered long stretches of undulating sand dunes and only reached the Via Balbia at 1300 hours. The British, states the Panzerarmee war diary, "avoided action and sought to withdraw as quickly as possible in the general direction of Msus."[8]

---

[4]*KTB, Panzerarmee Afrika*, 21 January 1942, NZT.
[5]*Hitler had raised Rommel's command to the status of an army.*
[6]*Rommel began his offensive with 117 German and 79 Italian tanks.*
[7]*KTB, Panzerarmee Afrika*, Appendix 563, 21 January 1942, NZT. See Also Army Corps, *KTB, DAK, T-314, 21, #000179-000180.*
[8]*KTB, Panzerarmee Afrika*, 22 January 1942, NZT.

Rommel persisted with his plans to encircle and destroy the British armor facing him. While the Italian Motorized Corps held the Agedabia area, Crüwell's Afrikakorps was to establish a cordon along the line Agedabia-Antelat-Saunnu; Group Marcks, advancing southeast of Saunnu, was to close the ring on the eastern flank. "It was an ambitious plan," concludes von Mellenthin, " and was only partially successful. Owing to a serious lapse in staff work at Afrikakorps headquarters, Saunnu was not occupied by 21 Panzer after the departure of Group Marcks, and the enemy took advantage of this gap to extricate the bulk of 1 Armored Division."[9]

Smoke and dust rise above British positions as they are subjected to intense German gunfire.

The disgruntled Italians now dispatched the chief of their high command, General Cavallero to Panzerarmee headquarters - to "remonstrate with Rommel" about his independent action. Accompanied by Kesselring, he handed Rommel a directive from Mussolini. "Make this no more than a sortie and then come straight back," Cavallero hissed. But Rommel, who now had Hitler's firm backing, thumbed his nose at the agitated Italian. "Nobody but the Führer could change [his] decision," he riposted, for the bulk of the fighting would be done by German troops. Cavallero "went off growling."[10]

On the 25th the Panzerarmee badly defeated Messervy's 1 Armored Division. Advancing on the right 21 Panzer encountered little opposition; but 15 Panzer collided with superior tank forces northwest of Saunnu. Messervy's inexperienced tank crews never had a chance as 8 Panzer Regiment "broke into the enemy at a tearing speed and threw

---

[9]Von Mellenthin, _Panzer Battles_, pg. 104.
[10]See Kesselring, _Soldat_, pp. 162-63.

While Count Cavallero was visiting an Italian unit, General Kesselring visited his Luftwaffe units and the German supply units. Later, as an intermediary between the Commando Supremo and Rommel, he met with the "Desert Fox."

him into complete confusion."[11] "At times the pursuit attained a speed of 15 miles an hour, and the British columns fled madly over the desert in one of the most extraordinary routs of the war."[12] At 1100 hours 15 Panzer's spearheads reached Msus airfield.

Rommel had inflicted a punishing blow. At little loss to himself, his army had destroyed or captured 299 tanks and armored vehicles and taken nearly 1,000 prisoners.[13] "We have had four days of absolute success," he exclaimed. "Our blow struck the enemy between the eyes."[14]

Goodwin-Austen, 13 Corps commander, decided the time had come to bail out of Cyrenaica; he ordered 4 Indian Division to abandon Benghazi and Messervy to move the battered rump of 1 Armored to Mechili. But Auchinleck and Richtie suddenly intervened. "Interpreting Rommel's moves as yet another 'reconnaissance in force,' they cancelled the instructions for 13 Corps' withdrawal."[15]

[11]*KTB, 15 Panzer Division*, 25 January 1942, NZT.
[12]Von Mellenthin, *Panzer Battles*, pg. 104.
[13]Army Corps, *KTB, DAK*, T-314, 21, #000201. From January 21-25 DAK war diary records the following as destroyed or captured: 299 tanks and armored vehicles, 24 airplanes, 147 guns, 751 motor vehicles and 933 prisoners. Its own losses during the period amounted to 3 officers and 14 men dead; only 3 tanks were totally destroyed.
[14]*Rommel Collection*, T-84, 274, #000579.
[15]Lewin, *Rommel*, pg. 105.

From wireless intercepts by 3./56 Signals Unit, Rommel gleaned his opponent's indecisiveness; he would exploit it through a daring and unexpected stroke. While Crüwell feinted towards Mechili, Rommel, with Group Marcks and 3 and 33 Reconnaissance Battalions, would thrust straight through to Benghazi and destroy the Indian division.

Rommel's small force set out at dusk on the 27th. It struggled forward "under the severest weather and terrain conditions - heavy rainstorms, cloudbursts and deep wadies."[16] Ritchie swallowed the bait and moved Messervy off to Mechili to intercept the phantom German thrust. The next day, like a "clap of thunder," Rommel burst upon his unsuspecting foe. "In less than an hour," writes Lieutenant Alfred Brandt, "the Indian Division has been smashed. Our troops capture hundreds of trucks: we have done the seemingly impossible - we have overcome every obstacle, driven by our commander's spirit through the marshy wilderness and across the red and slippery mountains of Cyrenaica; and we have struck right into the enemy's flank just as they think they are safe at last."[17] Over 1,000 prisoners were taken.[18]

Rommel in the Italian army corps HQ on 28 January 1942, meeting with General Navarrini (far left). Directly behind Rommel is Colonel Diesener (the liaison officer), and to his left is General Gause.

[16]*KTB, Panzerarmee Afrika*, 28 January 1942, NZT.
[17]As quoted in Irving, *The Trail*, pg. 157.
[18]*KTB, Panzerarmee Afrika*, 29 January 1942, NZT.

Rommel discusses defense positions with an Italian officer. At far left is von Mellenthin.

Word of the victory was promptly passed to Berlin; Hitler promoted his favorite to Colonel General. No one else had ever reached the exalted rank so young.

General Ritchie drew the inescapable conclusion from the battering he had taken. He relinquished all of the Cyrenaican bulge and retired to positions south of Gazala.[19] Goodwin-Austen, disgusted with his superior's clumsy conduct of operations, tendered his resignation.

But Rommel, too, had problems; he was again at loggerheads with the Italians. His plan to exploit his triumph through an advance on Tobruk and then on Egypt was squashed by Mussolini. In a telegram from Cavallero to Bastico (1 February) the Duce outlined his operational instructions: "the main object with all operational plans remains at all times the defense of Tripolitania by the German-Italian troops in Libya." The result was a compromise. Rommel positioned a thin skin of mobile troops before the British Gazala line and held the main force of the Panzerarmee far back to the west - around Antelat and Mersa Brega. "This," writes Bayerlein, "concluded the winter fighting. Both sides now prepared for the approaching decisive battle of the summer."[20]

---

[19]In the Panzerarmee's KTB "Appreciation" for 4 February, it states "the enemy appears to be reforming for defense with the bulk of his forces in a line north of Bir Hacheim-Acroma-Tobruk, whilst units of 1 Armored Division and reconnaissance units are covering the building of the position along a general line Bir Hacheim-Ain el Gazala." KTB, Panzerarmee Afrika, 4 February 1942, NZT.
[20]Hart, Rommel Papers, pg. 183.

In mid-March Rommel flew to Rastenburg to discuss his plans for future operations. He met an "indifferent" Führer who was engrossed in his preparations for the forthcoming summer offensive in Russia. Hitler and his staff had little time for the Desert Fox and his "colonial war." Rommel was informed not to expect reinforcements in the near future. He returned to Africa a frustrated and bitter man: "The German High Command, to which I am subordinate, still failed to see the importance of the African theatre. They do not realize that with relatively small means, we could have won victories in the Near East which, in their strategic and economic value, would have far surpassed the conquest of the Don Bend. Ahead of us lay territories containing an enormous wealth of raw materials: Africa, for example, and the Middle East - which could have freed us from all our anxieties about oil. A few more divisions for my Army, with supplies for them guaranteed, would have sufficed to bring about the complete defeat of the entire British forces in the Near East. . . . But it was not to be. . . . It was obvious that the High Command's opinion had not changed from that which they had expressed in 1941, namely that Africa was a 'lost cause.' "[21]

National Archives

Rommel is greeted by Hitler at Rastenburg.

It was clear, however, that Malta had to be eliminated. In late April Mussolini, Cavallero and Kesselring met with Hitler at the Obersalzberg. Cavallero pressed strongly for a joint German-Italian undertaking against the island, and Hitler agreed. Operation "Hercules," as it was called, was to "take place during the full-moon period in June, and

[21]*Ibid.*, pg. 191.

During the meeting with Hitler on 16 March 1942, Rommel found the Führer indifferent to the Panzer Army's problems. General Field Marshal Keitel (center) was annoyed at Rommel for his untimely visit.

Following his conference at Rastenburg, Rommel made a short visit to his home at Wiener-Neustadt. There he was congratulated for his award of the Oakleaves and Swords by ranking officials from the local NSDAP and affiliated organizations. Lucie Rommel has her back to the camera.

Rommel arrived back in North Africa in time to help celebrate General Crüwell's birthday. Here he is greeted by General Nehring.

U.S. Army Photograph

U.S. Army Photograph

Rommel congratulates General Crüwell on the occasion of his birthday and gives him a gift from "home." The location is 40 kilometers southeast of Derna, Cyrenaica.

as a preliminary Field Marshal Kesselring was ordered to soften up Malta by continuous air attacks."[22]

Kesselring then flew to Africa and arrived at Rommel's headquarters on 28 April. In a conference attended by Gause, Westphal and Air Commander *(Fliegerführer)* Africa, Lieutenant General Hoffman von Waldau, Kesselring informed Rommel of his conference with the Führer. He promised to do all in his power to fulfill the Panzerarmee's logistical requirements.[23] Later that afternoon, after Kesselring had flown back to his headquarters, "the Supreme Commander of Armed Forces in North Africa, Marshal Bastico, decorated [Rommel] with the Grand Order of the Colonial Star in the presence of the G.O.C. Italian Army Corps."

Rommel receives the Grand Order of the Colonial Star. From left to right: Rommel, Gambara, Calvi, Bastico and Crüwell.

At the Obersalzberg Hitler and Mussolini had agreed to let Rommel take the offensive before Hercules - "with the reservation that after capturing Tobruk he was to revert to the defensive, while the main axis effort was diverted to Malta."[24] This suited Rommel just fine. There was evidence that Ritchie was preparing to attack, and Rommel was determined to strike first. On 30 April he drafted a report to the Italian GHQ in North Africa in which he openly stated his intention to "attack and destroy the British forces in the area of Bir el Gubi-Tobruk-Ain el Gazala-Bir Hacheim during the first days of June." A few days later Marshals Bastico and Barbasetti,[25] on Rommel's invitation, arrived at

---

[22]Von Mellenthin, *Panzer Battles*, Pg. 107.
[23]*KTB, Panzerarmee Afrika*, 28 April 1942, NZT.
[24]Lewin, *Rommel*, pg. 108.
[25]General Curio Barbasetti was Gambara's successor as chief to the GHQ, North Africa.

Rommel discusses the joint German/Italian offensive against entrenched British positions with field commanders under him.

Panzerarmee headquarters to inspect the front of the Italian Corps. When Rommel broached his plans for a new offensive, "Marshal Bastico expressed complete agreement and promised [to]...make every effort possible to replenish the Italian formations."[26] As if to underscore his resolve, that very day the *SS Ankara* and *SS Monviso* arrived in Benghazi, and *SS Lerici* and *SS Bixio* at Tripoli. They delivered 272 vehicles, 27 field guns and 20 tanks.[27]

In the brutal heat of mid-May, the Panzerarmee was an anthill of activity, carefully arranging the final details of the impending offensive. Rommel's staff viewed the attack with mixed feelings. General Gause considered it a risk to Rommel's "entire reputation," while Westphal argued that "on the balance they had no option but to attack - to wait any longer on the defensive might put the entire Panzerarmee in danger."[28] But cracking Ritchie's Gazala line would be a formidable task. It stretched over forty miles into the desert - from Gazala to Bir Hacheim. Along its front were dense minefields of an unprecedented scale; the line itself was anchored by a series of fortified "boxes" - infantry strong points buttressed by artillery and surrounded by barbed wire and minefields.

The armored balance again favored the British. Eighth Army now fielded some 700 tanks in its front line strength. Included among these were 167 Grant M3's, about which Rommel had no intelligence.[29] These

---

[26]*KTB, Panzerarmee Afrika*, 2 May 1942, NZT.
[27]*Ibid.*
[28]Irving, *The Trail*, pg. 163.
[29]Von Mellenthin disputes this point. He insists that the Germans did know   **133**

American-built medium tanks possessed a 75mm main armament, which far out-classed the 220 Panzer III's which comprised the bulk of the German armor. The only tanks in Rommel's arsenal capable of competing with them were 19 Panzer III Specials (with a high-velocity 50mm gun) and 4 Panzer IV Specials. The Panzerarmee did have 48, 88mm guns, and these were more than a match for any British tank. In all, the Axis entered the Gazala battle with 332 German and 228 Italian tanks.[30]

Rommel's plan was as simple as it was audacious. The German 15 Rifle Brigade (from 90 Light Division) and the 10 and 21 Italian Corps were to assault the northernmost section of the Gazala line on early afternoon 26 May. General Crüwell, having returned from sick leave,[31] was to command this group; it was hoped that his attack, intended as a feint, would entice the British to shift their armor northwards. Rommel would lead the main striking force himself. This consisted of 15 Panzer Division (Lieutenant General Gustav von Vaerst), 21 Panzer Division (Major General Georg von Bismark), 90 Light Division (Major General Kleeman)[32] and the Italian 20 Motorized Corps (Ariete and Trieste divisions). The Afrikakorps, now commanded by General Walter Nehring, was to execute a "rapid night march, advance round the Gazala Line to the Acroma area, and then attack the British forces from the rear. 90 Light and the reconnaissance units were to advance to El Adem and cause disruption on the British supply routes." Operating on the northern flank of the *Schwerpunkt,* Ariete Division was to capture the Bir Hacheim strong point. But "events were to show," writes von Mellenthin, "that our attitude towards Bir Hacheim was far to casual, and that a capture of the place was a 'sine qua non' for any successful operation behind the Gazala Line."[33]

After the Axis heavy guns had completed their preparatory bombardment, Group Crüwell, at 1400 hours, advanced against the Gazala Line. Trucks which mounted aircraft engines and propellers raced across Crüwell's front to simulate an attack by the entire Panzerarmee in that sector - another ruse from the Desert Fox's bag of tricks.

At 2300 hours Rommel issued the code word "Venezia"; his steel phalanx of 10,000 vehicles began to rumble southwards, silhouetted against a bright moonlight. The advance of this column "had been prepared in minute detail; compass bearings, distances, and speeds had been carefully calculated; dim lights concealed in gasoline tins indicated the line of march, and with the smoothness of a well-oiled

---

about the Grant tanks; and that his Intelligence Appreciation of 20 May "included a full description." All objective sources, however, point to the contrary. The Grant, writes Heckmann, could destroy a German Panzer III at a range of 1 500 meters. Heckmann, Rommel's Krieg, pg. 302.

[30]They also fielded twenty-four captured British tanks. Von Esebeck, Afrikanische Schicksalsjahre, pg. 72.

[31]Crüwell had taken sick leave on 8 March due to jaundice.

[32]An air attack on 9 December had killed the division's former commander, Sümmermann.

[33]Von Mellenthin, Panzer Battles, pp. 112-13.

machine the regiments of the Afrikakorps swept on to their fueling point southeast of Bir Hacheim."[34]

Rommel's efforts to mask the *Schwerpunkt* of his offensive were only partially successful; the 4 South African Armored Car Regiment had detected the Afrikakorps columns - shrouded in a sea of whirling dust - pushing southwards that night and relayed the information to 7 Armored Division. But to Rommel's good fortune, the British were sluggish in reacting.[35]

Rommel and Major General Georg von Bismarck, commander of 21 Panzer Division.

At 0430 hours the armored fist wheeled to the north[36] - 21 Panzer on the left, 15 Panzer on the right. The tanks were now behind Ritchie's front and, two hours later, von Bismark's division plowed into 3 Indian Brigade. In a brief but violent engagement, 21 Panzer steam-rolled its opponent. At 0700 hours von Vaerst's Panzers carved clean through 4 Armored Brigade as it deployed for battle; 8 Hussar's was destroyed and 3 Royal Tank Regiment badly beaten up. "We had, in fact," remembers von Mellenthin, "inflicted a shattering defeat on the famous 7 Armored Division, which made off as best it could towards Bir el Gubi and El Adem."[37] On the right flank 90 Light Division swept over the Retma

[34]*Ibid.*, pg. 116.
[35]*Ultra provided the British with the precise X-Hour for the German offensive. The source was a deciphered message from Rintelen in Rome to OKH. Heckmann, Rommel's Krieg, pg. 305.*
[36]*Divisions, KTB, 21 Panzer Division, T-315, 768, #000639.*
[37]*Von Mellenthin, Panzer Battles, pg. 117.*

Box; General Messervy was captured by a German reconnaissance unit, but escaped the next day.

Rommel had smashed through the left wing of Norrie's 30 Corps; only slowly did his adversary begin to react. At 0845 hours 22 Armored Brigade motored southwards to counterattack; but a concentric thrust by the armor of both German Panzer divisions sent it reeling back. The British continued to hurl their tanks forward in dribblets. At noon it was 2 Armored Brigade's turn. It lunged at the Afrikakorps' spearheads as they crossed the Trigh Capuzzo east of the Knightsbridge Box; though

Gause, von Mellenthin, Rommel and Nehring attend a field conference on May 26, 1942 to discuss the final plans for the attack on Gazala.

the attack was poorly coordinated, it inflicted severe losses and brought the DAK advance to a temporary halt.

In the bitter fighting of the 27th, Nehring's tank crews suffered heavily. The new British medium tank - the Grant - came as a devastating shock. In one engagement that day, 40 of the 29-ton Grants had clattered forward and hit deep into the flank of von Vaerst's 15 Panzer - their stout 75mm guns spewing fire. A disaster was narrowly averted by the quick action of Colonel Alwin Wolz. He scraped together every available flak gun - 16 of them - and arranged them on a three kilometer front.   When the enemy tanks were within 1 200 meters, Wolz's Pak front opened a terrific counterfire and broke the attack. At dusk the burned-out skeletons of 24 Grants ringed the battlefield.[38]

Despite the tactical successes, by nightfall the Axis Army found itself in a critical situation. Ariete had failed to capture Bir Hacheim; Trieste Division was stuck in the minefields to the west; Crüwell's diversion had "made no real impression."[39] The Afrikakorps had lost a third of its tanks and von Vaerst's division was low on fuel and ammunition. III./104 Infantry Regiment (21 Panzer) was so badly decimated it had to be disbanded.[40] Rommel's striking force was now scattered over the Gazala line, wedged between British units which, "though battered, were by no means destroyed."[41] "90 Light Division under General Kleeman," records Rommel in his *Papers,* "had become separated from the Afrika Korps and was now in a very dangerous position. British motorized groups were streaming through the open gap and hunting down the transport columns which had lost touch with the main body. And on these columns the life of my army depended."[42]

15 and 21 Panzer Divisions established hedgehog positions between Rigel Ridge and Bir Lefa; Kleeman's 90 Light, pushed back during the day by 4 Armored Brigade, formed a front south of El Adem. As mentioned, Rommel's detachments were widely dispersed; a concentrated armored thrust by Eighth Army could now have swept Rommel's pawns right off the board. Eighth Army, records von Mellenthin, "in spite of its initial reverses of the day,... was in a position to win a crushing victory."[43] But the next day the British continued to waste their armor in "penny-packet" attacks, and thus squandered their opportunity to deal the Afrikakorps a deadly blow.

The failure of his opening move did not shake Rommel; he resolved to continue the battle in a northernly direction. Fierce armored battles raged throughout the 28th between Afrikakorps and 2 and 22 Armored Brigades in the Knightsbridge Box area. 15 Panzer was still immobilized due to fuel shortages, but von Bismark's tanks pushed aside a British column north of Rigel Ridge and climbed the escarpment overlooking the Via Balbia.[44] The day's fighting was inconclusive, though losses on both sides were considerable.

As the sun rose in the western desert on 29 May, Rommel's position had become desperate. The two Italian infantry corps had failed to attack with authority, enabling Ritchie to switch all his armored units south to meet DAK's advance. But as so often in times of acute crisis, Rommel's personal intervention and leadership would tip the scales in his favor.

[38]Karl Alman, *Panzer vor: Die dramatische Geschichte der Panzerwaffe und ihrer tapferen Soldaten* (Rastatt: Erich Pabel Verlag, 1966), pp. 268-69.

[39]Lewin, *Rommel,* pg. 114.

[40]KTB, 21 Panzer Division, 27 May 1942, NZT.

[41]C.B. Playfair, *The Mediterranean and the Middle East,* Vol. III: The British Fortunes Reach Their Lowest Ebb (London: Her Majesty's Stationery Office, 1960), pg. 225. Hereafter cited as *British Fortunes.*

[42]Hart, *Rommel Papers,* pg. 208.

[43]Von Mellenthin, *Panzer Battles,* pg. 120.

[44]Divisions, KTB, 21 Panzer Division, T-315, 768, #000643.

While his forces are embroiled near Bir Hacheim, Rommel plots his next strike towards Sidi Muftah.

His first activity that morning was to personally steer the overdue supply columns through a gap he had discovered in the minefields to the stranded 15 Panzer Division at Rigel Ridge. He then lashed out violently at 2 Armored Brigade, which was rolling west from Knightsbridge in an effort to drive a wedge between Ariete south of the Trigh Capuzzo and the DAK armor to the north. "The battle which followed was one of the most critical of the campaign... 'The Grants were shooting magnificiently and time after time brought the squat black Mark III's and IV's to a standstill.' 22 Armored Brigade came up to assist 2 Armored Brigade... A hot wind and whirling sandstorms added to the strain on the tank crews, and by evening both sides were glad to call off the battle."[45] When the dust settled, Rommel's position had noticeably improved; he had concentrated 90 Light and the Afrikakorps in the area between Sidra and Aslagh Ridges - the area soon to be immortalized as the "Cauldron." The pattern of the Gazala battle, records Lewin, "is in fact one of progressive failure by the British command to grasp what was happening and a steady imposition of his will by Rommel."[46]

But his forces were still tied to a vulnerable logistical tail which coiled its way around Bir Hacheim; by dusk the Afrikakorps had nearly exhausted its ammunition and was again low on fuel. Rommel made an inspired decision. He would strike westwards, towards Sidi Muftah, slice a path through the enemy minefields and reestablish his communications with Group Crüwell and his main supply lines. With his supplies intact he could then shift his armor back to the east and "seek a decisive victory over the Eighth Army."

---

[45]Von Mellenthin, _Panzer Battles_, pp. 121-22.
[46]Lewin, _Rommel_, pg. 116.

Earlier that day General Crüwell had climbed into a Storch to fly to the headquarters of the 10 Italian Corps. He had sent Colonel Krause on ahead, with instructions that a flare should be fired to prevent his aircraft from overshooting its mark and entering enemy air space. This arrangement proved a failure, however, and soon Crüwell's Storch was over the British positions. A quick burst of ground fire killed the pilot; providentially, the plane only damaged its undercarriage when it plunged to the ground. Crüwell was uninjured, but a prisoner.

Command on the northern front now devolved upon Rommel's chief intelligence officer, von Mellenthin. Fortunately, Field Marshal Kesselring has arrived, and though it took some coaxing, he agreed to take temporary command of Group Crüwell.[47] Kesselring, "one of the best staff officers and administrators produced by any service, ... was astounded at Rommel's loose battlefield control. 'From what eye witnesses told me about goings-on at Rommel's headquarters on the first day of the tank battle,' he later wrote, 'they just beggared all description.' "[48] Rommel's critics came down hardest on his preference for commanding in the front lines - often leading individual battalions or platoons in the attack. Such a technique, they felt, unduly exposed Rommel to minor fluctuations in the fighting, without yielding an accurate picture of the battle as a whole.[49]

The crew of this Pz.Kpfw. III rests during a lull in the fighting.

[47]Kesselring, _Soldat_, pp. 170-71.
[48]Irving, _The Trail_, pg. 172. See also Kesselring, Soldat, pg. 171.
[49]Kesselring, _Soldat_, pg. 171.

For the next three days Rommel concentrated his efforts on smashing a breach through the enemy minefields to link up with 10 Italian Corps. The operation began on 30 May and quickly brought an unpleasant surprise. German intelligence had failed to uncover the presence of a heavily-fortified box at Sidi Muftah; Rommel's push ran square into 150 Brigade, nestled behind its minefields and wire entanglements. After investing the box, Rommel attacked the next day with 90 Light, Trieste and battlegroups from the Afrikakorps.[50] Von Waldau's Stukas swooped over the enemy positions; later, Rommel personally led the breakthrough into the enemy perimeter. The Afrikakorps war diary noted the stubborn nature of the defense: "individual positions have to be taken dugout by dugout in close combat."[51] Around noon on 1 June, enemy resistance flickered out after a "short but violent attack."[52] Three thousand men emerged from their battered dugouts and shuffled into captivity.

"The elimination of the 150 Brigade greatly eased Rommel's position";[53] he had secured his supplies and torn a gap in the Gazala line. But the triumph had proven costly: Westphal, wounded in a mortar attack, was evacuated to Europe; that afternoon Rommel's indispensible operations officer, General Gause, was also badly injured.

On 2 June Rommel moved 90 Light and Trieste Divisions southwards with orders to crack the enemy strong-point at Bir Hacheim. The protracted struggle which followed provides one of the more extraordinary chapters of the desert war. Manning the crumbling fort at Bir Hacheim were some four thousand French troops, including a Jewish brigade and some legionnaires. They would resist fanatically - for days - while Stukas screamed down from the sky and terrorized them with tons of well-placed bombs. The diary of a captured British officer paints a vivid picture of the tortured scene:

> June 1. At noon there was a terrible hail of bombs from wave after wave of dive bombers. The trenches and walls of the fort caved in, burying men alive. It's a horrific sight...
>
> June 2. Another hail of bombs from twenty airplanes. They come right down low and machine-gun us. We can't hold on. More men are killed, many more...
>
> June 3. This afternoon we were bombed three times by German and Italian airplanes. We couldn't get any water until evening. There are more injured everywhere. Their screams of agony ring around the ruins of the fort...
>
> June 4. The air is full of smoke, and in this motionless

[50]KTB, 90 Leichte Division, 30 May 1942, NZT.
[51]KTB, DAK, 31 May 1942, NZT.
[52]KTB, 90 Leichte Division, 1 June 1942, NZT.
[53]Von Mellenthin, Panzer Battles, pg. 125.

hot air it just lies in coils around us. I'm dying of thirst, but nobody's got any water to give...

June 5. We don't have any stretchers, we've got no water, we can't even bury our dead. The choking stink of the exploding bombs mingles with the foul smell of rotting bodies - just to see them leaves our nerves in shreds.[54]

That day, June 5, 1942, Auchinleck put in his long-awaited counter-punch in an attempt to hurl the Afrikakorps back out of the Cauldron. After an artillery barrage, Eighth Army's tanks burst forward at 0530 hours.[55] The attack - code named "Aberdeen" - was a dismal failure. 22 Armored Brigade (156 Grants, Stuarts and Crusaders) ran into withering artillery fire and pulled back. 32 Tank Brigade forfeited 50 of its 70 tanks in a futile assault on von Bismark's 21 Panzer at Sidra Ridge. This latter thrust was "one of the most ridiculous attacks of the campaign." Without adequate infantry or artillery support, the brigade's armor simply advanced into an unexpected mine belt where it was "shot to pieces."[56]

Rommel quickly counterattacked. The Afrikakorps overran the tactical headquarters of 7 Armored and 5 Indian Divisions; by dusk it had slaughtered 10 Indian Brigade, badly shaken 9 Indian Brigade, and destroyed over 100 enemy tanks.[57]

The fierce actions of the 5th had turned the tide in favor of the Axis forces. Rommel now sent a strong battlegroup from 15 Panzer southwards to support the stalled attack on Bir Hacheim. The fort's "ferocious defense," led by Colonel Pierre Koenig, "was raising problems for the whole Mediterranean campaign. Marshal Kesselring watched with mounting impatience - knowing that the battle was using *Luftwaffe* planes he would soon need for his German-Italian assault on Malta... On 7 June Kesselring flew by Stuka dive bomber to Rommel's headquarters. The heat was unbearable. There was a new, violent argument. By the time he left, Kesselring had extracted a firm timetable from Rommel: he would wipe out Bir Hacheim the next day, thrust through to the coast on the 9th or 10th, pry open the Gazala line, let the infantry divisions pour through to the east and then - the long-sought prize itself": Tobruk.[58] And Tobruk, Kesselring insisted, must fall at the very latest by the 25th.

Bir Hacheim did not go under on the 8th. For several more days Stukas atomized the indomitable, though dying, fort. Then, late on 10 June, Koenig began a breakout attempt. Sheets of fire, laid down by 606

[54]As quoted in Irving, *The Trail*, pg. 174.
[55]Divisions, *KTB, 21 Panzer Division*, T-315, 768, #000652.
[56]Von Mellenthin, *Panzer Battles*, pp. 132-33.
[57]21 Panzer alone registered 49 tank kills that day. Since the 26th, the division had shot up a total of 214 enemy tanks.
[58]Irving, *The Trail*, pg. 175.

Flak and 605 Antitank Battalions, tore great gaps in the withdrawing enemy columns; but large forces succeeded in breaking through the Axis ring and escaping. The next morning 90 Light Division occupied the fort, taking prisoner some 500 French legionnaires.[59]

With the fall of Bir Hacheim, Rommel once again sent his Panzers chugging northwards, for a final reckoning with the Eighth Army. Ritchie's position was still strong; he had established a series of defensive posts bristling with minefields in the area north of the Cauldron. 201 Guards Brigade held the Knightsbrigde Box while 29 Indian Brigade

After the fall of Bir Hacheim, Rommel races northward to personally direct envelopment of the enemy behind the Gazala line.

was firmly entrenched at El Adem. Von Vaerst's 15 Panzer along with 90 Light and Trieste moved northwest; their objective was El Adem - "that small strip of sand and stone which, as so often in the desert war, acquired a significance which bore no relation to its relative insignificance."[60] Simultaneously, 21 Panzer and Ariete demonstrated against the British forces in the Knightsbridge area. In essence, Rommel had reverted to his original plan of enveloping enemy resistance behind the Gazala line. His tank forces were now greatly reduced in

[59]*KTB, 90 Leichte Division*, 11 June 1942, NZT.
[60]Lewin, *Rommel*, pg. 119.

number. Afrikakorps had only 124 battle tanks remaining; Ariete could still muster 60 of its "steel coffins."[61] The decimated 90 Light was down to battle strength of 1,000 men. But in the ensuing 48 hours, he would again benefit from Ritchie's clumsy tactical combinations.

On June 12 and 13, Afrikakorps' Panzers grappled with the British Cruisers and Matildas. By the end of the first day I./5 Panzer Regiment alone had rendered 43 enemy tanks "hors de combat";[62] the remnants of 90 Light had reached the high ground north of El Adem. When the fire-fight ended on the 13th, 150 British tanks were smoking wrecks on the battlefield; Eighth Army's armored backbone was shattered. The next day Ritchie's beat-up columns began to evacuate the Gazala positions and to limp back towards the frontier. At Tobruk a large British garrison still held out. Rommel was on the verge of his greatest victory.

On the road to Tobruk, Rommel samples of captured British "selected fruit."

[61]Heckmann, _Rommel's Krieg_, pp. 345, 348.
[62]Army Corps, _KTB, DAK_, T-314, 21, #000426.

The Capture of Tobruk to First El Alamein
June-July 1942

Rommel immediately launched a vigorous pursuit of his beaten enemy. On 14 June, Rommel writes in his *Papers:* "the German Panzer divisions moved off and rolled northwards. Full speed was ordered, as British vehicles were now streaming east in their thousands. I rode with the tanks and constantly urged their commanders to keep the speed up. Suddenly we ran into a wide belt of mines. Ritchie had attempted to form a new defense front and had put in every tank he had. The advance halted and our vehicles were showered with British armor-piercing shells."[1]

But Ritchie's desperate attempt to parry the Panzerarmee's advance on the general line Acroma-El Adem-El Gubi was doomed to sudden failure. The Gazala fighting had reduced Eighth Army to some 70 tanks; Rommel now disposed of over twice that number. He moved quickly to mop up British resistance around the Tobruk perimeter, prior to an attack on the fortress itself. On 15 June 90 Light Division moved against El Adem, the southern cornerstone of the Tobruk defenses. Defending the strongpoint were two battalions of 29 Indian Brigade and they successfully beat back the German attacks that day. On the 16th 21 Panzer advanced on Sidi Rezegh and Belhamed, while 90 Light renewed its attacks on the stubbornly defended El Adem Box. The furious German assaults forced the Indian infantry to withdraw from El Adem during the night. By the next evening Sidi Rezegh was in the clutches of von Bismark's Panzers, but not before a desperate engagement. British fighter bombers, armed for the first time with 40mm cannon, had shuttle bombed 21 Panzer and caused considerable losses.[2]

Rommel now ordered the Afrikakorps and Ariete Division to advance on Gambut and its airfield. Shortly after midnight on 17-18 June, 21 Panzer severed the coast road east of Tobruk, and thus completed the isolation of the fortress. A few hours later the division seized the Gambut airfield.[3] Rommel, with his *Kampfstaffel,* arrived in Gambut with his

---

[1]Hart, <u>Rommel Papers</u>, pg. 222.
[2]Divisions, <u>KTB, 21 Panzer Division</u>, T-315, 768, #000701. The war diary erroneously puts the calibre of the new British weapon at 20mm.
[3]<u>Ibid.</u>, #000704.

German infantry marching towards Tobruk.

awesome prehistoric monsters, flinging shells into the Tobruk harbor itself. At 1900 hours, the port and the city proper were firmly in German hands.[13] 15 Panzer, now led by Colonel Crasemann, advanced on Pilastrino Ridge.[14]

By nightfall the battle was a foregone conclusion. It remained only to extinguish the flickering resistance in the coming morning. A bright glow and dense clouds of black smoke settled over the crumbling fortress; violent explosions rocked the night air as the British hurriedly demolished their fuel and ammunition dumps. Long lines of prisoners marched into the German POW cages.

Rommel, strutting triumphantly inside Tobruk, must have felt an exhilerating release: "For months his troops had crouched outside this malicious parcel of Libyan desert, tortured by flies and plagues, tormented by sub-zero temperatures and baking sun, unable to raise their heads or seek cover between dawn and dusk - and now here he was, standing in the midst of the fortress."[15]

Shortly after dawn, on 21 June, the curtain dropped on the final act of the Tobruk drama. General Klopper emerged from his headquarters and met with Rommel on the Via Balbia west of Tobruk. The men quickly arranged the capitulation of the garrison. Rommel immediately signaled Berlin that the fortress had fallen; with over 25,000 prisoners. Numbed by the excitement he wrote home: "Tobruk the battle was magnificent. Much activity in the fortified area. I must get a few hours

[13]Divisions, _KTB, 21 Panzer Division_, T-315, 768, #000710.
[14]Von Vaerst was injured during the Gazala battles.
[15]Irving, _The Trail_, pg. 181.

149

A mixed grouping of Italian armor and German supply units pause during the advance against Tobruk.

An assault team pauses at a captured British strong point.

sleep after all this."[16] Evidently the fall of Tobruk had made an impression upon Hitler, too, for that evening Rommel heard over radio of his promotion to Field Marshal.

A Field Marshal at 50! It was a dazzling honor. A flood of congratulatory mail poured into the Rommel home in Wiener-Neustadt. "The news that I was made Field Marshal came like a dream," he confided to Lucie. "In fact, all the events of the last few weeks are like a dream."[17] For some, however, Rommel's good fortune loomed like a nightmare. Count Galeazzo Ciano, the Italian Foreign Minister, confessed in his diary: "Rommel's promotion to Field Marshal, which Hitler evidently made to accentuate the German character of the battle, causes the Duce much pain."[18]

But even as the news of Rommel's tremendous victory blared ostentatiously over the German radio, President Roosevelt was driving the first nails into the Panzerarmee's coffin. Churchill was visiting with Roosevelt in Washington, D.C. when the bitter news of Tobruk's capitulation reached him. When the American President queried, "What can we do to help?" Churchill was quick to reply: "Give us as many Sherman tanks as you can spare, and ship them to the Middle East as quickly as possible."[19] In the desperate days of November 1942, these tanks would help to break the back of Rommel's El Alamein defenses.

Rommel wasted no time savoring his long-sought victory. "We are moving up and hope to strike the next blow soon," he confessed to Lucie. "Speed is essential now." For the Desert Fox, it was now a matter of "letting slip the dogs of war - his armor. The frontier, Cairo and Alexandria, the Canal and the oilfields in the Persian Gulf seemed glittering and attainable prizes."[21]

But first a sticky strategic dilemma demanded a solution. The issue was Malta. The Axis dictators had earlier decreed that after the fall of Tobruk the Panzerarmee was to stand on the defensive at the Egyptian frontier; every available *Luftwaffe* plane was to be hurled against Malta, to support the intended assault on the island.[22] On 21 June Kesselring flew to Africa to confer with Rommel. He reminded the Panzerarmee commander of the pressing need to stick to the original plan and eliminate Malta. Otherwise, he argued, the army's supply lines would be fatally compromised. But the impetuous Rommel emphatically disagreed. Eighth Army was in head-long retreat, he asserted; there now

[16]*Rommel Collection*, T-84, 274, #000740.
[17]*Ibid.*
[18]Galeazzo Ciano, *Ciano's Diary*, 1933-1943 (London: William Heinemann Ltd., 1947), pg. 485.
[19]Francis L. Lowenheim, Harold D. Langley, and Manfred Jones, eds., Roosevelt and Churchill: Their Secret Wartime Correspondence (New York: E. P. Dutton, 1975), pg. 678.
[20]*Rommel Collection*, T-84, 274, #000740.
[21]Lewin, Rommel, pg. 129.
[22]For details of operation Hercules, see Kesselring, Soldat, pp. 173-74. The rejection of this undertaking, reflected Kesselring, "was a mortal blow."

No time was wasted in pursuing the Eighth Army towards Egypt.

existed a "unique opportunity" to sweep right up to the Suez Canal. The conference ended with both men still at loggerheads. But the crafty Rommel had no intention of dropping his plans of pursuit into Egypt. He quietly dispatched a member of his personal staff to Berlin to represent his views before the Führer. This stratagem carried the day for Rommel. Hitler agreed to allow the Panzerarmee to push on into Egypt and resolved to postpone operation Hercules. He had lost faith in the propsed airborne attack anyway. Hitler then wired Mussolini: "The Goddess of Victory approaches commanders in battle only once... If they do not clutch her then, she often never again comes within their reach."[23] This decision would have far-reaching consequences in the days to come.

Rommel flung his spearheads across the frontier wire on 23 June. Ritchie had no intention of making a stand in the defensive posts along the frontier and had already started to withdraw to the east - to positions around the port of Marsa Matruh. In the next two days the Afrikakorps bolted dramatically forward, encountering little resistance from Eighth Army ground forces. But in the air an ominous change had occurred. The British Desert Air Force, dramatically revived, began to tackle the rolling Axis columns with greater frequency and telling effect. In fact, "Rommel never again enjoyed the advantage of air superiority, and the enemy's air forays grew with terrifying strength. It

[23]Irving, _The Trail_, pg. 185.

was the beginning of a process which was to alter the whole balance of the war, and which reached its culmination in the annihilating battles of Mortain and Falaise [in Normandy]."[24]

The Panzerarmee was besieged by other difficulties as well. Many units were running short on petrol and lagged far behind. Afrikakorps, moreover, had dwindled to 44 tanks. But Rommel remained undaunted; he had his enemy on the run and he was determined to deliver a final, knock-out punch.

Reconnaissance detachments of 15 Panzer reached Mersa Matruh late on the 25th. Rommel intended to attack the next day. The night passed violently as RAF bombers repeatedly blasted and dispersed the Axis columns.[25] Enemy fighter planes even peppered Rommel's own headquarters.

Rommel and von Bismarck plan the role of the 21 Panzer Division in the upcoming advance on British defenses.

General Auchinleck now took personal command of Eighth Army. He had already decided not to make a final stand at Mersa Matruh. Auchinleck's motive "was his desire to gain time - time to bring up more tanks from the workshops, time for the RAF to settle down and work from new airfields, time to bring up 9 Australian Division from Syria, time to concentrate all the remaining field and medium artillery

---

[24]Von Mellenthin, _Panzer Battles_, pp.152-153. DAK also noted the heavy air activity on its front. Army Corps, _KTB, DAK_, T-314, 21, #000468.
[25]Army Corps, _KTB, DAK_, T-314, 21, #000472-000473.

under centralized command."[26] Thus his orders to his corps commanders - Generals Gott and Holmes - warned them to avoid encirclement at Marsa Matruh at all costs. Auchinleck would keep the battle mobile and try to blunt Rommel's sword in the area between Matruh, El Alemein and the Qaltara Depression.[27]

The Eighth Army defensive positions extended some fifteen miles and were screened by thick minefields. The 10 Indian Division of 10 Corps was situated in Marsa Matruh proper. 13 British Corps held the southernmost side of the Sidi Hamza escarpment. The Corps' armored division, the 1st, possessed 159 tanks, including 60 Grants.[28] But the British defenses were painfully weak in the center, protected only by thin mine fields and two weak columns - Gleecol and Leathercol. Thus it "appears that [Auchinleck's] dispostions were designed to protect his army from envelopment, rather than as a means of destroying the enemy."[29]

Rommel attacked on the afternoon of 26 June. His appraisal of Eighth Army's defenses proved entirely erroneous and purely by good fortune he struck the weakest point in their line. 90 Light Division, operating on DAK's northern flank, traversed the enemy minefield at 1915 hours and squashed the Leathercol group.[30] 21 Panzer pulverized Gleecol. The Panzerarmee had broken clean through the British center at one fell swoop. At dawn the next day the advance continued. By mid-afternoon, 21 Panzer had attained the high ground south of Bir Shineina;[31] and at 1900 hours elements of 90 Light cut the coast road some twenty miles west of Matruh.

National Archives

Rommel observes the joint air and ground strikes on the retreating Eighth Army.

[26]John Connel, _Auchinleck: A Biography of Field Marshal Sir Claude Auchinleck_ (London: Cassell and Co. Ltd., 1959), pg. 614.
[27]_Ibid._
[28]_Ibid._, pg. 615.
[29]Von Mellenthin, _Panzer Battles_, pg. 154.
[30]_KTB, 90 Leichte Division_, 26 June 1942, NZT.
[31]Army Corps, _KTB, DAK_, T-314, 21, #000480.

Rommel's lightning advance had led his greatly diminished army right between "the jaws of Eighth Army." 21 Panzer found itself in a perilous position. It had only 23 tanks and some 600 men remaining; unknown to Rommel, on the division's flank lurked the entire 13 British Corps around Minqar Qaim. At the coast road sat 1,600 men of 90 Light Division - dangerously exposed and fifteen miles from the nearest Afrikakorps unit.[32] But the Desert Fox was in fine fettle and brimming with confidence; he "had a complete contempt for the enemy, and no idea of the perils of his position."[33]

These "perils" were more imagined than real, for the British, their fighting spirit conquered by the speed and confidence of the Axis advance, were already pulling back. General Gott ordered 2 New Zealand and 1 Armored Divisions to retire to the Fuka Line. In this manner Eighth Army forfeited a golden opportunity to crush the life from Rommel's army once and for all.

On 28 June 90 Light and the Italian divisions closed the ring around Mersa Matruh; that night the bulk of the encircled British 10 Corps successfully broke through the Axis perimeter and escaped to the east. 21 Panzer, meanwhile, stormed the high ground around Fuka and annihilated 29 Indian Brigade. At the close of the day's fighting the Afrikakorps was down to 41 tanks.[34] The next day 90 Light entered Mersa Matruh. In all, Rommel's army took 8,000 prisoners during the battle. "Rommel may have been lucky," writes von Mellenthin, "but Mersa Matruh was certainly a brilliant German victory, and gave us great hope of 'bouncing' Eighth Army out of the Alamein Line."[35]

On the afternoon of 29 June, Rommel once more had his exhausted troops on the move. The men were at the end of their tether; sometimes they fell asleep in broad daylight and were only awakened by the ominous thunderclap of enemy guns. The Panzerarmee's supply lines were stretched to the breaking point. The Desert Air Force grew daily in strength and effectiveness. The writing was on the wall as far as Rommel's army was concerned, but he would push it forward for a final, desperate attempt to reach the Nile.

90 Light motored down the coast road, followed by the 21 Italian Corps, and Littorio Division. By nightfall 90 Light had reached a point fifteen miles west of the El Alamein Box. The Afrikakorps advanced on El Quseir in an unsuccessful attempt to cut off British forces withdrawing from Mersa Matruh. In the German camp it was believed that Eighth Army had "constructed to the west and southwest of El Alamein his last, though strongly fortified, line before the crossing of the Nile, and he

---

[32]The fighting on 27 June was uncommonly brutal; the Afrikakorps war diary records violations of international law committed by New Zealand troops against III./104 Rifle Regiment, such as the murder of wounded men. Army Corps, KTB, DAK, T-314, 21, #000481. These allegations, however, proved exaggerated.

[33]Von Mellenthin, Panzer Battles, pg. 156.

[34]Army Corps, KTB, DAK, T-314, 21, #000487.

[35]Von Mellenthin, Panzer Battles, pg. 158.

will probably defend it to the very last with all the troops at his disposal."[36]

The Alamein "line" was really not a line at all, but a number of fortified boxes that ran from El Alamein to the "impenetrable, sunken, dried salt marshes of the Qattara Depression 38 miles inland. The wildness of the depression was a spectacle that Rommel never tired of seeing. A dozen times in July 1942 we find him drawn to the high rim looking down on the vast cavity, with its dunes rolling like flat waves into the shimmering distance, out of which rose silent and forbidding flat-topped mountains on which, perhaps, no human foot had trod."[37]

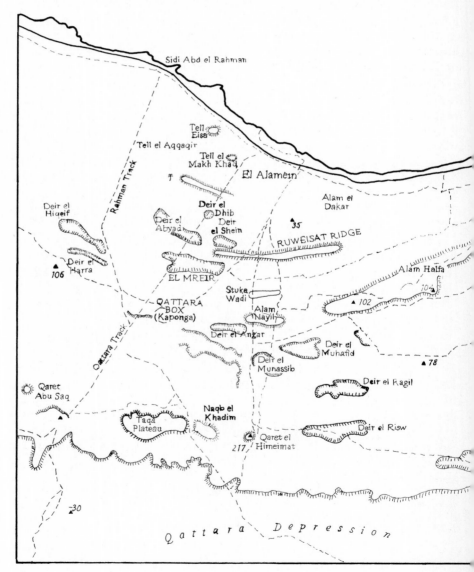

The next day, 30 June, Rommel prepared his troops for an assault on this last ditch line of resistance. He decided to repeat his successful tactical combinations of the Matruh battle. "Under cover of darkness the Afrikakorps was to penetrate between the boxes at Alamein and Deir el Abyad and get in the rear of 13 Corps. 90 Light Division was to swing south of the Alamein Box and cut the coast road to the east of it - exactly the same orders as at Mersa Matruh."[38] Late that evening 21 Panzer reported a strength of 26 battle tanks;[39] overall the tank situation had slightly improved as DAK now fielded 55 runners.

Swallowed in a twisting sandstorm, 90 Light commenced its attack at 0320 hours. "Mounted in desert formation," it raced for the gap between the El Alamein Box and Deir el Shein. Then, unexpectedly, it ran square into strongpoints manned by 1 South African Division about which the Germans had no intelligence. The division recoiled in panic. Rommel personally attempted to urge 90 Light forward, but was himself pinned down by a ferocious artillery barrage.

[36]KTB, _90 Leichte Division_, 30 June 1942, NZT.
[37]Irving, _The Trail_, pg. 194.
[38]Von Mellenthin, _Panzer Battles_, pg. 160.
[39]Divisions, _KTB, 21 Panzer Division_, T-315, 768, #000727. This broke down as 19 Panzer III's, 6 Panzer III Specials and 1 Panzer IV.

The German armor also ran into trouble. At Deir el Shein 18 Indian Brigade held a fortified box. Neither Rommel nor Nehring knew of its existence. Early in the afternoon elements of 104 Rifle Regiment (21 Panzer) broke through the position;[40] by nightfall the Indian Brigade had melted away. But the heroic resistance of the defenders of Deir el Shein broke the impetus of the Panzer attack - 18 more precious Afrikakorps tanks crackled and burned in the desert night.

"Both wings of the German advance were thus brought to a halt. Oscillating between them Rommel experienced the full rigor of the battle. Late in the afternoon, up with *Kampfstaffel* Kiehl in support of 90 Light, he and Bayerlein had another narrow escape."[41] In his *Papers* Rommel writes, "Furious artillery fire again struck into our ranks. British shells came screaming in from three directions, north, east and south; antiaircraft tracers streaked through our force. Under this tremendous weight of fire, our attack came to a standstill. Hastily we scattered our vehicles and took cover, as shell after shell crashed into the area we were holding. For two hours Bayerlein and I had to lie out in the open."[42]

Rommel's momentum was broken - the impetus of his army shattered. Weeks of gruelling combat across a parched and tortured landscape, obstinate Eighth Army counterthrusts and the incessant RAF shuttle bombing had ground the once-glorious Panzerarmee to a nub of its former self. On 2 and 3 July Rommel renewed his attacks with little success, for Afrikakorps was down to 26 tanks. Auchinleck riposted with a move of his own when he suddenly belted Ariete Division. The New Zealanders advanced with fixed bayonets and wrestled away 380 prisoners and all of the division's artillery.[43] "When darkness fell," recollects von Mellenthin, "Rommel ordered the Panzer divisions to dig in where they stood; everyone realized that the offensive which opened on 26 May, and which had achieved such spectacular victories, had at last come to an end."[44]

The war in North Africa had reached an irrevocable turning point. As the burning July days paraded past, the mobile battle, at which, perhaps, Rommel knew no peer, yielded to a brutal war of attrition. For the Desert Fox the days of daring maneuver, of lightning sweeps into the enemy's flanks and rear were gone forever. And with his tattered army and modest resources he could hardly hope to prosper upon a static battlefield. "One loses all idea of time here," he wearily wrote

[40]*Ibid.*, #000730.
[41]Lewin, *Rommel*, pg. 135.
[42]Hart, *Rommel Papers*, pg. 246.
[43]The Ariete was operating on 15 Panzer Division's southern flank and moving on Alam Nayil when four batteries of New Zealand artillery brought it under fire. The subsequent infantry attack "so unnerved the Italians that, waving pieces of paper or white cloth, they came forward to meet the New Zealand infantry now advancing on foot with fixed bayonets." J.L. Scoullar, The Battle for Egypt: The Summer of 1942 (Wellington: Department of Internal Affairs, 1962), pg. 170. The Italians lost at least 44 pieces of heavy artillery and some 20mm guns.
[44]Von Mellenthin, Panzer Battles, pg. 162.

home. "The struggle for the last positions before Alexandria is hard. I've been up in the front area for a few days, living in a car or a hole in the ground. The enemy air force gave us a bad time. However, I hope to manage it."[45]

Rommel began to pull his remaining armor from the line, in an attempt to create a small mobile reserve. By 6 July his situation had improved somewhat; Afrikakorps now had 44 tanks. But his divisions were down to 1,200-1,500 men, and most of his line was defended by badly demoralized Italian infantry.

In Auchinleck, Rommel faced an Eighth Army commander determined to succeed where others failed. "These damn British," remarked Rommel's pugnacious opponent, "have been taught for too long to be good losers. I've never been a good loser, I am going to win."[46] He recognized the Italian infantry divisions as the weak links in Rommel's front; systematically, he began to sever these links with dramatic results.

"The next morning, 10 July," Rommel writes, "we were awakened at about 0500 hours by the dull thunder of artillery from the north. I at once had an inkling it boded no good."[47] No good indeed! After a *Trommelfeuer* (drum-fire) reminiscent of World War I, the fierce soldiers of 9 Australian Division cleaved clean through the Italian Sabratha Division, which covered the western face of the El Alamein Box.[48] Von Mellenthin led a desperate counterattack, throwing elements of 382 Regiment (part of 164 Infantry Division now arriving from Europe) into the gap. Thus a disaster was narrowly averted, but Sabratha had ceased to exist. The battle cost Rommel his brilliant wireless intercept unit. Captain Seebohn, its commander, succumbed with over 100 of his men in a savage but forlorn defense of their priceless equipment and code books. This was a terrible loss, for, as British wireless experts determined after an inspection of the captured equipment, "a great deal of the foxiness of the Desert Fox was due entirely to good German intelligence and poor British wireless security."[49]

---

[45]Hart, *Rommel Papers*, pg. 249.

[46]Lewin, *Rommel*, pg. 133.

[47]Hart, *Rommel Papers*, pg. 252.

[48]Some of the Italians did fight bravely this day, as evident from a notation in the diary of Major Renzo Rastrelli:

"The enemy was close at hand; their patrols and armored-cars were all over the road. Without hesitation the battery commander, Captain Comi, opened fire at minimum elevation on the level ground in front of his position, handling his massive 149's as if they were machine guns. The space before the leveled guns was swept clear in no time. The ground was ploughed up in front of the guns for a distance close on twenty yards, and there rose up an inferno of dust, smoke, sand and stones. The guns became red-hot, and many of the handlers were burnt; emulsified glycerine spurted from the recoil-brakes. The area in front of Comi was deserted, except for blazing vehicles and dead Australians." Paolo Caccia-Dominioni, *Alamein 1933-1962: An Italian Story* (London: Allen and Unwin, 1966), pg. 72. Hereafter cited as *Alamein*.

[49]Anthony Cave Brown, *Bodyguard of Lies* (New York: Harper and Row, 1975), pg. 116.

159

At first light on the 11th, the Australians assaulted Tell el Eisa and captured the strongpoint along with 350 Italians from Trieste Division. Between 14 and 17 July, Rommel's wavering line was again shaken, this time by stinging jabs against Pavia and Brescia Divisions. 2 New Zealand Division and 5 Indian Brigade broke through the positions of Brescia Division on Ruweisat Ridge and advanced on Deir el Shein, threatening Rommel's entire line. Only a vigorous counterpunch by 3 and 33 Reconnaissance Battalions and elements of 15 Panzer threw them back.[50]

"The Panzerarmee," records von Mellenthin, "was passing through a dangerous crisis. We had only been able to save the front by throwing in the last reserves; the Italian units seemed to be falling to pieces and the whole burden of the battle was borne by the sorely tried German divisions."[51] German frustration occasioned by these "regrettable symptoms of disintegration" among their allies knew no boundaries. "The Italians ought to be whipped," declared Rommel's interpreter, Armbruster. "This nation of shits deserves to be shot. And we still have to fight for them! Now of all times, just before the finish, these guys turn yellow."[52]

The fighting in Africa had, indeed, taken an untoward turn. For the first time it was the British who were calling the shots and Rommel dashed from one sector of his brittle line to another to shore up the enemy breakthroughs. Rommel, too, stung his opponent with limited counterattacks, but the initiative had passed once and for all to Eighth Army. His letters to his wife during this period mirror his growing anxiety and despair in fulsome detail:

> 11 July: No day passes without a grave crisis. The Italians are completely unreliable in combat and suffer one defeat after the other. German troops must always be interspersed with them. I could cry![53]
>
> 14 July: My expectations in yesterday's attack were sadly unfulfilled. We were not granted success. We must pocket the blow bravely and continue operations.[54]
>
> 17 July: I'm in a pretty bad way at the moment. The enemy, especially superior in infantry, is swallowing up one Italian unit after the other. The German troops are much too weak to hold by themselves. I could cry![55]

[50]Army Corps, KTB, DAK, T-314, 21, #000541-000543.
[51]Von Mellenthin, Panzer Battles, pg. 168.
[52]As quoted in Irving, The Trail, pg. 195.
[53]Rommel Collection, T-84, 274, #000766.
[54]Ibid.
[55]Ibid., #000780.

18 July: The whole day was especially critical. Once
more we pulled through. But it must not go on like
this for long or the front will crumble. These days are,
of course, the very hardest of my life.[56]

But reinforcements were slowly trickling in to Africa, and on 21-22
July Rommel scored a major defensive success that once more bouyed
his flagging spirits. During the night the raw 161 Indian Motor and 6
New Zealand Brigades attacked on Ruweisat Ridge towards El Mireir.
The enemy air activity, the Afrikakorps war diary recorded, "exceeds
anything hitherto experienced. Telephone communications are frequently broken and there is no contact with the divisions."[57] The attack
at first made good headway and in the morning the New Zealanders
reached the El Mireir Depression. But the tanks of 23 Armored Brigade
were late in launching their supporting thrust. When they did go
forward, in "what has been described as 'a real Balaclava charge,' they
came under terrific antitank fire, ran onto a minefield, and were
overwhelmed by a counterattack of 21 Panzer."[58] Colonel Müller's 5
Panzer Regiment alone claimed over 40 tank kills.[59] The attack cost
Auchinleck over 100 tanks and 750 prisoners.[60]

Colonel
Gerhard
Müller

[56]*Ibid*.
[57]Army Corps, *KTB, DAK*, T-314, 21, #000558.
[58]Von Mellenthin, *Panzer Battles*, pg. 169.
[59]Kurowski, *Die Geschichte des Panzerregiments 5*, pg. 35. *Müller received the
Knight's Cross for his actions.*
[60]Army Corps, *KTB, DAK*, T-314, 21, #000563. *Von Mellenthin, however, puts the
number of prisoners at 1,400. Von Mellenthin, Panzer Battles, pg. 169.*

General Warlimont arrived at Rommel's headquarters on the 27th "to get a picture of the situation." In his book *Inside Hitler's Headquarters 1939-45,* Warlimont states that "by the time I arrived Rommel was once more thinking of taking the offensive, thereby achieving the rare feat of being in agreement with both the German and Italian Supreme Headquarters at the same time." Warlimont briefed Hitler on the situation and pointed out that Rommel's army was facing an opponent "who had become considerably superior on land, on sea and in the air." This fact was also obvious to Rommel and he knew that the British would not remain inactive for long. On 29 July Rommel issued this order:

29/7/42

Panzerarmee
C. in Co.
To: Afrikakorps, etc.

I order every man - including those at HQ to remain at his post and not to retreat. Retreat means destruction. If positions are held the nightly battles can be withstood victoriously and with a minimum of losses. Enemy units which break through must be dealt with by reserves held ready. Thrusts similar to those that have occurred in recent days must be expected in the near future.

Anyone deserting his post is to be charged with cowardice in the face of the enemy. Court martial proceedings will be taken in every individual case.

Rommel[61]

At the end of the month the fighting on the Alamein front flickered out. Both sides were exhausted and in need of substantial reinforcements. The roar of battle gave way to a numbing routine. During the days the men of both armies lay uncomfortably in their miserable trenches and dugouts, tormented by a sweltering sun. The nights, in contrast, bustled with activity as dust-caked soldiers emerged from their shelters to lay or lift mines, to carry out patrols or to resupply or exercise. First light was reveille for the Alamein flies and they swarmed over the men in thick droves. These sordid little creatures craved moisture and they clung by the hundreds to any stain on one's clothing. They attacked one's mouth and, if not constantly swished away, made breathing difficult. The official historian of Eighth Army ammunition company writes: "[The flies] fastened on our food and accompanied it into our mouths and down our throats, scorning death when there was an advantage to be made. They drowned themselves in our tea and in our soup." To the west, the sun-baked warriors of Rommel's Panzerarmee shared equally the discomforts loosed by this undiscriminating pest; they would soon be battling droves of Eighth Army tanks as well.

---

[61]KTB, _Panzerarmee Afrika_, 29 July 1942.

Alma Halfa: The Gambler's Toss
August-September 1942

By the summer of 1942, Rommel's aura of invincibility had reached staggering proportions. He had cracked the mighty fortress of Tobruk in one day; he had again routed Eighth Army in the open field; and he had swept across Egypt to the very gates of Alexandria. To be sure, the month of July had brought a swift reversal in his fortunes, but his army was still intact and undefeated. Rommel's spreading fame had even caused Auchinleck reason for embarrassment and concern. "There exists a real danger," he had earlier written, "that our friend Rommel is becoming kind of a bogey-man to our troops who are talking far too much about him. He is by no means a superman, although he is undoubtedly very energetic and able. Even if he were a superman, it would still be highly undesirable that our men should credit him with super human powers.... I wish to dispel by all possible means that Rommel represents something more than an ordinary German general, quite an unpleasant one though, as we have heard from his own officers. The important thing now is that we do not always talk of Rommel when we mean the enemy in Libya. We must refer to 'the Germans,' or 'the Axis powers,' or the 'enemy' and not always keep harping on Rommel... P.S. I am not jealous of Rommel."[1]

At 10 Downing Street, England's feisty Prime Minister contemplated this growing infatuation with the German Field Marshal with a mixture of admiration and despair. The Desert Fox had outwitted each of his Eighth Army commanders in swift succession; and with each Rommel victory, a swell of indignation had surged through parliament and had threatened to sweep the embattled Churchill from office. To ensure his political survival, he needed a major victory in North Africa, and he needed it now. "Rommel, Rommel, Rommel," he cried, "what else matters but beating him!"

In early August Churchill flew to Cairo for a high-level conference. It ended with the dismissal of Auchinleck as Eighth Army's commander. The tactical shadow boxing of the preceeding month had shattered Churchill's faith in his commander: Auchinleck had blunted Rommel's spearhead but had accomplished nothing of a decisive nature.

[1]*Rommel Collection, T-84, 273, #000009.*

To show his appreciation for the supply efforts (especially petrol) exerted by Italian submarine crews, Rommel visits one of them and shares a drink with its crew.

169

"General Field Marshal Rommel suffers the results and symptoms of low blood pressure with a tendency towards fainting spells. The present condition dates back to a stomach and intestine disorder existing for some time, which is being intensified by the excessive physical and psychological demands of the last weeks, especially considering the unfavorable climactic conditions. A *full* employment, especially under heavy stress, is at present not advisable at all, and only to be expected again after a prolonged home leave under medical care. A temporary treatment on African soil seems reasonable."[14]

"The state of my health," Rommel dutifully wrote home, "is such that I can be up from time to time. However, I won't be able to get around that 6 weeks cure in Germany. This blood pressure business must be taken care of once and for all. I will certainly stay on the job here until a substitute arrives... Considering the turnover of five generals per division these 1 and ½ years in Africa it is not surprising that my turn has also come for an overhaul."[15]

Rommel radioed Berlin and recommended Heinz Guderian as a worthy substitute. According to Ulrich von Hassell, this sober suggestion brought forth "a burst of fury from Hitler."[16] Guderian was still in the Führer's dog-house for his actions during the brutal Russian winter of 1941-1942. The Field Marshal then decided to stay at his post during the coming offensive; when it was over, he could return to Germany for treatment.

Rommel's plan of attack was daring, if repetitive. "He intended to hold in the north, feint against the Ruweisat Ridge in the center, and press hard on his right with 15 and 21 Panzer Divisions of Nehring's Afrikakorps. The main striking force was to concentrate between Bab el Qattara and the El Taqa plateau and to advance eastwards at 2300 hours on 30 August. After penetrating the British minefields, it was to wheel to the left, pause, and prepare for the main action. Rommel calculated that his line of battle would now be formed by Reconnaissance Units 3 and 33 on his eastern flank; next the Afrikakorps; then 20 Italian Corps and 90 Light Division, while a mixed group under 10 Corps would provide a pivot of maneuver on the left. Next morning at 0600 hours his army would drive to the north and encircle the enemy."[17]

For his "gambler's last throw" he could field 229 German and 243 Italian tanks, as against some 700 British tanks.[18] The disparity was diminished by the fact that Panzerarmee Afrika now had 70 Panzer III and 27 Panzer IV long-barrelled "specials." But Montgomery enjoyed

[14]*Rommel Collection*, T-84, 277, #000052.
[15]*Ibid.*, 274, #000835.
[16]Ulrich von Hassel, *The von Hassel Diaries, 1938-1944* (London: Hamish Hamilton, 1948), pg. 240.
[17]Lewin, *Rommel*, pg. 152. See also Panzer Armies, *Panzerarmee Afrika*, T-313, 467, #8765512-8765514. Ia Anlage zur Lagekarte, Stosslinien ab 30.8.18.00.
[18]*21 Panzer began the offensive with 111 battle tanks, including 53 "specials."* Divisions, *KTB, 21 Panzer Division*, T-315, 768, #000957.

an overwhelming superiority in the air and his front bristled with hundreds of brand new six pounder antitank guns.

By 29 August Rommel's fuel supply had failed to improve. This compelled him to change his plan. Gone was the alluring dream of a Panzer thrust to the Suez Canal, unless he could capture some British supply dumps: "Owing to the unsatisfactory fuel situation, I have decided to limit the objective of the proposed operation to the defeat of the enemy in the field." Even this limited objective, he continued, "has only been made possible because [Kesselring] had lent the army 1,000 tons of fuel ... from his stock."[19]

On the morning of the attack, Rommel left his sleeping truck with a "very troubled face." Professor Horster accompanied him. "The decision to attack today," he confided to his doctor, "is the hardest I have ever taken. Either the army in Russia succeeds in getting through to Grozny and we in Africa manage to reach to Suez Canal, or ..." he made a gesture of defeat.[20] He wrote Lucie: "Today has dawned at last. How eagerly I have waited for and worried about this day, wondering whether I would be able to gather my forces and strike again."[21]

His soldiers also waited impatiently as their watches ticked towards X-hour; they drew nervously on their cigarettes. Then, at 2300 hours, the whine of engines and the crunch of tank tracks ripped the stillness of the pale, moon-lit night. Off they roared - to the east. Rommel's men worshipped him and they would follow him anywhere - even, as it turned out, into the yawning abyss of a deadly trap.

The Panzerarmee advanced toward the enemy minefields - the Afrikakorps on the right wing, the Italian armor (Littorio and Ariete) in the center and 90 Light on the left. Almost at once everything went wrong. The minefields existed in much greater depth than Rommel had anticipated. The Panzers halted. Sappers rushed forward to clear passages through the deadly ground and were met by devastating machine gun, mortar and artillery fire. The entire time-table of the attack was thrown off. Then, at 0230 hours, the Desert Air Force pounced on the straded Axis columns and pounded them with bombs.[22] A new British magnesium flare lit the battlefield as bright as day. A short time later RAF bombers blasted the Afrikakorps command post and wounded General Nehring. General von Bismarck, pressing forward with his lead battalion, was killed by a mortar round.[23]

The dawn of 31 July found the attackers still tightly wedged in the enemy minefields. At 0805 Rommel arrived at Afrikakorps headquarters where he conferred with Bayerlein. Only then did he learn of the bitter setback his army had suffered.[24] Greatly disturbed, his first impulse was

[19]KTB, Panzerarmee Afrika, Appendices, 29 August 1942, NZT.
[20]Hart, Rommel Papers, pg. 275.
[21]Rommel Collection, T-84, 274, #000835.
[22]Army Corps, KTB, DAK, T-314, 21, #000621.
[23]Divisions, KTB, 21 Panzer Division, T-315, 768, #000958.
[24]Army Corps, KTB, DAK, T-314, 21, #000622-000623.

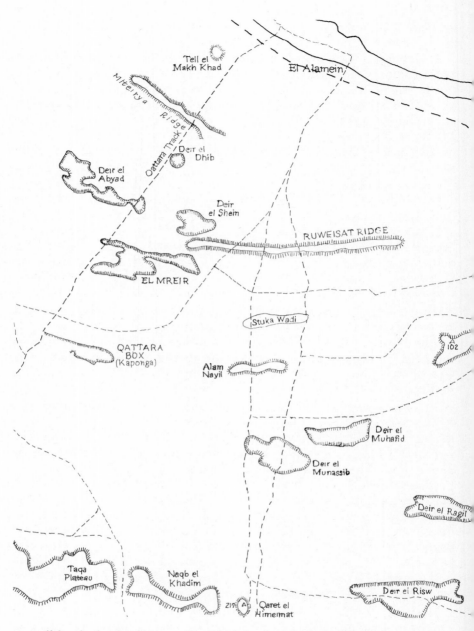

to pull back: he had not succeeded in surprising his enemy; somehow Montgomery had devined his intentions.

That 'somehow' was Ultra. "Before [Rommel] attacked at Alam Halfa, Montgomery possessed through Ultra not only a clear picture of Rommel's 'thrust line' - the direction in which the bulk of his armor would advance - but also a sufficiently accurate knowledge of the date when the Panzerarmee would assault." Ultra intercepts also provided "the

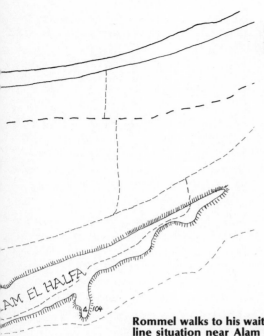

Map of the El Alamein/Alam el Halfa area.

Rommel walks to his waiting command car to inspect the front line situation near Alam Halfa.

E.C.P. Armies

general and his staff with solid evidence about the morale, supplies and order-of-battle of their opponents.... In his first command of an army in action Montgomery grasped Ultra's significance, applied it triumphantly in battle and 'believed it afterwards.' For Alam Halfa was a model. Rommel was allowed to enter a trap. Everything was prepared in advance."[25]

[25]Lewin, _Ultra_, pp. 264-65.

But at 0830, Bayerlein, in temporary command of Afrikakorps, reported triumphantly that the German Panzers had broken through and were advancing rapidly eastwards. Rommel decided to continue the offensive; at the same time he fatally altered his plan. Instead of sweeping some 20 miles further to the east and then wheeling north to strike Eighth Army in the rear, he would send his tanks north much sooner. This new "Stosslinie" (line of thrust) would hurl his divisions directly at Hill 132 - Alam Halfa.[26] Montgomery had anticipated this move and he had turned the ridge into an impregnable fortress. Two brigades of infantry (from 144 Division) were entrenched there; the Grant tanks of 22 Armored Brigade lurked in "hull down" positions on the ridge's western rim. To the north waited 23 Armored in mobile reserve and on the eastern flank sat another armored brigade - the 8th.

At mid-day the tanks of 15 and 21 Panzer resumed their advance eastwards and made good progress.[27] A sudden sandstorm choked the air and cut visibility to 100 meters, thus hiding the rolling German columns from the fighters and bombers of the Desert Air Force. At about 1630 they wheeled northwards, but were soon bogged down in deep sand which caused a further delay and wasted precious gasoline.[28]

Not until evening did the Afrikakorps launch its desperate charge. It smashed forward with its Panzer IV specials in the van. 15 Panzer ran smack into 22 Armored Brigade and a violent slugging match, tank versus tank, was the result. The long-barrelled 75's of the Panzer IV's brewed up one British tank after another. Soon all twelve Grants of "A" Company were blazing wrecks. But then the massed Eighth Army firepower on Alam Halfa Ridge was brought to bear; an inferno of fire cascaded down on the attacking German armor. "After dusk, the bombers came. It was sheer slaughter, but with only 30 miles' fuel supply left - as the new Afrikakorps commander, General von Vaerst bluntly told Rommel - they were stuck. They could not attempt to bypass the ridge to the east, where the going was far better, unless more fuel was brought up during the night... All night long the slaughter went on. Rommel drove out at dawn, September 1, to watch: the cramped terrain was littered with the wreckage of his tanks; many were still burning."[29]

At 0815, 15 Panzer renewed its assault on the ridge.[30] It was a forlorn gesture. The RAF again carpet-bombed the courageous attackers; its

---

[26]Panzer Armies, KTB, Panzerarmee Afrika, T-313, 466, #8764475.

[27]The Italian armor - Littorio and Ariete - were still stuck in the vast belts of enemy mines.

[28]It appears that the British planted a false "going map" - crumpled and dirty and covered with tea and ink stains, but quite readable - in no man's land for the Germans to discover. "I can confirm," writes von Mellenthin, "that this map was accepted as authentic and served its purpose in leading the Afrikakorps astray." Von Mellenthin, Panzer Battles, pg. 175.

[29]Irving, The Trail, pg. 209.

[30]21 Panzer, low on fuel, could offer no support.

The pressures of the situation are evident on Rommel's face as he faces the imminent destruction of his Afrikakorps.

devastating effect magnified by the hard, rocky ground that increased bomb fragmentation.

Rommel jumped into his Horch car and raced to Afrikakorps' advanced headquarters. It was a frenetic journey, for he was strafed and bombed "no less than six times." He arrived at 1110 and met with the Korps' chief of operations. The British, Rommel discovered, had repulsed the assault by 15 Panzer and had themselves attacked, unsuccessfully, with 100-150 tanks.[31] It was clear, however, that the acute fuel shortages made a continuation of the Panzerarmee offensive an impossibility. Earlier in the day the British had blasted the Italian tanker *San Andrea* - with its 2400 tons of gasoline - out of the water.

Suddenly "the whole existence of the Afrikakorps was in jeopardy. Throughout 1 September the Panzers lay immobile, unable to advance or retire, and under constant bombardment from guns and aircraft. On the morning of 2 September Rommel decided to retreat, but shortages of gasoline prevented any large-scale withdrawal during the day, and the Afrikakorps had to remain where it was under ceaseless bombing and shellfire. The circumstances were extremely propitious for a British

---

[31]*Army Corps, <u>KTB, DAK</u>, T-314, 21, #000630.*

counterattack, but Montgomery made no move, apart from the harassing operations of 7 Armored Division north and west of Qaret el Himeimat "[32]

The next day Rommel's bloodied army reeled back in head-long retreat. It left behind 50 tanks, 50 guns and 400 lorries on the battlefield; losses in manpower (German and Italian) amounted to 570 dead, 1,800 wounded, and 570 prisoners.[33] British losses were considerably higher, but unlike those of the Axis, would be quickly replentished.

Rommel had suffered a decisive defeat. Montgomery had handled his numerically superior forces with skill and determination, if also with undue circumspection. But the main reason for Rommel's setback was, undoubtedly, Ultra. And his failing health can hardly be overlooked. Rommel was a sick man during the battle and it showed: his decision to renew the attack on 1 September was pure folly. "Very bad days lie behind me," he lamented to Lucie. "The Army's offensive had to be halted.... It can't be helped. I am at the [Panzerarmee main headquarters]... for the first time since the beginning of the attack. I even managed to get my boots off my feet and take a bath. I hope the situation can be cleared up."[34]

The Panzerarmee completed its withdrawal on 6 September. Rommel immediately began to strengthen his El Alamein defenses to meet Montgomery's inevitable offensive, which would, he calculated, probably come during the full moon period of October. The enemy's growing air superiority disturbed him greatly; he knew it would impose rigid guidelines on his conduct of the forthcoming battle: "Anyone who has to fight, even with the most modern of weapons, against an enemy in complete command of the air, fights like a savage against modern European troops, under the same handicaps and with the same chances of success. And since there was no foreseeable hope, with the German *Luftwaffe* so severely stretched in other theatres, of Kesselring receiving aircraft reinforcements in any way comparable with those flowing to the British, we had to face the likelihood of the RAF shortly gaining absolute air superiority. We therefore had to try to put our defense against the forthcoming British attack in such a form that British air superiority would have the least effect. For the first and most serious danger which now threatened us was from the air. This being so, we could no longer rest our defenses on the motorized forces used in a mobile role, since these forces were too vulnerable to air attack. We had, instead, to try to resist the enemy in field positions which had to be constructed for defense against the most modern weapons of war... The fact of British air superiority threw to the winds all the tactical rules which we had hitherto applied with such success... In every battle to

---

[32]Von Mellenthin, Panzer Battles, pg. 176.
[33]These figures are Rommel's own estimates.
[34]Rommel Collection, T-84, 274, #000848.

come the strength of the Anglo-American air force was to be the deciding factor."[35]

Rommel prepared his defenses in great depth. Stretching from the rocky hillock of Tel el Eisa on the Mediterranean coast to the 600-foot pyramid of Qaret el Himeimat near the edge of the Qattara depression, they could not be outflanked.[36] Montgomery would have to hit them head on.

The Axis front was to be protected by a series of mined boxes, which, though unoccupied, were studded with thousands of mines and deadly obstacles, and covered by infantry. Two thousand yards behind the boxes sat Rommel's main line of infantry; behind that, waited his anti-tank and heavier guns; back further still were the mobile reserves.

Rommel's "Devil's Garden"

Bundesarchiv

Bundesarchiv

[35]Hart, _Rommel Papers_, pp. 285-86.
[36]Fritz Bayerlein, "El Alamein," in _The Fatal Decisions_, Ed. by William Richardson and Seymour Freidin, (London: Michael Joseph Ltd., 1956), pg. 85.

New Zealand's Brigadier Clifton (far left) shortly after his capture on 4 September 1942.

Rommel's elaborate maze of mines, christened the "Devil's Garden," was an extraordinary and creative achievement. Panzerarmee supply trucks brought forth load upon load of German, French, British and Egyptian mines; troops stripped the frontier of its wire entanglements and steel posts and incorporated them into the line. Engineers laid the German Teller antitank mines in several tiers. A sweep might reveal the first mine, but then the second would go off. An experienced sapper might spot the second after lifting, carefully, the first, but then the third one would prove fatal. Italian hand grenades were strewn about and linked into the "T" mine system as booby-traps. *Luftwaffe* bombs were placed in chessboard patterns and concealed by battlefield debris; they were connected by trip wires and hooked up to push-pull igniters. Upon detonation, these 50 and 250 pound bombs could wipe out an entire platoon of enemy troops. A small percentage of this Devil's Garden consisted of deadly antipersonnel mines. When touched off, they jumped into the air and burst chest-high, sending steel pellets whizzing in all directions. "From 5 July to 20 October," records the Panzerarmee war diary, "German and Italian pioneers installed 264,348 Teller and Schuh mines. In addition to these, there were the captured enemy minefields in the fortified front (Deir el Shein and Bab el Qattara and also on the new southern front) with about 181,010 mines of all types. In all, mines installed on the Alamein front totalled 445,358 (all types)."[37]

On 11 September Jodl received a rambling situation report from the Panzerarmee's distressed commander. The report set down the reasons for the sharp reversal at Alam Halfa, and warned that a "large scale enemy offensive must be expected soon, probably in October. It will not be possible to hold an attack of these proportions with the German troops available and the weak spirited Italian troops."[38] Rommel

On 15 September Rommel flew to Tobruk to inspect the damage done by British forces on the previous day when they attempted to destroy the dock installations and sink the ships in the harbor.

[37]*KTB, Panzerarmee Afrika*, 20 October 1942, NZT.

[38]*In paragraph three of his report, Rommel deals at length with the reasons for the collapse of the Italian ground forces in North Africa. The authors of this book have decided to quote this paragraph in full; it casts a revealing light on the insufferable obstacles that plagued the Italian soldier in Africa:*

"The Italian troops have failed once more - exactly as during the last offensive. The reasons for this are as follows: the command is not equal to the mobile direction of battle in desert warfare.... The training of Italian units does not correspond to the demands of a modern war. For example, units brought up to replace lost batallions for a division fired for the first time near the front. Officers who had not served since the end of World War I were detailed as battalion commanders. The arms of Italian units do not permit the Italian soldier to withstand British attacks without German assistance. Apart from the well known faults of Italian tanks - short range and feeble engines - the artillery, with its lack of mobility and inadequate range (6km - maximum 8km), is absolutely inferior to the British artillery, which is known to be good. Also, weak equipment with antitank weapons gives the Italian soldier a feeling of inferiority. Supply of the Italian troops is not adequate. Troops have no field kitchen and quantities of food are small. For this reason the Italian soldiers, who are usually extremely contented and unassuming, often come to their German comrades to beg something to eat and drink. The great difference in food allocation to officers and men has an adverse effect on morale of the troops. The Italian soldier is not equal to the bayonet attacks of British infantry. He has not got the nerve to hold on when enemy tanks have broken through. Continual bombing attacks and artillery fire quickly wear down his will to resist. The Italian soldier therefore can maintain defense only with German support, and then only if the German soldier bears the brunt of the fighting." See AHBT.

emphasized the "extremely critical supply situation of the Army" and complained that "the requirements of the German troops of the Panzerarmee are continually being held up in favor of the Italian forces and the *Luftwaffe*. This crisis is not only having an effect on the fuel and ammunition situation, but also on the food supply situation. Bread rations had to be cut by half and the transport of additional food supplies foregone. The consequences are undernourishment of the troops and a high sickness rate."[39]

In conclusion, he listed his "relevant proposals," designed to bring his weak army up to strength and ease the burdensome supply difficulties. These included: "a) Dispatch of 30,000 tons of supplies in September and 35,000 tons in October. b) Reinforcements numbering about 5,200 men; 2,000 vehicles and 70 field guns, as well as reinforcements numbering about 6,000 men and 1,200 vehicles (including 120 tanks), which are still in Germany."[40]

Rommel's health had failed to improve. On 19 September his temporary replacement arrived - Panzer General Georg Stumme. "Kesselring found him more even tempered than Rommel and watched approvingly as Stumme set about repairing the bruised relations between German and Italians and between commanders and troops. Rommel briefed him extensively, and showed him the letters he had written appealing for reinforcements and supplies..."[41]

A general shake-up of the German unit commanders had also occurred about this time. Colonel Heuthaus took over the 90 Light Division. Von Vaerst returned to 15 Panzer and Major General von Randow assumed command of 21 Panzer Division. To replace the injured Nehring, General von Thoma took command of the Afrikakorps.[42]

With a "heavy heart," Rommel flew to Derna on 23 September, where he switched planes for his flight to Rome. The next afternoon, after a frank discussion with Mussolini, he flew to Germany, but he vowed to return to Africa when the shooting started in ernest, regardless of his health.

---

[39]On September 1, 21 Panzer complained in its war diary about moldy bread rations and the fact that hepatitis was increasing among the men. Divisions, *KTB, 21 Panzer Division*, T-315, 768, #000964.

[40]*AHBT*.

[41]Irving, *The Trail*, pg. 212. Stumme, it seems, had recently been involved in Hitler's grotesque game of musical generals. Von Hassel notes in his diary: "Stumme, commanding general of a tank corps, was sentenced to five year's imprisonment because a staff officer from one of his divisions carrying plans for the deployment of his troops, fell into the hands of the Russians. He was immediately pardoned, with Göring promising him a new command, and is now being sent to Africa as a substitute for Rommel." Von Hassell, *Diaries*, pg. 240.

[42]Army Corps, *KTB, DAK*, T-314, 21, #000660-000661.

Second El Alamein - The Turn of the Tide
October-November 1942

On 26 September Rommel drove to Hitler's East Prussia headquarters and received his Field Marshal's baton. After a brief ceremony, Rommel "outlined to the Führer the course of [his] attack on the Alamein Line and the cause of its failure."[1] He described in some detail the strength of his own defenses, producing "scaled sketches of [the] so-called 'mine orchards' which he himself had planned";[2] and he repeated his demand that the Panzerarmee receive 30,000 tons of supplies in September and 35,000 in October to withstand successfully the coming Eighth Army onslaught. He also levelled bitter barbs at his unreliable and "traitorous" Italian allies.

Hitler greets Rommel on September 26, 1942.

---

[1]Hart, <u>Rommel Papers</u>, pg. 294.
[2]Eckhard, Christian, "The El Alamein Crisis and Its Aftereffects in the OKW," MS D-172, pg. 4.

(above) Rommel is presented his Field
Marshal's baton. (right & below) Details of
the baton.

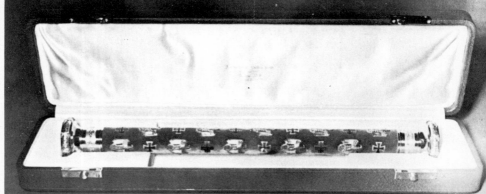

"During the conference," records Bayerlein, "Rommel could not help noticing that the atmosphere at Supreme Headquarters was one of extraordinary optimism. Göring in particular tended to pooh-pooh the difficulties which confronted us in Africa."[3] When Rommel broached the subject of the new Allied tank-busting aircraft, and pointed out that their 40mm cannon had knocked out many German tanks, Göring became indignant. This was "quite impossible," the Reich-Marshal retorted, and "nothing but latrine rumors. All the Americans can make are razor blades and refrigerators." "I only wish, Herr Reich-Marshal," Rommel snapped back, "that we were equipped with similar razor blades."[4] To drive home his point he produced one of the armor-piercing rounds that his troops had salvaged from a disabled German tank.

Hitler proceeded to rattle off a stream of promises to the Field Marshal: the Panzerarmee's supplies would be "constantly increased"; new shallow draught ferries *(Siebelfähren)* would be added to the Mediterranean transport fleet; a *Nebelwerfer* (Multiple Rocket Launcher) brigade, as well as 40 new Tiger tanks and self-propelled guns, would soon be dispatched to Africa. For the most part, these "promises" proved quite empty.

Bundesarchive

Rommel is featured, on 30 September 1942, at the Berlin Sports Palace during the official beginning of the 1942/1943 War Winter Help program. Dr. Goebbels is to Rommel's left.

[3]*Richardson, Fatal Decisions, pg. 91.*
[4]*Ibid.*

The morning of 3 October, at the request of Propaganda Minister Goebbels, Rommel "attended a press reception for international journalists at the propaganda ministry. As Rommel stepped into the auditorium, all eyes were on him. Deliberately he stopped with his hand on the doorknob. Movie cameras began softly whirring. 'Today,' he calmly announced, 'we stand just fifty miles from Alexandria and Cairo, and we have the door to all Egypt in our hands. And we mean to do something with it, too! We haven't gone all that way just to get thrown back again. You can take that from me. What we have, we hang on to.' "[5] He would later "bitterly regret" the incident.

Rommel attends a press conference at the Propaganda Ministry on 3 October 1942. Dr. Goebbels is in the center (back to the camera) addressing the new Field Marshal. Rommel at the Berlin Sports Palace on 30 September 1942.

◀ **Rommel at the Berlin Sports Palace on 30 September.**

[5]Irving, _The Trail_, pp. 215-26.

That afternoon Rommel left Berlin and flew to Semmering - a mountain resort near Wiener Neustadt - to begin his convalescence. His new lodging provided a halcyon contrast to the roaring guns and pitiless heat of the Egyptian desert. "Up on the Semmering," he writes in his Papers, "I was completely cut off from the outside world, except from the radio, newspapers and occasional letters from General Stumme and Colonel Westphal. But with my army in such a plight I was, of course, incapable of attaining real peace of mind. I followed the operations of our submarines in the Atlantic with particular anxiety."[6]

The reports from North Africa were hardly encouraging. The British were beefing up their attacks on Axis shipping with telling effect. A British submarine sank the SS Barbaro on 28 September, along with its badly needed cargo of food, ammunition, tanks and vehicles.[7] For the month of September, in fact, the Panzerarmee received only 16,200 tons of supplies - 54% of its requirements.[8] The food situation was particularly appalling: "No fat whatsoever available. Flour supplies should hold out another 11 days with the reduced bread ration. Vegetables, fruit - lemons in particular - not available, or in very short supply. The consequences are undernourishment, greatly reduced efficiency and a high rate of sickness."[9] On the plus side, the Afrikakorps' tank strength had risen slightly; by 4 October 15 Panzer had 110 runners and 21 Panzer, 122.[10]

Throughout October Eighth Army was alive with ominous energy as it feverishly prepared for its grand offensive. Luftwaffe reconnaissance flights revealed thousands of vehicles of all shapes and sizes crammed behind the enemy front.[11] Montgomery planned to make his principal effort on the northern sector of the front. Here Lieutenant General Sir Oliver Leese's 30 Corps (9 Australian, 51 Highland, 2 New Zealand, 1 South African and 4 Indian Divisions) was to tackle the Axis infantry and bore corridors through Rommel's Devil's Garden. 10 Armored Corps, commanded by Lieutenant General Lumsden and consisting of 1 and 10 Armored Divisions, was to pour through the gaps and hammer the Axis armor. In the south, Lieutenant General Sir Brian Horrock's 13 Corps (50 and 44 Infantry and 7 Armored Divisions) was to launch two secondary thrusts - one against Himeimat and the Taqa feature, the other in the Gebel Kalakh and Qaret el Khadim area. The 13 Corps operations were designed to mask the true Schwerpunkt of Montgomery's operation, and to pin down Axis forces - principally 21 Panzer and Ariete - that might otherwise intervene on the decisive northern flank.

[6]Hart, Rommel Papers, pg. 296.
[7]Panzer Armies, KTB, Panzerarmee Afrika, T-313, 466, #8764505.
[8]Ibid., #8764513.
[9]Ibid., #8764521.
[10]Army Corps, KTB, DAK, T-314, 21, #000679.
[11]Aerial photographs from 13 October revealed, according to Panzerarmee estimates, 13,400 vehicles of all types - an increase of 3,400 since 17 September. Panzer Armies, KTB, Panzerarmee Afrika, T-313, 466, #8764542.

The British made every effort to hide the weight, direction and timing of their attack. "The first problem," writes Guingand,[12] "was to try to conceal our concentration as much as possible from the enemy. The staff worked out the complete layout on the day of the attack - the number of guns, tanks, vehicles and troops..We then arranged to reach the eventual density as early as possible, and to maintain it up to the last moment, so that the enemy's air photography would show no particular change during the last two or three weeks. To achieve this we used spare transport and dummy transport. These were gradually replaced by those belonging to the assault units and formations as they came up to take over their allotted sectors."[13] "Various refinements of camouflage were developed, such as devices known by the code name 'sunshields,' an erection of canvas over a framework, resembling a truck but capable of housing a tank or gun. Boxes of ammunition and other stores were either hidden underground or openly piled up in the shape of trucks, the Eighth Army's camouflage units becoming so expert that, even from a short way off the ground, it was difficult to tell the dummy from real." In a further attempt to deceive the Panzerarmee, Eighth Army began construction of a "dummy pipeline leading from the coast inland towards the southern sector, and prolonged at such a set and steady pace that it appeared unlikely to be completed until well into November."[14]

These extraordinary measures were unprecedented in the desert war, and showed that Montgomery was taking no chances, though his army was far superior to Rommel's in every respect. Eighth Army had over 1,000 tanks, including some 400 American-built Shermans, outfitted with a powerful 75mm cannon. To oppose this the Panzerarmee could muster 211 German and 275 virtually worthless Italian tanks - mostly M 13/40's. Thus Montgomery enjoyed a numerical superiority of 5 to 1 over the German armor. This superiority was now also qualitative, for Rommel had only 38 tanks armed with 75mm guns. Eighth Army, moreover, had 195,000 men fit for combat; the Axis only 24,173 German and a number of disspirited Italian troops. The German divisions were well below establishment: 15 Panzer, for example, had only 3,940 men; 90 Light, 2,827; and 21 Panzer, 3,972.[15]

In spite of the obvious handicaps that crippled the Panzerarmee in October 1942, its morale was high. "We're all itching to give the enemy a real thrashing," Westphal wrote to Rommel. General Stumme had also written: "The Tommies are bound to attack - for political reasons

    [12]Brigadier-General Sir Francis de Guingand served as Eighth Army's chief-of-staff at this time.
    [13]Kershaw, "Desert War," pg. 40.
    [14]Ronald Walker, Alam Halfa and El Alamein (Wellington: Dept. of Internal Affairs, 1962), pg. 217.
    [15]The troop strength of the other divisions was as follows: 164 Infantry Division, 6,343; Ramcke Brigade, 3,376; Army artillery, 2,331; 19 Flak Division, 4,384. Von Esebeck, Afrikanische Schicksalsjahre, pg. 118.

**Rommel
and Gause.**

**Rommel
photographing the
aftermath of a desert
battle.**

**Rommel presents
the German Cross in
Gold to Bayerlein in
the field.**

The inspection of positions and the morale of his men were two duties which kept Rommel continually near the front.

Kesselring, during one of his numerous fact-finding visits to North Africa.

Siegfried
Westphal

Georg Stumme, Rommel's replacement while on leave in September/October 1942.

they've got no choice. But they are none too happy about it. We're going to wipe the floor with the British."[16]

The "victory" celebrations were woefully premature. The 19th found the Axis army down to 3,900 cubic meters of gasoline - enough for eleven days average consumption.[17] The problem assumed crisis proportions that same day when a Wellington bomber, alerted by Ultra, sank the tanker *Panuco* with its 2,600 tons of fuel. For the entire month of October, 44% of Axis cargo and gasoline destined for Africa would be sunk[18] - Churchill's "golden eggs" paid large dividends. The effects of this "energy crunch" on Rommel's conduct of the El Alamein battle cannot be overemphasized.

23 October: in faraway Russia, at that meatgrinder on the Volga known as Stalingrad, von Paulus' 6 Army struggled desperately against determined Soviet resistance; in the North Atlantic, beefed-up German U-boat packs scoured the sea lanes in search of Allied convoys. In North Africa, the day passed uneventfully, punctuated only by sporadic Eighth Army artillery fire. Colonel Ulrich Liss, the chief of Foreign Armies West, the concerned *Wehrmacht* intelligence branch, toured the El Alamein defenses with General von Thoma. Contrary to the views of the Panzerarmee, Liss declared confidently, OKH did not expect a major enemy attack on the Alamein line in the immediate future.[19]

Then, at 2040 hours, a furious Eighth Army barrage opened up along the entire Axis front. Over 1,000 enemy guns pummelled the positions of the Panzerarmee and eventually concentrated their drum-fire on the northern sector of the front. Waves of RAF bombers, some specially equipped to jam the Axis signal system, added to the deafening cacaphony. This crushing bombardment, the prelude to Montgomery's

[16]Irving, _The Trail_, pg. 220.
[17]Panzer Armies, _KTB_, _Panzerarmee Afrika_, T-313, 466, #8764544.
[18]Lewin, _Ultra_, pg. 266.
[19]Army Corps, _KTB_, _DAK_, T-314, 21, #000699.

big offensive, ripped down telephone lines and shattered the defender's communications network. Shells rained down on the mine gardens and, as each impacted, it was followed by a concatenation of violent roars as the mines themselves detonated.

More than an hour later the infantry of 30 Corps swept forward, supported by tanks and bombers. They attacked on a 10 kilometer front, steamrolled the forward defense posts and cut deep through the mineboxes. At 0100 hours they stood before the defender's main battle line. Unnerved by the terrific weight of the barrage, elements of 62 Infantry Regiment (Trento Division) had already fled to the rear. When the British tanks thrust forward they overran the remnants of the regiment and smashed into the German line. Two battalions of 382 Infantry Regiment (164 Division) melted away.[20] On the southern part of the front, 13 Corps launched its diversion with 44 Infantry and 7 Armored Divisions. This attack also punched a hole in the covering mineboxes.[21]

As the night wore on, however, the Axis resistence stiffened; the attackers failed to reach many of their objectives. The density of the mine belts had proven a greater obstacle than anticipated by Eighth Army - the corridors cleared through mines too narrow to assist a rapid deployment of the mass of 10 Corps' armor. "So at dawn on the 24th the British tanks had to deploy as best they could - cramped among the mines, tactically in bad positions, and unable to maneuver."[22] At 0700 the mass of 15 Panzer, supported by Littorio, unloosed a sharp counterpunch and recaptured part of the main battle line.[23]

General Stumme had spent a restless night in his headquarters' van, listening to the rumbling *Trommelfeuer* as it spattered the Panzerarmee. His own slim stocks of ammunition did not permit, he felt, counter-fire against Montgomery's tanks and infantry - which were crammed restlessly in their assembly points. By dawn Stumme had yet to receive more than a trickle of isolated reports from his forward units; the situation remained obscure. He decided to drive up to the front himself.

Motoring along an "emergency track towards the center of the battle...," Stumme "suddenly found himself surrounded by British infantry with many guns and antitank weapons. Colonel Buechting, the only officer with him, was immediately shot through the head. The driver [Corporal Wolf] turned the car about at once. General Stumme had jumped out, but now he managed to cling to the outside of the car while the driver, going flat out, succeeded in escaping the enemy fire. At this point General Stumme must have fallen off. The driver noticed nothing. Later the general was found dead beside the track - heart attack."[24]

---

[20]*Panzer Armies, 1a Panzerarmee Afrika, Schlachtbericht*, T-313, 470, #8768505.

[21]At 0700, 5 Panzer Regiment reported a penetration by 30 enemy tanks. *Divisions, KTB, 21 Panzer Division*, T-315, 769, #000013.

[22]Lewin, *Rommel*, pg. 175.

[23]*Panzer Armies, 1a Schlachtbericht*, T-313, 470, #8768509.

[24]Richardson, *Fatal Decisions*, pg. 96.

That afternoon Lieutenant Berndt placed an urgent phone call to the Field Marshal. "Montgomery's offensive has begun," he blurted into the receiver, "last night. And General Stumme has vanished without a trace!" A short time later a dour Hitler telephone the Semmering: "Rommel, the news from Africa sounds bad. Nobody appears to know what happened to General Stumme. Do you feel capable of returning to Africa and taking command of the army again?" Rommel replied affirmatively.

Rommel flew out of Wiener-Neustadt airfield the next morning in his specially converted Heinkel 111 bomber and touched down in Rome at 1100 hours. Von Rintelen met him at the airfield and briefed him on the latest reports from Africa. The losses in the north had been particularly high, Rommel learned, and the Panzerarmee was down to three issues of gasoline. The latter news struck him like a thunderbolt: "This was sheer disaster, for with only 300 kilometers worth of petrol per vehicle...prolonged resistance could not be expected; we would be completely prevented from taking the correct tactical decisions and would thus suffer a tremendous limitation in our freedom of action. I was bitterly angry, because when I left there had been at least eight issues for the army in Egypt and Libya, and even this had been absurdly little in comparison with the minimum essential of thirty issues."[25]

Rommel climbed back into his Heinkel and flew to the airfield at Herakleion, Crete. Here General von Waldau - now commander of 10 Air Corps - greeted Rommel with more bad news: the enemy had been attacking all day with masses of tanks up and down the front; a search party had recovered the body of General Stumme.

After refueling, Rommel began "to climb back aboard [his aircraft] but von Waldau checked him. 'I cannot permit you to fly on a Heinkel in broad daylight - it's asking for trouble.' Rommel borrowed a sleek, modern Dornier 217 bomber instead of the slower plane and took off for Egypt without further protest. The Dornier landed at the sand-swept airfield of Qasaba at 1750, where Rommel's Storch was waiting. He flew on east until darkness forced him to land, and then he continued along the coast road by car. The horizon ahead was ablaze with the flash of bombs and artillery. Again and again he asked himself: Has Stumme already lost the battle? Then he was back at Panzerarmee headquarters - the familiar faces, the operations bus, the same barren desert strewn with stones, the same stifling heat, the same scorpions and flies, the same lean, brave troops that he left just 32 days before."[26]

It was the evening of 25 October when Westphal and von Thoma reported to Rommel on the course of the bitter struggle of the past two days. The *Schwerpunkt* of the enemy effort lay in the north, von Thoma informed him, where Eighth Army had attacked with large waves of tanks. The British had punched numerous small holes in the Panzerar-

[25]Hart, Rommel Papers, pp. 304-05.
[26]Irving, The Trail, pg. 219.

mee front, but vigorous and repeated counterattacks by the German and Italian armor had often hurled the attackers back. Losses had been frightful: most of the Trento Division was wiped out; two battalions of infantry and two of artillery had vanished from 164 Division's order of battle. RAF bombers and fighters roamed the desert at will shooting up the Panzer columns as they prepared to counterattack. 15 Panzer was down to 31 of its 119 tanks.[27]

The RAF tormentors were again over the Axis positions that night, smothering them with bombs; they pulverized the Afrikakorps headquarters for over three hours.[28] Shortly before midnight Eighth Army captured the important patch of high ground known as Kidney Ridge (Hill 28). The British then pushed reinforcements forward to the hill, from which they planned to attack in the morning in the hope of extending their bridgehead to the west of the minefield.

National Archives

Rommel and Westphal atop his Mammoth command vehicle as plans are made to thwart the British advances.

Rommel slept only a few hours and was back in his Mammoth by 0500. For the next two days, his efforts were dominated by desperate attempts to recapture Hill 28. At daybreak he launched an attack with elements of 15 Panzer, Littorio and a Bersaglieri battalion. "The British resisted desperately," he records, "Rivers of blood were poured out over miserable strips of land which, in normal times, not even the poorest Arab would have bothered his head about."[29] Rommel watched the attack go in through his fieldglasses as the RAF sprayed tons of bombs on his advancing columns. In the evening the Bersaglieri

[27]Panzer Armies, 1a Schlachtbericht, T-313, 470, #8768514.
[28]Army Corps, KTB, DAK, T-314, 21, #000708.
[29]Hart, Rommel Papers, pg. 306.

Battalion succeeded in snatching footholds on the eastern and western rims of the hill, but the hill itself remained in enemy hands.

Eighth Army, too, had attacked vigorously around Hill 28. "The British," writes Rommel, "were continually feeding fresh forces into their attack...and it was clear that they wanted to win through to the area between El Daba and Sidi Abd el Rahman... Late in the afternoon German and Italian dive-bomber formations made a self-immolating attempt to break up the British lorry columns moving towards the northwest. Some 60 British fighters pounced on these slow machines and forced the Italians to jettison their bombs over their own lines, while the German pilots pressed home their attack with very heavy losses. Never before in Africa had we seen such a density of antiaircraft fire. Hundreds of British tracer shells criss-crossed the sky and the air became an absolute inferno of fire."[30]

At 1700, 160 British tanks and armored fighting vehicles rolled over the already badly mauled III./382 Infantry Regiment south of Hill 28. Only a well-aimed counterjab by the remaining Axis tanks was able to throw the attackers back.[31]

That evening Rommel made a grim decision. He transferred 21 Panzer and elements of Ariete up to the north - to concentrate his battered armor against Montgomery's main effort. This was a gamble, for he well knew that his dwindling gasoline reserves would never allow him to send these divisions back southwards.[32]

On the afternoon of the 27th, Rommel renewed his assault on the hill: "Our dive-bombers swooped down on the British lines. Every artillery and antiaircraft gun which we had in the northern sector concentrated a violent fire on the point of the intended attack. Then the armor

Knight's Cross holder Lieutenant Theo Schwabach (far left) directing fire on British concentrations of armor.

moved forward. A murderous British fire struck into our ranks and our attack was soon brought to a halt by an immensely powerful antitank defense, mainly from dug-in antitank guns and a large number of tanks. We suffered considerable losses and were forced to withdraw."[33] The failure of this attack was a bitter disappointment:

> Dearest Lu:
> Nobody can ever know the load that weighs on me. Everything is stacked against us. But I hope we'll pull through. You know I'm giving my last to achieve this.[34]

The Panzerarmee's fuel reserves continued to plunge. The tanker *Proserpina* with 2,500 tons of gasoline, was sunk outside Tobruk harbor;[35] the transport vessel *Tergestea*, carrying 1,000 tons each of ammunition and fuel, was also sunk. The effect of these sinkings on Rommel's operations loomed very large indeed, for without adequate stocks of gasoline to feed his armor he was doomed to fight a static battle of attrition - to forego the wide-open maneuver battle at which he excelled.

> Dearest Lu:
> Who knows whether I'll ever have a chance to write to you again in peace. I have a chance to do so now. The battle is raging. Perhaps we will survive in spite of all that goes against us. If we fail it would have grave consequences for the entire course of the war, for in that case North Africa would fall to the British almost without a fight. We do our utmost to succeed, but the enemy's superiority is tremendous and our own resources very small. If we fail, whether or not I survive the battle will be in God's hands. The lot of the vanquished is hard to bear. I have a clean conscience, as I have done everything to gain a victory and have not spared my own person. Should I remain on the battlefield I would like to thank you and our boy for all the love and joy you have given me in my life.[36]

Ceaseless bombing attacks hammered the Panzerarmee throughout the 28th. 21 Panzer Division alone suffered through eleven separate aerial bombardments that day.[37] In the afternoon it became apparent that throngs of British tanks were massing in the deep breach in the

[30]*Ibid.*, pp. 306-07.
[31]Panzer Armies, 1a *Schlachtbericht*, T-313, 470, #8768521.
[32]21 Panzer received orders to move north at 2000 hours. Divisions, KTB, 21 Panzer Division, T-315, 769, #000014.
[33]Hart, Rommel Papers, pg. 310. The number of operational tanks left in the Panzerarmee by the end of the day was as follows: 15 Panzer (23); 21 Panzer (91); Littorio (44); Ariete (128); Trieste (34). Panzer Armies, 1a *Schlachtbericht*, T-313, 470, #8768533.
[34]*Rommel Collection*, T-84, 274, #000876.
[35]Hart, Rommel Papers, pg. 307.
[36]*Rommel Collection*, T-84, 274, #000876.
[37]Divisions, KTB, 21 Panzer Division, T-315, 769, #000016.

minefields that they had conquered at such a terrible cost. Rommel held his breath. The British, he thought, were about to launch a big new attack.

At 2105 hours the horizon lit up like a ball of fire as hundreds of Eighth Army guns began to plow under the positions of 90 Light Division and II./125 Panzer Grenadier Regiment north of Hill 28.[38] Forty-five minutes later the hardened veterans of Morehead's 9 Australian Division went forward. This attack was designed to "pinch off' the northern flank of Rommel's line, which now projected forward like a balcony, and to clear the way for a drive along the Via Balbia towards Daba and Fuka.

The fighting raged with unabated fury well into the morning. The German grenadiers fought on savagely until overrun after a six-hour battle; a battalion of Bersaglieri infantry fought until exterminated.[39] Rommel observed this nightmarish dance of death from a position astride the coast road: "We could see the flash of bursting shells in the darkness and hear the rolling thunder of the battle. Again and again British bomber formations flew up and tipped their death-dealing loads on my troops, or bathed the country in the brilliant light of parachute flares. No one can conceive the extent of our anxiety during this period."[40]

But the Australian assault was brought to a halt, with stiff losses for the attackers. One company of German infantry wiped out 17 enemy tanks. Rommel now shifted von Sponeck's 90 Light Division to the coastal sector to guard against further breakthroughs.

Montgomery spent the morning of 29 October steeped in contemplation. For five full days he had bludgeoned his stubborn foe with hundreds of tanks, guns and planes; and he had still failed to achieve the decisive breakthrough. In London, Churchill was growing ornery. "Why did Montgomery tell us he would be through in seven days," he barked at General Alan Brooke, chief of the Imperial General Staff, "if all he intended to do was fight a half-hearted battle? Have we not got one single general who can win one single battle?"[41]

But Montgomery had concocted a new scheme of attack. In his memoirs he writes:

> During the morning it became increasingly evident that the whole of Rommel's German forces were grouped in the northern part of the front. The actions of 1 Armored Division in the northern corridor, and the operations of 9 Australian Division northwards towards the coast had clearly made him think that we intended to break out in the north along the coast,

---

[38]Army Corps, _KTB_, _DAK_, T-314, 21, #000719.
[39]Panzer Armies, _1a Schlachtbericht_, T-313, 470, #8768544.
[40]Hart, _Rommel Papers_, pg. 312.
[41]Irving, _The Trail_, pg. 224.

despite his superiority must also be at the end of his strength. It would not be the first time in history that a strong will has triumphed over the bigger battalions. As to your troops, you can show them no other road than to victory or death.

signed Adolf Hitler[56]

At 1105 Jodl personally telephoned Hitler's signal to von Rintelen's adjutant in Rome. Twenty-five minutes later it was radioed, encoded by the Enigma machine, to Panzerarmee headquarters. Shortly thereafter, the complete text of the dramatic message was also in British hands. In fact, all of the major signals between OKW and Rommel during these frantic few days found their way to Churchill's desk; they provided percise and detailed data about the dire straits of the Panzerarmee. At the Foreign Office, Sir Alexander Cadogan noted in his diary on 3 November, "C. had news, which he phoned to me this morning, which certainly seems to show that Rommel is in a fix."[57]

Rommel returned to his command post about midday, "only just escaping by some frantic driving a carpet of bombs laid by 18 British aircraft." At 1330 hours an officer on Westphal's staff handed him a copy of Hitler's famous order. "We were completely stunned," Rommel writes, "and for the first time during the African campaign, I did not know what to do." But given the Field Marshal's loyalty to Hitler, his freedom of action was necessarily limited: "...We issued orders for all existing positions to be held on instructions from the highest authority. I forced myself to this action, as I had always demanded unconditional obedience from others, and, consequently, wished to apply the principle to myself. Had I known what was to come I should have acted differently, because from that time on, we had continually to circumvent orders from the Führer or Duce in order to save the army from destruction."[58]

Rommel then radioed OKW a graphic account of his army's crumbling position: "The German losses are almost 50% in infantry, antitank and engineer troops. The Afrikakorps is down to 24 tanks. Littorio Armored and Trieste Motorized Divisions are virtually wiped out."[59] He also dispatched Berndt to Hitler's East Prussia headquarters, to induce the Führer to revoke his senseless order.

Throughout the morning of 4 November, Rommel's army clung stoically to the miserable strip of sand and rock that Hitler had ordered be defended to the death. At 1255 Rommel learned that the British had captured von Thoma. Disheartened by the untoward turn of events, von Thoma had pinned on all his medals, climbed into a tank, and rumbled off into the vortex of the battle, presumably to seek his own death.

---

[56]*Rommel Collection*, T-84, 296, #000885.
[57]Lewin, *Ultra*, pg. 268.
[58]Hart, *Rommel Papers*, pg. 321.
[59]*Rommel Collection*, T-84, 296, #000886.

At 1100 hours Bayerlein had raced off in an armored reconnaissance car to find him. "Suddenly," Bayerlein recalls, "a hail of armor-piercing shot was whistling all about me. In the noontime haze I could see countless black monsters far away in front. They were Montgomery's tanks, the 10 Hussars. I jumped out of the armored car and beneath the midday sun ran as fast as I could towards Tel el Mampsra. It was a place of death, of burning tanks and smashed flak guns without a living soul. But then, about 200 yards away from the sandhole in which I was lying, I saw a man standing erect beside a burning tank, apparently impervious to the intense fire which criss-crossed about him. It was General von Thoma... Von Thoma stood there, rigid and motionless as a pillar of salt, with his canvas bag still in his hand. A bren carrier was driving straight towards him with two Shermans just behind. The British soldiers signalled to von Thoma. At the same time 150 vehicles poured across Tel el Mampsra like a flood."[60]

A dazed von Thoma stands by his captor, Montgomery, shortly after being seized by British troops.

---

[60]Richardson, <u>Fatal Decisions</u>, pp. 106-07. Von Thoma's last words to Bayerlein had been "Bayerlien, Hitler's order is a piece of unparalleled madness. I can't go along with this any longer. Go to the El Daba command post. I shall stay here and personally take charge of the defense of Tel el Mampsra." <u>Ibid.</u>, pg. 122.

That afternoon the roof caved in on the battling remnants of the Axis army. From his command post Rommel could see angry balls of smoke and dust rising in the south. Here, the pitiful armor of the Ariete Division fought on pugnaciously in a desperate attempt to beat back the British tanks that had poured around its open flank. But it was soon over - 20 Italian Motorized Corps wiped out almost to the last tank.

A 12-mile gap yawned in the Panzerarmee's front. Eighth Army tanks streamed westwards and threatened to encircle the Axis forces in the north. Rommel took the bull by the horns; without waiting for word from Hitler, he commenced the retreat.[61] It was too late to save the unmotorized infantry, but at least, he hoped, his few remaining mobile troops might survive. And so he began a hellish 2,000 mile withdrawal. The next morning a signal arrived from Hitler allowing Rommel to do what he had already done - to begin to fall back.

---

[61]*All this time Rommel was at his headquarters waiting for Field Marshal Kesselring. When Kesselring arrived he told Rommel that he also considered Hitler's "victory or death" order nonsense. After much discussion they agreed that as long as Rommel was the man on the spot, command of the army should be left to him. They also discussed the possibility of "circumventing" Hitler's order; Kesselring told Rommel that he "would accept joint responsibility for not carrying out the order and would immediately send Hitler a message to that effect." Albert Kesselring, A Soldier's Record (New York: William Morrow and Company, 1954) pg. 159.*

The Retreat
November 1942-January 1943

That night, 4 November, the Axis army continued its retirement towards the Fuka position. An endless motor convoy jammed the coast road. RAF planes smothered the road in the dazzling light of parachute flares and bombed and strafed the vast armada of vehicles. Most of the Panzerarmee contrived to avoid this chaos as they made their way back through the open desert. The next day large elements of the Afrikakorps, 90 Light Division and the residue of the Italian Motorized Corps reached the Fuka line. Montgomery's timerous attempts to cut off and destroy his fleeing enemy failed on each occasion.

Farther south the doomed Italian infantry was in its death throes. Mussolini insisted that every effort be made to salvage these troops, but such a rescue, Rommel knew, was hardly possible. The Italians had no motor transport and the surviving mobile elements of Rommel's army, themselves struggling to avoid extinction, were much too weak to render assistance.[1] The result was an unavoidable tragedy, which Caccia-Dominioni describes vividly in his memoirs: "Names steeped in history passed out of existence alongside others, newer but no less glorious. The infantry of the Pavia had had a hundred years or more of life, though they really dated back to the French-named regiments of Savoy; the Brescia had originally been composed of volunteers of 1848; the Bologna of men recruited in Venetia and Romagna in 1859. Nothing was left of them. Nor of the youthful Ariete and Littorio. Nor of the new-born Folgore, reduced finally to the most painful of all sacrifices. They suffered a cruel misfortune and were powerless to stave off humiliation; it was like an ant-hill being overwhelmed by a flood."[2]

Rommel had no intention of staying at Fuka. Strong British forces had engaged the Afrikakorps' rear guards and a large contingent of enemy armor was attempting to sneak around Rommel's southern flank. To avoid encirclement the Axis columns resumed their retrograde movement. The confusion was indescribable as the mixed German and Italian transport reeled back in utter disorder. Thousands of trucks

---

[1]*According to Afrikakorps records the two German armored divisions now had 38 tanks between them - 15 Panzer had 8 and 21 Panzer, 30. In guns and infantry they were also sorely reduced. Army Corps, KTB, DAK, T-314, 21, #000753.*

[2]*Caccia-Dominioni, Alamein, pg. 242.*

204

choked the road in bumper-to-bumper fashion; sudden sandstorms frequently cut visibility to zero; the smouldering steel carcasses of burnt-out vehicles marked the path of the beaten army and attested to the prowess of the RAF.

During the morning, 6 November, 15 Panzer and 90 Light reached an area to the south of Mersa Matruh.[3] 21 Panzer, its tanks out of gasoline, had no choice but to dig in southwest of Quasaba. Throughout the morning and afternoon a force of 50-60 Eighth Army tanks launched repeated assaults against the immobilized division. The attacking armor smashed a breech in 21 Panzer's line and rumbled on towards the division's artillery. The heavy German guns resisted savagely and blasted the enemy tanks over open sights until crushed by the overpowering weight of the attack. The division had little choice but to scuttle its immobilized Panzers and beat a fighting retreat westwards down the Telegraph track with its wheeled transport. By the next morning its Panzer regiment had 4 tanks left.[4]

On the afternoon of the 6th, an emissary of Cavallero, General Gandin, visited Rommel and probed him about the army's future plans. The Field Marshal didn't hold his punches: "I told him point-blank that with the present balance of forces there was not a chance of our making a stand anywhere, and that the British could keep on going right through to Tripolitania, if they choose to.... We could attempt no operation with our remaining armor and motorized forces because of the petrol shortage; every drop that reached us had to be used for getting our troops out. Gandin left my H.Q. visibly shaken."[5]

Rommel continued to cast his glance westwards; soon his columns were approaching the frontier. Torrential rains on 6-7 November transformed many of the thin desert tracks into unnavigable quagmires and the retreat slowed to a crawl. The downpours also reduced the speed of Eighth Army's pursuing tanks and lorried infantry to a snail's pace. In his memoirs, in fact, Montgomery states that only the rain saved Rommel's forces "from complete disaster."[6] Montgomery's statement, however, is self-defensive and conceals a much larger truth, which is that Eighth Army's methodical and overapprehensive pursuit had handed Rommel numerous well-exploited opportunities to get away. This fact is all the more incredible when one realizes that Allied code-breakers provided Montgomery with every detail of Rommel's desperate plight. The Desert Fox had scarcely any tanks, guns or gasoline, but still Montgomery was unable to administer a knock-out blow. In his Papers, Rommel does not hide his contempt for his opponent's bungling: "The British commander [showed] himself to be over-cautious. He risked nothing in any way doubtful and bold solutions

[3]Army Corps, KTB, DAK, T-314, 21, #000755-000756.
[4]Divisions, KTB, 21 Panzer Division, T-315, 769, #000023-000024.
[5]Hart, Rommel Papers, pg. 341.
[6]Montgomery, Memoirs, pg. 129.

were completely foreign to him.... I was quite satisfied that Montgomery would never take the risk of following up boldly and overrunning us, as he could have done without any danger to him.... Montgomery had an absolute mania for always bringing up adequate reserves behind his back.... The speed of reaction of the British command was comparatively low."[7]

At 1000 hours, 7 November, General Ramcke arrived at Panzerarmee headquarters. Rommel had given up Ramcke and his men for killed or captured, for, like the Italian infantry, they were completely unmotorized. Not to be left behind, the brigade had ambushed a British convoy, captured its trucks and raced on through to rejoin Rommel's force. Now here they were, General Ramcke and 600 of his arrogant, tough-skinned paratroopers. Rommel had never felt much affection for these men. Crack *Luftwaffe* troops, they had always demanded special privileges. But the Desert Fox could not help but marvel at their spectacular achievement.

With the rains over, the Axis army ground its way down the road to Halfaya and Sollum. The 30 to 40-mile-long procession of tanks, trucks, guns and troop carriers trudged wearily up the passes and disappeared in their serpentine twists and turns. Enemy fighters and bombers were constantly overhead, but the retreat was more orderly now and did not become a rout. On the morning of the 8th, Rommel met Bayerlein and informed him that an Allied convoy - 104 ships - was nearing northwest Africa. Operation Torch was in the wings; a large Anglo-American force was about to land in Algeria and Morocco. Soon Rommel would have a lavishly equipped army of 100,000 men advancing on him virtually unopposed from the rear. He realized that the end for his Panzerarmee could not be far away. He became convinced that the only feasible long-range policy was to abandon North Africa altogether. Hitler, however, had no intention of surrendering an entire theatre of war. As early as 10 November he began to pump the first elements of what would become a new army (5 Panzer) into Tunisia to form a front against the invasion force.

Mussolini had demanded that Rommel hold the Sollum Line, but such a course of action proved impossible. The army's handful of troops and guns could not hope to make a determined stand along a line that offered an open southern flank. The British would inevitably outflank the position, and Rommel had neither the requisite motorized troops nor the gasoline to banish such a threat.

> Dearest Lu:
> Since the enemy breakthrough at Alamein I have had no chance to write. I want to send you a few lines today. When an enemy has broken through an army, that army is in bad shape. It has to fight its way

[7]Hart, *Rommel Papers*, pp. 360, 395.

through and looses whatever striking power still remains. We can't go on much longer because a superior enemy is chasing us."[8]

The Panzerarmee retired through Cyrenaica. In rapid succession the bitterly contested battlefields of 1941-42 loomed up and then vanished to the east - Sidi Rezegh, Gazala and, of course, Tobruk, where the bleached bones of von Ponath's brave machine gunners lay buried forever beneath the sand and rock. On 13 November the first Axis contingents reached the Mersa el Brega line.[9] The Eighth Army pursuit still lacked verve; German rearguards parried all attempts to bottle up and destroy the Panzerarmee. The army also had a new engineer officer, Major General Karl Buelowius, who proceeded to discomfit greatly the advancing enemy with deviously-placed mines and booby-traps.

By mid-November the crushing pressures of a humiliating retreat had again brought Rommel's health to the breaking point. The Field Marshal was worn out and depressed. "I wish I were just a newspaper vendor in Berlin," he intimated to Armbruster, "then I could sleep nights, without the responsibility I have now." On the 14th his aid Berndt observed: "In consequence of the many upsets and his interrupted cure, the C in C's health is very poor. Several bouts of fainting."[10]

Rommel's catastrophic fuel situation was hardly calculated to enhance his tenuous well-being. His army required 250 tons of gasoline a day just to keep going,[11] but the average daily deliveries were well below this figure; on some days not a drop was delivered. Things went from bad to worse when, on 17-18 November, British submarines - alerted by Ultra - struck savagely at the Axis convoys and torpedoed seven vessels laden with thousands of tons of gasoline. "All the tankers have been sunk," von Waldau scribbled in his diary. "How R. is going to keep moving now is a mystery."[12]

But keep going he did - somehow. His little army retreated down the Cyrenaica bulge. By the 19th, 90 Light Division had evacuated Benghazi, but not before an orgy of destruction had rendered the port temporarily useless to the British. Four days later the Panzerarmee was sitting snugly behind the Mersa el Brega line. It had withdrawn 800 miles in the face of a vastly superior enemy, and had hardly lost a man.

Dearest Lu:

The last few days have been quiet as far as actual fighting is concerned. It's been pouring with rain on and off, which hasn't made life particularly comfortable, especially as I've been camping out in my car.

[8]*Rommel Collection*, T-84, 274, #000883.
[9]*Panzer Armies, 1a Schlachtbericht*, T-313, 470, #8768653.
[10]Irving, *The Trail*, pg. 241.
[11]Von Esebeck, *Afrikanische Schicksalsjahre*, pg. 132.
[12]Irving, *The Trail*, pg. 243.

Today I have a roof over my head again, and a table. That is great luxury. I've written you some thoroughly miserable letters, which I'm sorry for."[13]

Rommel quickly surveyed the new defensive line. It was a hundred miles in length and abutted on an extensive salt marsh, which made it difficult to be turned from the south. The Italians were already busy at work strengthening the defenses under the supervision of Bastico, to whom Rommel was once more directly subordinated.[14] The Italian division's "Young Fascist," Pistoia and Spezia had occupied the line, while elements of the newly-arrived Centauro Armored Division provided a reserve. Both Hitler and Mussolini had ordered Rommel to hold at Mersa el Brega at all cost.

But the Field Marshal had other ideas. His plan was to abandon Tripolitania altogether and retreat, hundreds more miles down the jagged African coastline - to Tunisia. There, at Gabes, was a twelve-mile stretch of land that ran from the sea to a chain of lakes and marshes known as the Shott el Jerid (or Fejaj). This line, Rommel felt, offered ideal possibilities for the defense; it should be the ultimate destination of the Panzerarmee - short of a complete evacuation to Europe.

On the 24th Rommel, Kesselring and Cavallero met at the Arco dei Fileni. The Panzerarmee records describe this conference in some detail. Rommel was blunt and to the point. The Mersa el Brega line, he contended, could not be held, at least not with the meager forces at his disposal. To make a stand against a major Eighth Army attack he would need the following, and within 10 days: 50 75mm Pak guns, 50 Panzer IV specials and 78 guns of large caliber. In addition he would need at least 4,000 tons each of gasoline and ammunition.[15] Rommel also broached the thorny subject of a retreat from Tripolitania, but "came up against the solid opposition of Kesselring and Cavallero." For the Panzerarmee commander the results of this meeting were far from satisfactory. "Me," writes Rommel, "they regarded as a pessimist of the first order, and they were probably the source of the legend which later went the rounds back in the rear - and was swallowed whole by certain office-chair soldiers only too anxious to delude themselves - that I was 'cock-a-hoop in victory but a prey to despair in defeat.' In any case it was quite obvious that neither of the Marshals would ever support my case."[16]

Two days later he harvested the bitter fruit of this conference. Bastico radioed Rommel and informed him that Mussolini now wanted the

---

[13]*Rommel Collection*, T-84, 274, #000909.
[14]On 22 November the liaison group Delease (Delegazione del Commando Supremo in Africa Settentrionale) formed originally to function as a channel of communications between Rommel and Commando Supremo, was placed under Bastico's Superlibia. This change in the command apparatus brought Rommel once again under Bastico's command.
[15]Panzer Armies, 1a Schlachtbericht, T-313, 470, #8768703.
[16]Hart, Rommel Papers, pg. 364.

Panzerarmee to attack the British advance guards; under no circumstances was Rommel to withdraw further without the Italian High Command's explicit approval. But his superiors' threats had never deterred Rommel in the past and they did not deter him now. He spoke with General Navarrini and ordered him to prepare the army for another leap backwards, to the Buerat line. This position lay 250 miles to the west, across an immense, barren track of desert.

At loggerheads with Kesselring and the Italian High Command, Rommel committed a highly impulsive - though characteristic - act. Without notifying Bastico, or OKW for that matter, he boarded his Heinkel and flew to Germany. He planned an audience with the Führer "to ask him personally for a strategic decision...and to lay before him the operational and tactical views of the Panzerarmee."[17]

At 1700 hours, 28 November, he was ushered into the Führer's presence. Rommel could not have chosen a more unpropitious moment for his meeting, for Hitler was in a foul mood. In Russia the front had started to crumble; von Paulus' 6 Army was trapped at Stalingrad. The *Luftwaffe* was airlifting supplies to the army, and Hitler was planning a relief attack under General von Manstein. Rommel's uninvited appearance from a relatively quiet theatre of war did not please the Führer.

As usual, Rommel did not mince his words. He carefully listed the weakensses of his army, and stated that if it remained in Africa it would be destroyed. He recommended that the North African theatre be abandoned entirely and the Axis troops withdrawn to Europe. The latter statement was more than Hitler could bear and he flew into a frenzy. Undaunted, Rommel continued. His men, he said, had lost most of their weapons during the retreat; thousands of troops were completely unarmed. Hitler fulminated. He accused Rommel's men of throwing their weapons away. The brave Field Marshal protested vehemently, "but there was no attempt at discussion. The Führer said that his decision to hold the eastern front in the winter of 1941-42 had saved Russia and that there, too, he had upheld his orders ruthlessly. I began to realize that Adolf Hitler simply did not want to see the situation as it was, and that he reacted emotionally against what his intelligence must have told him was right. He said that it was a political necessity to continue to hold a major bridgehead in Africa and there would, therefore, be no withdrawal from the Mersa el Brega line. He would do everything possible to get supplies to me. The Reich-Marshal [Göring] was to accompany me to Italy. He would be vested with extraordinary powers and was to negotiate with the Italians and all responsible authorities."[18]

There is little doubt that the tumultuous conference was a turning point in Rommel's relationship with his supreme commander - "a most important stage in the diminution of his loyalty to Hitler. The seed was

[17]*Ibid.*, pg. 365.
[18]*Ibid.*, pg. 366.

sown at El Alamein."[19] But it was more than that; it was another link in the chain of events that had gradually shifted Rommel's outlook on the war as a whole. He had, in fact, come to consider the war as a lost cause for Germany.

Shortly after this disastrous conference, Rommel was rolling south towards Rome, aboard Göring's lavish special train, *Asia*. The trip took almost two days and Rommel "was compelled to witness the antics of the Reich-Marshal.... The situation [in Africa] did not seem to trouble him in the slightest. He plumbed himself, beamed broadly at the primitive flattery heaped on him by imbeciles from his own court, and talked of nothing but jewelry and pictures. At other times his behavior could perhaps be amusing - now it was infuriating."[20] Göring attempted to "curry favor" by presenting Rommel with the Golden Pilot's Badge with Diamonds - the *Luftwaffe's* highest military honor.

Once in Rome, Rommel conferred with Mussolini.[21] The Duce, for a change, supported Rommel's tactical recommendations; he agreed that a last ditch stand at Mersa el Brega, as Hitler had ordered, could only end with the destruction of the army. Rommel received permission to build a defensive line at Buerat, and to pull back the unmotorized Italian infantry to this position. The motorized troops, however, were to remain at Mersa el Brega, and only to withdraw in the event of an Eighth Army attack.

After the conferences Rommel attended a luncheon at Rome's opulent Hotel Excelsior. Field Marshal Erhard Milch, who was also present, recorded in his papers: "During lunch Göring savagely insulted Rommel, which cut him to the quick. Rommel asked me up to his room afterward, and for several hours I tried to console him. But he was such a nervous wreck deep down inside, that he finally buried his head in my right shoulder and wept for some time."[22]

Rommel returned to Africa on 2 December - wounded and depressed. Hitler's lack of support, his unwillingness to recognize the tremendous hardships that beset the Panzerarmee, had badly disillusioned the Desert Fox. That Rommel expected the worst, total defeat or even capitulation to Montgomery's army, is evident in a letter home shortly thereafter:

> Dearest Lu:
> Little news. There is more activity at the front now.
> Our supply problems are still not solved by any means

---

[19]Lewin, <u>Rommel</u>, pg. 194.
[20]Hart, <u>Rommel Papers</u>, pg. 366.
[21]Kesselring's observations at this point are instructive: "I myself noticed Rommel's tired demeanor [this was after Rommel had spent almost 41 hours on the train with Göring]; he looked almost more in need of a rest than he did before he went on leave. Göring and I were convinced that Rommel in this state was not able to do what was expected of him and what the difficult situation required. His thoughts were already retreating to Tunis and thence to the Alps." <u>AHBT</u>, VII/104.
[22]Irving, <u>The Trail</u>, pg. 248.

and give me a great headache. I wonder whether you would be kind enough to send me by courier an English-German pocket dictionary. I have an idea that I'll be able to make good use of it."[23]

The Panzerarmee was now out of range of the *Luftwaffe* bases in Sicily, thus the fuel crisis had grown even worse. And although 5,000 tons of gasoline had reached the army during November, the British had sunk considerably more than that - 8,100 tons.[24]

By 5 December the quickening pace of Eighth Army activity along the front pointed to an imminent offensive. The following night Rommel began to truck the Italian infantry back to Buerat. He had taken numerous precautions in an effort to conceal the shift in forces from the British. The Italians, however, roared off to the west as if on a holiday - with blazing headlights and blaring horns. Somehow, the British failed to detect the movement, which swallowed up most of the army's remaining stocks of gasoline.

Around midnight, 11 December, Eighth Army artillery began to rake the Axis front - Montgomery's long awaited offensive on the Mersa el Brega line had begun. The Italian infantry was now out of the line, and, in accordance with a pre-arranged signal, Rommel's armored troops began to retire as well. By morning the front was empty.

Once again Rommel's Panzer divisions were rolling back in retreat - this time across the "arid and monotonous wastes of the Great Sirte." The divisions came close to annihilation on 15 December when the Afrikakorps' rearguard ran dangerously low on gasoline. General Gustav Fehn, the Afrikakorps' new commander, ordered 21 Panzer Division to turn over its remaining fuel to 15 Panzer, so that the latter division's tanks would continued the fight and protect the others until more fuel could be trucked forward. As usual, Montgomery failed to exploit his chances, and pursued the retreating army with his customary caution. But there was evidence that Eighth Army, too, was beset by supply difficulties. Rommel's logistical woes could not have been worse. In the last four weeks the enemy had sunk nine out of ten transports destined for Tripoli.[25]

Rommel drove off to Buerat on the 17th. The countryside here, dotted with meadows of fragrant flowers, was strikingly different from the lunar landscape of the Great Sirte. He inspected the Buerat defenses the next day. A deep antitank ditch covered the line, and Axis engineers had strewn some 80,000 mines along its front, though these were mostly of the antipersonel variety and harmless to tanks. But it was the same old story, for no matter how imposing were the fixed defenses, the position could be outflanked in the south. Besides, the army had little

---

[23]*Rommel Collection*, T-84, 274, #000936.
[24]*As of 1 December the Afrikakorps' Panzer strength had risen slightly - to 46 Panzer III's and IV's. Panzer Armies, 1a Schlachtbericht, T-313, 470, #8768725.
[25]Ibid., #8768787.*

ammunition or gasoline, and almost no tanks or guns to speak of. Rommel met with Bastico and advocated that another step back be taken, to the Tarhuna-Homs line; and his eyes were still riveted on Gabes as his army's final destination. Bastico supported Rommel's thinking in all its essentials, but this scarcely mattered, for a frantic signal arrived from the Duce: "Resistance to the uttermost. I repeat, resistance to the uttermost, with all the troops of the Panzerarmee in the Buerat line."[26]

By 29 December the Axis army was firmly ensconced behind the Buerat line. Rommel bowed to Mussolini's directive and began to fortify the position, but he had no intention of immolating his army there if Montgomery attacked in strength; in that case, he would defy his orders and beat a retreat. What he did not know, or would not believe, was that Montgomery's very real logistical difficulties would preclude an attack at Buerat until mid-January 1943.

For Rommel, the closing days of 1942 were charged with grave anxieties. His nightmare was that the Anglo-American army in Tunisia might crash through the Gabes bottleneck and drive a wedge between him and General Hans Jürgen von Arnim's 5 Panzer Army. He radioed dark signals to Rome and to OKW, in a desperate attempt to gain some understanding for his plight. His efforts only succeeded in further alienating the Italian High Command. "I'm against giving Rommel any freedom of action at all," Cavallero exclaimed to Kesselring. "Just look how he behaves when he does get it. It's quite clear that all he wants is to get to Tunis as fast as his legs will carry him." The same day Cavallero jotted in his diary, "we've got to get rid of Rommel."[27]

On the last day of 1942, a heated conference took place between Bastico, Kesselring and Rommel. Mussolini, Rommel learned, had decided that the army could retire to the mountain passes at Homs, but only when sorely pressed by the enemy. Resistance in Tripolitania, the Duce maintained, must be kept up for another two months to gain time to prepare a thorough demolition of the port of Tripoli. Rommel insisted that the vulnerable Italian infantry be pulled back at once. Bastico demurred. The conference ended in a deadlock and Bastico radioed the unsatisfactory results to Rome. Several days later an order arrived from Bastico: Rommel could begin shuttling the Italian infantry back to the Tarhuna-Homs line. "But there was still a string attached to it," Rommel writes, "for it charged us with the task of holding up the British

---

[26]*Ibid.*, #8768791.

[27]Irving, *The Trail*, pg. 254.   *Agents for the Allies learned of the "strictly confidential discussions" and passed them on. The report finally got back to the OSS as file No. CID 29411 (classified B-good; 2-probably true report). "According to this extremely reliable source, Rommel is in disgrace with both the officer corps and Hitler. The reputation that Rommel enjoys with the United States is evidently not understood by the German military people, for they consider him as only good for offensive knockout tactics and also as one of their worst generals. Rommel's advance past Halfaya Pass was oppsite to specific instructions and directly responsible for subsequent defeat, for it created an impossible German supplies situation. It is unlikely that Rommel will be given command in Tunis operations."*

in front of the Tripoli defenses for at least six weeks. I had already shown how pointless it was to fix such targets."[28]

The front was quiet at the turn of the new year, 1943, as Montgomery prepared another set-piece battle. Rommel spent several days with Bayerlein, exhaustively reconnoitering the peaceful countryside that would soon be torn by bombs and shredded by tank tracks. He even took time to visit the Roman ruins of Leptis Magna - the crumbling legacy of a civilization buried deep beneath the pages of history. At the ruins, Rommel's A.D.C., Leiutenant von Hardtdegen, "particularly distinguished himself by falling asleep between two pieces of feminine statuary. Bayerlein photographed him there."[29]

At dawn, 15 January, Montgomery's new offensive went forward. 150 tanks and 100 armored cars plunged head-on into 15 Panzer Division. The attack continued into the afternoon; 15 Panzer knocked out 32 Eighth Army tanks, with a loss of only two.[30]

And so the same dreary scene repeated itself: Rommel's army jerked backwards in retreat, while the probing fingers of the Eighth Army pursuit groped tentatively forward. By 18 December the Panzerarmee was positioned in the new line. It had not been an easy withdrawal, for the shortages of fuel and ammunition had produced the usual hardships. The lack of gasoline had even forced Centauro Armored Division to tow its tanks back. "The enemy outnumbers us 8 to 1," Rommel wrote to Lucie.[31]

The next day, 19 January, was worse. "Toughest day since we left Buerat," Armbruster wrote. "We drove several times to the Afrikakorps. We stood aloft on a 'warlord's hill,' watching the enemy divisions foregathering for the attack. We had never seen anything like it before. When we were visiting 20 Corps, their heavy artillery - 15 centimeter guns - was already shelling the road and us. It stank, and I didn't like it at all. We just got out at the last moment."[32]

An even blacker episode was now in store for Rommel, for, by evening, an enormous column comprised of thousands of enemy vehicles had flooded around his desert flank and crossed the Tarhuna-Garian road. This column, he realized, threatened his army with encirclement and total annihilation if it remained at Homs. He sounded the retreat; he had no alternative but to abandon the rump of Tripolitania and move back to Tunisia - to the Mareth line.

This unauthorized withdrawal brought down a chorus of protests from the Italian High Command. On the 20th Cavallero shot off a thunderbolt of his own to Rommel:

---

[28]Hart, *Rommel Papers*, pg. 382.
[29]*Ibid.*, pg. 383.
[30]Panzer Armies, *1a Schlachtbericht*, T-313, 470, #8768879.
[31]*Rommel Collection*, T-84, 274, #000986.
[32]Irving, *The Trail*, pg. 259.

The Duce is not in favor of the steps at present being taken, because they are not in accordance with his instructions to hold the Tarhuna-Homs position at least three weeks. He does not believe the thrust from the south to be very pressing and considers the orders that have been given unjustified and over hasty. The Duce is of the opinion that the withdrawal will certainly develop into a break-through if all the moves are speeded up, as army [Rommel] intends to do. The Duce insists on the line laid down by him being held.[33]

Rommel "gasped" when he received this signal, for there could be no question of holding a position completely turned on its open flank. Late that afternoon the embattled Field Marshal drove to Bianchi, a small Italian colonial village. Three angry men - Kesselring, Bastico and Cavallero - were waiting for him. The encounter was a stormy one. "You can either hold on to Tripoli a few more days," Rommel challenged Cavallero, "and lose the army, or lose Tripoli a few days earlier and save the army for Tunis. Make up your mind."[34] By 25 January the first elements of the Panzerarmee were motoring into Tunisia.

Dearest Lu:
Yesterday I was busy from morning till night. Grave reproaches from Rome because we do not hold out longer against enemy pressure. We do what we can. The development of the situation yesterday has fully vindicated my actions. Shall we be able to continue fighting much longer with this state of supply? We want to and will fight as long as possible. You can imagine what troubles I have with our dear allies. It was inevitable that they would falter. I don't think they will be with us much longer.   People and nations don't change.[35]

On 26 January Rommel reconnoitered the Mareth front, which lay 80 miles inside the Tunisian frontier. The Tunisian landscape, he pleasantly discovered, was lush and green, and bejewelled with flowers, trees, plantations - even fresh water wells. The line itself, which ran from the sea to the Matmata Hills, was somewhat more prosaic: It "consisted of a line of antiquated French block-houses which in no way measured up to the standards required by modern war.... The southern part of the line could be regarded as completely proof against tanks. Its center was given some protection against tanks by a steep wadi, but this obstacle could be overcome by well-trained tank crews. Its northern end was covered to the front by a salt marsh, but most of this was negotiable by

[33]*AHBT*, VII/80-81.
[34]Hart, <u>Rommel Papers</u>, pg. 389.
[35]<u>Rommel Collection</u>, T-84, 274, #001010.

vehicles.... In view of [the line's weakness], I demanded occupation of the [Gabes Line].... This line [40 miles back from the Mareth line] could not be outflanked and would have, therefore, enabled us to make effective use of the non-motorized infantry.... But our superiors could not see it."[36]

The Italians, OKW and Kesselring, meanwhile, had been scheming for Rommel's dismissal.[37] At midday on the 26th, a signal arrived at the Panzerarmee's new Tunisian headquarters informing Rommel that he was to be relieved from his command, but the actual date was left for the Field Marshal himself to decide. General Giovanni Messe, a veteran of the Russian front and an Italian, was to be his successor.

The news of his impending release could hardly have shocked Rommel. "The sooner the better," he acidly commented. His health was again failing him, for between his own insensitive superiors, the African desert and the rigors of a long retreat, he was fighting more battles than any one man could bear. During a discussion of the Mareth line, 28 January, General Fritz Krause, Rommel's artillery commander, noted that the Field Marshal "gave the impression of a broken man." He did not speak naturally, "but read every word. His chief of staff [Bayerlein] who sat next to him at the conference, feared that Rommel would fall asleep from fatigue."[38] The steady erosion of his health and his plunging spirits are graphically recorded in his letters home during this period:

24 January

Dearest Lu:
You will know from the High Command communique that we had to abandon Tripoli. Now we hope to succeed in joining the army in the west. That will be a very different mission, considering the supply situation, the terrain and road conditions. I had to make a report on the state of my health. After two years in Africa I regret to say that I am not strong enough to continue much longer in this responsible position.[39]

25 January

Dearest Lu:
I cannot describe to you how hard such a withdrawal, with all the things connected with it, is for us. Day and

---

[36]Hart, Rommel Papers, pg. 392. In reference to Mareth line, Rommel remarked that "on the basis of his World War I experiences in mountain warfare, he, if he were an infantryman, would rather attack than defend such a position. He pointed out that there were many approaches that offered cover and concealment, and that one could easily infiltrate through the gaps between the individual forts especially at night." Fritz Krause, "Studies of the Mareth Position," MS D-046, pg. 3. Hereafter cited as "Mareth Position," D-046.

[37]In his memoirs, Kesselring becomes increasingly critical of Rommel's lack of offensive spirit. Kesselring, Soldat, pg. 198.

[38]Krause, "Mareth Position," D-046, pg. 8.

[39]Rommel Collection, 274, #001010.

night I am haunted by the fear of complete failure in Africa. I am so depressed, I can hardly work at all. Perhaps somebody else considers the situation more favorable and can still make something out of it. Kesselring for example is full of optimism and probably thinks I am the reason why the army did not hold out longer.[40]

28 January

Dearest Lu:

...in a few days I will turn over the command of my army to an Italian, as the state of my health permits me no longer to exercise it. There are other reasons too, of course, especially the question of prestige. I have exerted the greatest efforts to hold my own despite many difficulties. I pity my soldiers from the bottom of my heart. I cling to them with the greatest affection.[41]

So Rommel prepared to say farewell to Africa; to leave behind 10,000 of his devoted soldiers - men who had fought to the death for their beloved "Erwin." Their shallow graves criss-crossed the North African wastes from Tripoli to El Alamein.

The "Desert Fox" gives words of encouragement to his troops as they retreat into Tunisia. Standing at his left is Bayerlein.

[40]Ibid., #001023.
[41]Ibid.

Last Acts in Africa: Kassarine and Medenine

It was now early February 1943 and the Axis army was moving into position along the Mareth line; the long and brutal path from El Alamein had almost reached its end.[1] For three months - how unending they must have seemed! - the Desert Fox had maneuvered his suffering little army down a 2,000 mile strip of coastal highway, harrassed the entire way by immensely superior enemy air and ground forces, and brought it safely into the green and undulating hills of southern Tunisia. The retreat was a marvelous technical achievement and demonstrated the breadth of Rommel's prowess as a military leader.

Rommel's infantry march westward to the temporary haven of Tunisia.

All at once a great change came over Rommel and his personal morale began to soar again. He decided to remain in Tunisia until specifically relieved by the German High Command. "Everything in me," he wrote Lucie on the 7th, "revolts against leaving the scene of

---

[1] *The last elements of the Axis army, the rearguard of 15 Panzer, would reach the Mareth line on 15 February.*

battle as long as I can stand upright."[2] On the next day he wrote: "I've decided only to give up my command of the army on orders, regardless of my health. With the situation as it is, I intend to stick it out to the limit.... The man [General Messe] that Rome has sent to take my place will just have to wait his turn."[3] Fortunately, Messe and Rommel hit it off well, and the Italian declared that he was in no great hurry to take command.

Rommel recognized that the new theatre of operations offered strategic possibilities of the highest order; for the first time since the previous summer he was itching to attack again. At the present he had little to fear from Montgomery; for he was methodically stock-piling for an attack on the Mareth front that was still weeks away. Thus Rommel envisaged a two-fisted stroke, calculated to exploit his advantage of interior lines and Montgomery's deliberateness. He planned to hit the Allied army in western Tunisia with the first blow, for the Field Marshal doubted the capacity of the relatively inexperienced Americans to stand up to the seasoned German troops.[4] Elements of the two Panzer armies would burst through the enemy-occupied passes of the eastern and western Dorsale - the two mountain ranges that run down the country's spine - and smash the American assembly areas. Farther west, inside the Algerian border, the important Allied supply center at Tebessa offered a tempting target. 21 Panzer - now under von Arnim's command - had already dislodged a weak French garrison from the vital Fiad pass and thus established a viable bridgehead for a thrust through the mountains. If the offensive were successful, Rommel reasoned, it would be a devastating blow to American morale and eliminate the threat of an Allied attack westwards from Gafsa to the sea, with the object of severing communications between the Panzer armies. After he had humbled the Americans, Rommel intended to switch his troops back to the Mareth front and strike violently at Montgomery.

Such was Rommel's plan, but it encountered stiff opposition from the commander of 5 Panzer Army. Von Arnim had been in Africa since December, but unfortunately, notes Rommel, "very little coordination existed between this new command and ourselves. We badly felt the need during this period of a single authority on African soil which could have welded together under a common command the two armies whose fates were so closely dependent on each other."[5] Von Arnim was reluctant to surrender any of his forces to support Rommel's operation; he was preparing his own attack, albeit on a more modest scale. In an effort to establish a uniform policy, Kesselring ordered the two Panzer generals to meet him at the *Luftwaffe* base at Rhennouch on 9 February.

---

[2]*Rommel Collection*, T-84, 274, #001032.
[3]*Ibid.*, #001048.
[4]*The Americans in Tunisia were so lacking in combat experience that the British and French called them their "Italians." Helmuth Greiner, "Greiner Diary Notes," (August 12, 1942-March 12, 1943), MS C-065A.*
[5]*Hart, Rommel Papers, pp. 372-73.*

The Tunisian Battleground

(above) Faid Pass, Tunisia. (below) Sidi Bou Zid, Tunisia

Rommel had never liked von Arnim and the conference certainly did not enhance his estimation of the man. A mustachioed aristocrat from Silesia, conservative in outlook and a veteran of the eastern front, von Arnim was cast from an entirely different mold than Rommel. He counselled caution, for he doubted whether the two Panzer armies were strong enough to execute Rommel's ambitious design. In its stead he

Jürgen
von Arnim

proposed a limited operation, with the objective of capturing Sidi Bou Zid and securing the Axis hold on the eastern Dorsale. Thus "division produced compromise - two virtually independent operations. Von Arnim in the north would launch 'Frühlingswind,' with a center-line through the Faid pass directed on Sidi Bou Zid, while Rommel's 'Morganluft' followed in the line Gafsa-Feriana-Kasserine. After this meeting Kesselring had a private word with Rommel and told him that, should these moves make possible the 'big operation' against Tebessa, Rommel would become Generalissimo."[6]

The principal effort would initially be made by von Arnim, who would have the lion's share of the German armor under his control - Baron Fritz von Broich's 10 Panzer and Colonel Hans-Georg Hildebrandt's 21 Panzer Divisions. Together, these two divisions comprised some 200 tanks, including a dozen of the new, heavy Tiger tanks with their powerful 88mm cannons (501 Panzer Battalion).[7] Von Arnim placed his deputy, Lieutenant General Heinz Ziegler, in direct command of Frühlingswind, which was to commence on 12 February. Rommel was to launch Morgenluft two days later. Collectively, the forthcoming operations would be known as the Battle of Kasserine pass.

---

[6]Lewin, Rommel, pg. 200.
[7]10 Panzer fielded some 110 tanks; the re-equipped 21 Panzer now had, as of 7 February, 93 runners. Divisions, KTB, 21 Panzer Division, T-315, 769, #000225.

Kesselring and Rommel discussing the Tunisian situation.

Rain delayed Ziegler's operation for two days. At 0400 on the 14th, the tanks of 10 Panzer Division began to rumble through the Fiad pass. A sandstorm blew up and the German pioneers used flares to guide the tanks forward.[8] Farther south, 21 Panzer moved northwest through Maizila pass. General Hans Seidemann's air forces provided strong support.

The Panzers slammed into Combat Command A of 1 U.S. Armored Division, the only unit immediately available to resist the powerful German thrust. As expected, the inexperienced American tank crews were no match for their skilled opponents; soon the battlefield was strewn

---

[8]Toppe, "Desert Warfare," P-129. Anlage 10: <u>Panzerschlacht von Sidi Bou Zid</u>, 10 Panzer Division, pg. 290.

with the blazing wrecks of dozens of Grants, Lees and Shermans. Late that afternoon *Kampfgruppe* Stenkhoff (21 Panzer) made contact with 10 Panzer west of Sidi Bou Zid;[9] the American contingent reeled back in total defeat, leaving 44 destroyed tanks behind.[10]

The Americans had expected an attack but not in such strength; they persisted in underestimating the German effort and the next day launched Combat Command C in an ill-conceived counterpunch. As the spearheads of the attack reached their assembly areas the *Luftwaffe* blasted them with bombs. This delayed the assault until 1240 when the mass of tanks, guns and troop carriers swept forward towards Sidi Bou Zid in parade-ground precision. An hour later the Stukas again dived down on the attackers, who began to swerve from side to side in a desperate struggle to avoid the deadly gauntlet of bombs. A pincer attack by elements of the two Panzer divisions completed the massacre. The Americans lost another 39 tanks.[11]

In the south Rommel had also started his attack. The jittery Americans had abandoned Gafsa on the evening of the 14th; the next afternoon elements of the Afrikakorps and Centauro Armored Division occupied it without a fight.[12] Rommel set out for Gafsa on the morning of the 16th. Along the road he passed swarms of scavenging Arabs, their pack animals laden with loot plundered from the town's deserted dwellings. "The Americans," writes Rommel, "had blown up their ammunition in the citadel without any warning to the people living in the neighborhood and 30 houses had collapsed on their occupants. The bodies of 30 Arabs had been dug out of the ruins of their houses, and 80 were still missing. The people were consequently feeling very bitter towards the Americans and were noisily celebrating their liberation."[13]

Rommel quickly ordered Major General von Liebenstein - in charge of the Afrikakorps combat group - to push on north to Feriana (40 miles from Gafsa). After a spirited fight, the Germans crashed into the village on the morning of the 17th.[14] Later in the day they captured Thelepte and its important airfield, which was littered with the remains of 30 enemy aircraft. Farther north, Ziegler's attack continued to make progress; early that evening and after a vicious tank battle, 21 Panzer occupied the ancient Roman settlement of Sbeitla.[15]

Resounding success had crowned the first phase of the German offensive. The Panzerarmee had reached many of its objectives; and had routed the American armored troops opposing them. The German

[9]Divisions, *KTB, 21 Panzer Division*, T-315, 769, #000234.
[10]George F. Howe, *Northwest Africa: Seizing the Initiative in the West* (Washington, D.C.: Office of the Chief of Military History, Department of the Army, U.S. Government Printing Office, 1957), pg. 415. Hereafter cited as *Northwest Africa.*
[11]*Ibid.*, pg. 422.
[12]Army Corps, *KTB, DAK*, T-314, 21, #001198.
[13]Hart, *Rommel Papers*, pg. 400.
[14]Army Corps, *KTB, DAK*, T-314, 21, #001204.
[15]Panzer Armies, *KTB, 5 Panzer Army*, T-313, 416, #8709627.

losses had been astoundingly light, while the enemy had suffered heavily - 2,876 prisoners and 169 tanks destroyed on the northern sector alone.[16] In Rommel's view, the moment had come to implement his original design: "I wanted to push forward with all our strength to Tebessa, take possession of this important airbase, supply and transport centre, and strike on deep into the Allied rear.... I was convinced that a thrust beyond Tebessa by the combined armored and motorized forces of the two armies would force the British and Americans to pull back the bulk of their forces to Algeria, thus greatly delaying their offensive preparations.... Von Arnim was not prepared to recognize the possibilities of the proposed operation, probably because he wanted to keep 10 Panzer Division in his sector for a small private show of his own. Consequently, he pronounced himself firmly against the plan."[17]

Faced with von Arnim's intransigence, Rommel appealed directly to Kesselring and the Italian High Command:

> On the basis of the enemy situation as of today, I propose an immediate enveloping thrust from the southwest on Tebessa and the area to the north of it, provided Fifth Panzer Armee's supply situation is adequate. This offensive must be executed with strong forces. I therefore request that 10 Panzer and 21 Panzer Divisions be assigned to me and move immediately to the assembly area Thelepte-Feriana.[18]

In a "fever of impatience" Rommel awaited the decision of his superiors. At 0130 on the 19th, a signal arrived from Commando Supremo, which placed 10 and 21 Panzer Divisions under his command and provided authority for the operation. But the Italians had emasculated the plan, for Le Kef, not Tebessa, was to be the objective of Rommel's attack. "This," writes Rommel, "was an appalling and unbelievable piece of shortsightedness, which did, in fact, ultimately cause the whole plan to go awry."[19]

Rommel, however, could ill-afford to bellyache about the unfortunate change in his plan. The argument with von Arnim had cost valuable time; the Americans were reinforcing. Rommel would have to strike fast. He instructed the *Luftwaffe* to seize the bridges at Le Kef with paratroopers. He then ordered Buelowius, now in control of the Afrikakorps combat group for the injured Liebenstein, to advance on Kasserine pass. 21 Panzer was to move on Le Kef, via Sbeitla-Sbiba. Von

---

[16]*Ibid.*, #8709632.

[17]Hart, *Rommel Papers*, pp. 400-01.

[18]Howe, *Northwest Africa*, pg. 438.

[19]Hart, *Rommel Papers*, pg. 402. This change in plan "meant that the thrust had to be made northwards against the Allies' immediate rear instead of northwestwards towards their communications as Rommel had proposed and planned." Von Arnim, though he hardly approved Rommel's design, was equally disappointed with the new directive from the Commando Supremo. See Panzer Armies, KTB, 5 Panzer Army, T-313, 416, #8709635.

224

Broich's 10 Panzer was to remain in reserve at Sbeitla, ready to reinforce the column that made the most progress.

During the morning, under a misty, cloudy-grey sky, 33 Reconnaissance Battalion attempted to seize Kasserine pass in a coup-de-main. But the Americans, now strongly positioned on the high ground, beat back the assault.[20] Rommel threw in Menton's Panzer grenadiers in support but they, too, came under devastating shellfire and could make no headway.

Hildebrandt's tanks also ran into unexpected resistance. Slowed by heavy rainfall and wet, soggy roads, the attack got off to an unencouraging start. Six miles south of Sbiba, the Panzer division encountered a thin belt of mines. Pioneer troops quickly cleared the way, but shortly thereafter the tanks stalled before a second, more extensive minefield and stiffening enemy resistance. The defenders unleashed a tornado of artillery and antitank fire. By late afternoon ten of Hildebrandt's tanks were out of action.[21] He decided to break off the attack.

"What I had feared," comments Rommel, "had now happened at both points of attack. The enemy had had a chance of installing his reserves in hill positions which were difficult to assault, and was gaining time to bring up further reinforcements. In an offensive against Tebessa, we would probably have got well underway before meeting serious resistance.... In the belief that the Allies were weaker at Kasserine than at Sbiba, I decided to focus the weight of our attack in the Kasserine sector and bring up 10 Panzer Division."[22]

The next morning, 20 February, Rommel drove to Afrikakorps headquarters to meet with 10 Panzer commander, von Broich. On the way he passed the division's motorcycle troops as they buzzed down the road to the Kasserine pass, where they were to support the assault. From von Broich Rommel learned that von Arnim had not released two battalions of the tank division; he had held back the Tiger tanks, too. This blatant obstruction of his plans infuriated Rommel, though there was little he could do about it.

At 0830 Rommel resumed his attack on the pass,[23] determined to butt his way through the thickening American defenses. Throughout the day he fed fresh forces into the attack, including elements of Centauro Armored Divison and a contingent of the new *Nebelwerfer* rocket launchers. These six-barrelled launchers plastered the pass defenses with deadly high-fragmentation bombs. The Americans were badly shaken by the bombardment; many of them fled in panic. By 1700 Rommel had captured the pass.

---

[20]Army Corps, *KTB, DAK,* T-314, 21, #001210.
[21]Divisions, *KTB, 21 Panzer Division,* T-315, 769, #000243.
[22]Hart, *Rommel Papers,* pg. 403.
[23]Army Corps, *KTB, DAK,* T-314, 21, #001215.

Armored vehicles from 10 Panzer Division move into position for their next offensive against American positions.

That evening the Germans detected a large group of American tanks and armored vehicles gathering on the other side of the pass, apparently preparing a counterattack. Rommel sent forward 8 Panzer Regiment to attack the enemy force. The Panzers clattered across the hastily rebuilt Hatib River bridge and took their opponent by complete surprise. The seasoned German tankmen squeezed back the American armor and spattered it against the mountains. It was remorseless slaughter.

Early on the 21st Rommel inspected the carnage of the Kasserine battlefield. Shattered enemy half-tracks sat on the road, victims of their own mines. Captured half-tracks roared back through the pass, loaded with dour-faced American prisoners. Troop details dug graves for the dead. The ubiquitous Arabs scoured the ground for booty, adding to the ghoulish scene. Rommel examined the brewed-up American tanks and noted the impressive quality and standardization of the vehicles.

A strange lassitude gripped Rommel that morning; he did not renew his attack until the early afternoon, and the enemy put the intervening hours to good use. 10 Panzer advanced on Thala, the next town to the north, while Buelowius' assault group screened its eastern flank. The British 26 Armored Brigade retired in deliberate fashion, "bound by bound" before von Broich's pursuing armor.[24]

But the attack was not going forward with the necessary dispatch, so Rommel drove up to his leading infantry to get them moving. He found them struggling through a cactus patch beside an Arab village. "Heavy

[24]Lewin, _Rommel_, pg. 206.

artillery fire was falling in the village and confusion was complete, with every living creature, bird and beast, scattering in all directions."[25] The bodies of several British soldiers lay in the area, stripped naked by the Arabs.

Von Broich continued to make less than satisfactory progress; by 1600 he had already lost 15 tanks. Three hours later 10 Panzer actually broke into Thala and captured 700 prisoners; but the British hurried up reinforcements and forced the Germans to pull back. Buelowius' advance had also broken down in the face of stiff enemy artillery fire.

The offensive had lost its momentum; Rommel his desire to keep it going. The next day, 23 February, he resolved to call it off. Rommel's decision was less than pleasing to the habitually optimistic Kesselring; he drove to Rommel's command post to lodge a protest. He found Rommel deeply depressed, and unwilling to continue the battle. According to Kesselring's memoirs, Rommel was anxious to return his forces to the Mareth line for a final fling against his nemesis, Montgomery.[26]Kesselring changed the subject. He asked Rommel if he himself would be willing to take over the command of the two Panzer armies in Africa. Rommel declined, for he knew his days in Africa were numbered. The Italians wanted him out and were making no bones about it. His health was still poor and, in any case, Hitler had earmarked von Arnim for the big command.

Rommel's forces withdrew through Kasserine pass. During the afternoon of the 23rd the weather cleared. The Allied bombers again filled the skies and punished the German columns as they moved back through the valley bottoms. Rommel himself narrowly escaped a carpet of bombs that hit just one hundred yards in front of his convoy.

Later in the day a directive arrived from the Italian High Command giving Rommel command of the new Army Group Africa. Despite his misgivings, Rommel accepted the post, which placed under his command both von Arnim's 5 Panzer and Messe's 1 Italian Army - as his old Panzerarmee was now known. Unknown to Rommel, the promotion was little more than a propaganda device, calculated to show the world that the two Axis dictators still had faith in their tired desert warrior. But as Hitler well knew, his "favorite" would have to go - and soon. "Despite all their own shortcomings," Schmundt entered in his war diary, "the Italians have remained overbearing and highly sensitive. For political reasons, the Führer has decided that their request [for Rommel's departure] will have to be granted."[27]

Von Arnim recognized Rommel's "lame-duck" status and he quickly exploited it. He was about to begin an offensive of his own, "Ochsenkopf" (Oxhead), with the limited objective of expanding his army's bridgehead towards Beja. In preparing the attack he had gone

[25]Hart, *Rommel Papers*, pg. 405.
[26]Kesselring, *Soldat*, pg. 205.
[27]Irving, *The Trail*, pg. 276.

over Rommel's head and dealt directly with Rome and Kesselring. Rommel was rightly piqued; when he finally learned of von Arnim's plan he expressed grave reservations. *Ochsenkopf* went forward on 26 February. Rommel played no part in the affair.

> Dearest Lu:
> ...if we could only achieve a great defensive victory over here. I rack my brain day and night to that end. Unfortunately the means are lacking. Everything depends on supplies - has, for years. My health has kept going so far. Heart, nerves and rheumatism are giving me a lot of trouble. But I intend to stick it out as long as humanly possible.[28]

At first von Arnim's operation gained ground. Entries in the 5 Panzer Army war diary show that the enemy was taken by surprise and offered little resistance.[29] By the second day, however, the defenses had stiffened and the attack lost its impetus. Rommel was particularly critical over the way von Arnim had employed his armor: "It made me... angry to see how the few Tigers we had in Africa, which had been denied us

Bundesarchiv

One of the few Tigers sent to North Africa.

in our offensive in the south, were thrown in to attack through a marshy valley where their principal advantage - the long range of their heavy guns - was completely ineffective. The heavy tanks either stuck fast in the mud, or were pounded into immobility by the enemy. Of the 19

[28]*Rommel Collection,* T-84, 274, #001068.
[29]*Panzer Armies, KTB, 5 Panzer Armee,* T-313, 416, #8709658.

Von Arnim inspects his infantry's defenses in the hilly terrain of Tunisia.

Tigers which went into action, 15 were lost.... I very soon gave orders to 5 Army to put a stop to the fruitless affair at the earliest possible moment."[30]

Rommel still intended to sting Eighth Army with one last blow before Montgomery himself was ready to attack. On the 28th he held a commander's conference at the Wadi Akarit to devise the battle plan. Eschewing his standard approach of a right hook around the enemy's front, Rommel advocated a pincer attack. 10 and 21 Panzer would form the northern prong, while 15 Panzer and part of 164 Light moved through the mountains in the south. The objective would be Medenine.[31] Messe, however, protested vehemently against Rommel's plan. In its place he proposed a simple flanking operation in the south, across the Matmata mountain ridge. Rommel objected. The arguments went back and forth for hours, and ultimately Rommel acquiesced. Physically and emotionally he was at the end of the line; he would let

---

[30]Hart, _Rommel Papers_, pg. 410.
[31]Irving, _The Trail_, pg. 280.

Messe and Ziegler, in temporary command of the Afrikakorps, work out the arrangements on their own.

It was all just as well, for at Medenine the Axis walked into the deadly jaws of another well-laid trap. At Medenine, "Ultra intervened with devastating effect. Decrypts from Bletchley provided ample forewarning of an attack. By a considerable feat of organization and down the single coastal road a Guards Brigade, the New Zealand Division and a brigade of tanks were rushed up to Medenine in reinforcement. A position was calmly prepared in text-book fashion for antitank defense. The date of attack, 6 March, was precisely known."[32]

At 0600 Rommel began his last desert tank attack. Clouds blanketed the sky and a thick mist hung over the battlefield. From his forward command post, high atop Hill 713, Rommel watched as his tanks and motorized infantry moved across the broad, level plain toward Medenine. But they did not get far, for Montgomery had packed some 500 antitank guns and 350 artillery pieces into his front. Shell after shell slammed into the advancing Panzer divisions; by early afternoon, 21 Panzer alone had lost 20 tanks.[33] The attackers threw in Stuka dive-bombers to support the assault, but with little effect. By 1700 hours Rommel had had enough; he called off the operation. He had lost 50 of his 145 tanks.

Rommel had incurred a brutal defeat; and done nothing to unhinge Montgomery's offensive preparations. In a dark mood, he surveyed the deteriorating Axis position in Tunisia. Supplies were suddenly reaching the Army Group in hitherto unimaginable quantities - 46,000 tons in January and 53,000 in February. But these figures were still well below the minimum requirements of 69,000 tons needed to sustain his two armies in the field. In a situation report to Rommel, von Arnim had estimated that if his supplies were not stepped up, it would all be over in Tunisia by 1 July. Rommel drew the obvious conclusion from these unsettling facts: "For the Army Group to remain longer in Africa was now plain suicide."[34] He decided to fly to Hitler to tell him so.

At 0750 hours, 9 March, Rommel boarded a plane at Sfax airfield.[35] He would fly to Rome first, then to Hitler's Werewolf headquarters in the Ukraine. Soon his aircraft was gliding over the Mediterranean, where so many of his tanks and guns had found a watery grave. Rommel had departed Africa forever.

---

[32]Lewin, _Ultra_, pg. 275.
[33]Divisions, _KTB, 21 Panzer Division_, T-315, 769, #000262.
[34]Hart, _Rommel Papers_, pg. 416.
[35]Only a few days earlier, on the 3rd, Rommel had written Lucie "I can't get away for the time being. I must go on for a little while yet. I wish I would receive a different mission. I am hindered by Rome with every step I take, yet I have to bear the full responsibility. I can't stand that. Often I think my nerves will break. At the moment one has to pursue a course verging on the edge of an abyss. If we fail the consequences will be tremendous." _Rommel Collection_, T-84, 274, #001085.

The Atlantic Wall

On the afternoon of 10 March, Rommel arrived at Hitler's secret headquarters in southern Russia. That evening he was able to speak with Hitler in private, but the results of this tete-a-tete were singularly unrewarding. Africa, Hitler insisted, must be held; and Rommel was to go on sick leave. The Field Marshal pleaded to return to Africa for a few weeks, but Hitler refused. The next day Rommel was decorated with the highest order of the Iron Cross - the Oakleaves with Swords and Diamonds. He then flew back to Germany to begin his long-overdue treatment at the Semmering. At this time the Führer's headquarters issued orders to keep Rommel's departure from Africa a strict secret - his military reputation was still to serve as a deterrent. "It will, of course," Goebbels jotted in his diary on 7 May 1943, "be very difficult to explain to the people that Rommel is no longer in North Africa. Rommel is put in a very painful position. He has received the diamonds to his Oakleaf Cluster and the people know nothing about it; he has been on the Semmering for several weeks and nobody has the faintest idea of it! Everybody thinks he is in Africa. If we now come out with the truth, when the catastrophe is so near, nobody will believe us."[1]

The following months - to November 1943 - were a frustrating and unrewarding chapter in Rommel's life; they can be quickly told. He observed with despair the inevitable collapse in Tunisia. His son, Manfred, describes how, "as the battle raged round the Mareth line and the Akarit defenses, [Rommel] paced restlessly up and down the big study which had been provided for him by the hospital authorities. He had no doubts about its outcome. He was bitter in his criticisms of the Supreme Command, without sparing even Hitler himself."[2] During this phase Rommel's loyalty to Hitler declined steadily. "If the German people are incapable of winning the war," Hitler remarked to Rommel, "then they can rot." "Sometimes," Rommel confided to his son, "you feel that he's no longer quite normal."[3]

[1]Joseph Goebbels, The Goebbels Diaries 1942-1943. Edited by Louis P. Lochner (New York: Doubleday and Company, Inc., 1948), pg. 352.
[2]Hart, Rommel Papers, pg. 425.
[3]Ibid., pg. 428.

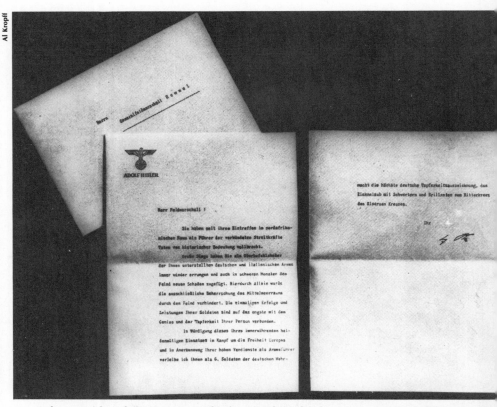

(Above) Hitler's letter to Rommel informing him that he was a recipient of the prized Oakleaves, Swords and Diamonds to the Knight's Cross of the Iron Cross. (Right) The document for the above award.

Hitler, however, soon had Rommel employed again; first by "attaching [him] to his own staff as a 'military advisor,' then, in May, ordering OKW to prepare Plan *Alarich* - an insurance against an Italian surrender - in which Rommel was earmarked to run an Army Group north of the Alps whose function would be to provide both a firm base for the German troops in Italy and also a service of reinforcement; next by dispatching him on 23 July to Salonika to 'report in detail and direct to him on conditions in Greece'; and finally, following Mussolini's arrest on 26 July, by recalling him to Rastenburg to tell him that 'I am to prepare the entry into Italy ... without being myself allowed, for the present, to cross the old 1938 frontier.' "[4]

During his "Italian Period" Rommel clashed with Kesselring over defensive strategy. In Rommel's view the German defenses should be withdrawn to the baseline of the Alps. But Kesselring argued that Italy's rugged mountain chains offered emminently defensible positions farther south. In any event, Kesselring had his way; events would soon prove him correct. On 17 August Rommel's headquarters moved over

---

[4]Lewin, <u>Rommel</u>, pg. 210.

IM NAMEN
DES DEUTSCHEN VOLKES
VERLEIHE ICH
DEM GENERALFELDMARSCHALL
ERWIN ROMMEL
DAS EICHENLAUB MIT
SCHWERTERN UND BRILLANTEN
ZUM RITTERKREUZ
DES EISERNEN KREUZES

FÜHRERHAUPTQUARTIER
DEN 11. MÄRZ 1943

DER FÜHRER
UND OBERSTE BEFEHLSHABER
DER WEHRMACHT

the Alps; divisions from his army group were now marching southwards and establishing defensive positions between Pisa and Rimini, in the area later known as the Gothic Line. Two months later Hitler decided to unify the Italian theatre under Rommel's command, giving Rommel authority over Kesselring's forces as well as his own. But "whilst the cable [to Rommel, dated 25 October] was still being transmitted, [Hitler] changed his mind and ordered Field Marshal Kesselring to take

When Fritz Bayerlein was awarded the Oakleaves to his Knight's Cross on 6 July 1943, his old commander was present. Note Rommel and Keitel in the background.

Rommel in Northern Italy.

over the supreme command of the Italian war theatre from 21 November 1943."[5]

This decision left Rommel and his army group staff unemployed at a time when OKW and Hitler were struggling to build up an Atlantic front against the threat of an Allied invasion. Thus on 5 November he received instructions from Hitler for a new and important assignment.

[5]Hart, _Rommel Papers,_ pp. 446-47.

Rommel and his staff "were commissioned ... to examine the coasts of Denmark, Flanders, the English Channel, Normandy and Brittany as to their defensive capabilities. The results of the inspection were to be reported directly to Hitler. Rommel was to furnish OB West [Supreme Commander Western Theatre, Field Marshal von Rundstedt] with pertinent sections of the report."[6] In his new post the Field Marshal would exercise, at first, a purely advisory function, for he had no troops under his command. Later (mid-January 1944) Rommel would ask for, and receive command of the two armies defending the critical sectors of the invasion coastline from the Zuider Zee to the mouth of the Loire: 7 Army under Dollmann (western Normandy and Brittany) and 15 Army under von Salmuth (from Antwerp to the Orne.)[7]

General Gause, again a member of Rommel's staff, was asked to recommend someone to fill the post of naval expert. Gause thought immediately of Vice-Admiral Fredrich Ruge, whom he had met in the spring of 1943. Rommel approved the choice and requested that the Admiral be assigned to the staff as *"Marineverbindungsoffizier"* (Naval

Ruge/W.M. James

Frederich Ruge

Alfred Gause

[6]Bodo Zimmermann, "OB West: Atlantic Wall to Siegfried Line, A Study in Command," MS B-308, pg. 45.

[7]In this manner, Rommel was able to bring some thirty divisions under his direct command. See Friedrich Ruge, "Rommel und die Invasion." In: Europäische Wehrkunde XXVIII Jahrgang. München. Oktober 1979. Heft 10. pg. 510.

(Above) Rommel and Gause in northern Italy. (Right) The last meeting between Rommel and the ex-Duce, Mussolini, before Rommel's departure from Italy. At the far left is Ambassador Rahn, German envoy to Mussolini.

Liaison Officer) and advisor on naval matters. Getting the Admiral, however, was far more complicated than Rommel had anticipated, for Ruge was in disfavor with Hitler at the moment. Evidently Ruge had submitted a report to his superiors in which he wrote negatively about the Italians; the report had reached Hitler. It took three requests from Rommel before Ruge was finally transferred to his staff.

Rommel soon had second thoughts about his new job. In a letter to Lucie on the 9th he wrote, "I am in a depressed mood. I am not sure whether my new assignment does not mean that I have been shelved. It is being judged in that sense in several quarters. I refuse to believe it. The Führer spoke quite differently. But so many people are jealous of me. And yet the times are so serious that there is really no room for envy and quarrel."[8]

Ruge reported for duty at Rommel's headquarters in Verona the next day, 10 November. Rommel informed his staff that their assignment stemmed from Hitler's Directive No. 51, dated 3 November.[9] He instructed Ruge to proceed to Berlin, confer with the Navy War Staff and gather material pertaining to their mission - maps, charts, tide tables, etc. After that he was to rejoin the staff at Silkeborg in northern Jutland on 2 December.

On 21 November Rommel relinquished his command in Italy to Field Marshal Kesselring and flew to Austria to spend a few days with his family in Ulm. Ruge, meanwhile, was in Berlin trying to complete the last phase of his mission, when, on the night of 23/24 November, all the material so carefully compiled by the Admiral was destroyed in an air raid. He replaced as much as possible before leaving to rejoin Rommel at Silkeborg.

The inspection team, with the exception of Ruge, met on 1 December at the Munich train station. They boarded a special train and headed for

Ruge/W.M. James

Admiral Wurmbach, General Hannecken and Rommel inspect the defense location maps.

[8]*Rommel Collection*, T-84, 274, #001117.
[9]See H.R. Trevor-Roper, ed., *Blitzkrieg to Defeat*, (New York: Holt, Rinehard and Winston, 1965), pg. 149, for the full text of this directive.

Denmark. Ruge met Rommel and the team on the 2nd and informed the Field Marshal of the loss of the material. But, he quickly added, that "it made no great difference, as he knew practically all the coasts and ports of the area from personal experience.[10] With this, Rommel began his last command.

He assembled his staff in Copenhagen, meeting first with General von Hannecken, the Wehrmacht commander in Denmark, on 3 December. That evening Rommel ordered his train to move up to Esbjerg on Jutland's west coast. He notified his staff that the first inspection in Denmark would begin at "exactly" 0800 hours the following day. Ruge learned of Rommel's "absolute punctuality" the next morning when the long convoy of staff cars started off while he was still on the train finishing breakfast. It was precisely 0800. The day began with an inspection of the Esbjerg coastal defenses, or as Ruge put it, the lack of defenses. That afternoon the staff attended a demonstration landing on the island of Fano at the entrance to the port of Esbjerg. It was here that Rommel conceived the idea of using obsolete antitank obstacles, called Czech Hedgehogs *("Tschechenigel")*, as antiboat obstructions.

In all Rommel spent ten days in Denmark, touring the defenses and hearing reports from von Hannecken, representatives of the Navy, the Luftwaffe and Organization Todt (the civilian building corps). But the situation "left much to be desired." "Denmark," writes Ruge, "clearly showed how overtaxed the Wehrmacht was. A handful of modestly

While walking in and around the sand dunes, Rommel saw first-hand the lack of defenses on the Danish coast.

---

[10]Friedrich Ruge, "Rommel and the Atlantic Wall," MS A-982, pg. 2. Hereafter cited as "Atlantic Wall," A-982.

After the inspection tour, Rommel bids farewell to his hosts which included Dr. Werner Best, Reichskommissar in Denmark. It is interesting to note that Dr. Best saved several thousand Danish Jews by having them sent to Sweden.

trained and equipped static divisions [coastal defense units] had to defend hundreds of kilometers of excellent landing beach."[11] On the other hand, Rommel and his staff hardly expected the invasion to come in Denmark, for the distance from the Allied fighter bases in England was too great.

---

[11]Ruge, "Rommel und Die Invasion." Europäische Wehrkunde, pg. 508.

For a headquarters Rommel and the Army Group B staff were assigned a small château in Fontainebleau that had once been the property of Madame de Pompadour. While at the château Rommel usually dined with his immediate staff: Major General Gause (Chief of Staff), Major General Meise (chief engineer officer), Major General Gehrcke (chief signals officer), Colonel von Tempelhoff (Ia), Colonel Lattman (artillery expert), Colonel Krähe (Ic. Later replaced by Lieutenant Colonel Staubwasser), Colonel Freiberg (personnel officer), Lieutenant Colonel Queissner (*Luftwaffe* Ia), Lieutenant Colonel Olshausen (Deputy Transport Officer), Lieutenant Colonel Hammermann, Captain Lang, the Prince of Koburg and Ruge. The meals were the same as those served by the field kitchens to the other ranks. After dinner Rommel would often reminisce with his fellow officers. He usually retired early, around 22-2300 hours, but rose early the next morning.

At this time Rommel came under the command of Field Marshal von Rundstedt, an officer older than and senior to Rommel. Keitel at OKW assured von Rundstedt that "Rommel would never be considered as [his] successor. With all his capabilities," Keitel told von Rundstedt, "Rommel was not up to that job. Should a replacement become necessary," Keitel decreed, "it could only be Field Marshal von Kluge."[12]

On 15 December Rommel drove to Paris to confer with von Rundstedt at his headquarters in the King George V Hotel. After lunch von Rundstedt briefed Rommel on the situation in France and the difficult task they both faced. He noted sarcastically that although he was the Army's senior officer, and only outranked within the *Wehrmacht* by Göring of the *Luftwaffe*, his sole authority was to change the guard in front of his own headquarters. Hitler had reserved for himself the right to move units along the Atlantic Wall: any formation larger than a battalion could not be moved without his expressed authority.

On 20 December Rommel began his main assignment: the inspection of the Atlantic Wall. His boundless energy and enthusiasm, coupled with a flair for innovation "brought a new impulse to the preparations. He fundamentally altered the underlying idea, thus changing the atmosphere of despondency and vague hope to one of hard work and clear plans. He was untiring in his efforts to instill his ideas into his men and they took them up eagerly because they appreciated his personality, his experience and his common sense." Unlike von Rundstedt, who remained remote and impersonal, Rommel visited his soldiers often in an effort to build confidence and morale. Even so, as Ruge remembers, the Field Marshal "remained unassuming and modest, but he used his name and his fame as one more weapon. He once said to his Chief Cameraman, 'You may do with me what you like if it only leads to postponing the invasion for a week.' "[13]

[12]Zimmermann, "OB West," B-308, pg. 45.

Rommel stresses to his troops the importance of stopping the Allies on the beaches.

Beginning with his first inspection of the coastal defenses, Rommel was dissatisfied with what he found. Despite assurances from Hitler, the Atlantic Wall simply did not exist. Only between Bologne and Dunkirk, in fact, was the coast well-fortified. Here the German defenses included four heavy naval batteries in concrete bunkers (28 to 40.6cm), five heavy batteries of railway artillery and numerous guns of a smaller caliber. To von Rundstedt the "Wall" was little more than "an enormous bluff, less for the enemy, who of course knew all about it through is agents and many other circumstances than for the German people. Hitler never saw the Atlantic Wall, not even one part of it!"[14]

Rommel intended to change this, and quickly. He immediately ordered the construction of a large variety of beach obstacles, antiglider and air landing obstructions. "In the beginning [the obstacles] were only simple balks, planted in shallow water and slanted seawards. Later,

---

[13]Ruge, "Atlantic Wall," A-982, pg. 25.
[14]Zimmermann, "OB West," B-308, pg. 24.

The first beach obstacles consisted of balks planted in shallow water and slanted seawards.

More elaborate obstacles are evident in this photo taken during one of Rommel's inspection tours.

reinforced side props, mines and connecting wires were added."[15] When it was discovered that the surf and tide washed the balks away, they were anchored with concrete supports and blocks. Soon more elaborate obstacles were introduced: obsolete and captured tank traps as well as tripods of wood and iron, booby trapped with mines - all intended to split open the bottoms of the landing craft like can openers. Beach obstacles incorporating captured French artillery shells began to appear along the coast and the minelaying accelerated dramatically.

"When Rommel came to France, 1,700,000 mines had been laid in three years. In the few months of his activity, 4,000,000 mines were laid."[16] For what Rommel had in mind, this was only a drop in the

National Archives

This strip of beach between the obstacles and barbed wire was heavily laden with antitank and antipersonnel mines.

bucket. Rommel wanted 200,000,000 mines. He envisioned a continuous minefield 1,000 yards in depth for the entire coast, with a second strip further back from the beaches. But he quickly learned that the engineers in France lacked the creative skills of those in Africa who had planted the El Alamein "Devil's Gardens" or covered the retreat of Panzerarmee Afrika; and he fought "many a battle with engineers who adhered to their hard and fast patterns for minefields"[17] before he could persuade them to do things his way. Major General Wilhelm Meise - the officer in charge of the mine laying program - was ordered

[15]Friedrich Dihm, "Rommel's Views on Tactical, Technical and Strategic Problems of the Defense," MS B-259, pg. 32. Hereafter cited as "Rommel's Views on Problems of the Defense," B-259.
[16]Ruge, "Atlantic Wall," A-982, pg. 15.
[17]Ibid.

to lay four belts of underwater obstacles, described by him as "1) a belt in six feet of water at mean high tide. 2) a belt in six feet of water at half-tide of a twelve foot tide. 3) a belt in six feet of water at low tide and 4) a belt in twelve feet of water at low tide."[18] Even where the beach was considered too steep for a landing, or cut by cliffs, mines were to be laid. To supplement his "limited" stocks of mines, Rommel utilized captured explosives to manufacture anti-personnel mines; he also ordered the flooding of large areas of the French countryside. But "to avoid lasting damage [he] repeatedly gave orders to dam fresh water only. The lockgates to the sea were to be opened only in cases of utmost urgency."[19]

On 19 December Rommel met with von Rundstedt in Paris and presented his plans for defeating an invading enemy. From this meeting emerged a controversy that would fatefully undermine the *Wehrmacht's* ability to resist the Normandy invasion. "To Rommel the only hope of repelling the invasion seemed to lie in offering the strongest possible resistance to the actual landing. The first 24 hours would be decisive. Once the Allies had established a large beachhead, it would be impossible to drive them back into the sea because of the superiority of materials."[20] Rommel planned to declare the beaches the *"Hauptkampflinie,"* or main line of battle; he intended to place the Panzer units directly behind the coastal defenses, so that they could immediately bring their concentrated firepower to bear on the landings, or be shifted up or down the coast as needed. During one conference Rommel stated that "elements which are not in contact with the enemy at the moment of invasion will never get into action, because of the enormous air superiority of the enemy."[21]

Von Rundstedt and the commander of Panzergruppe West - General Geyr von Schweppenburg - opposed Rommel's plan. "Having studied every major landing that had occurred," von Rundstedt "had come to the conclusion that: a) the enemy would succeed in making the landing under any circumstances. b) There was absolutely no way to keep the enemy from making an air landing."[22] He wanted to strike the Allies at their weakest moment: when the landing forces were still on small, isolated beaches and had not yet been reinforced or re-supplied. Thus in von Rundstedt's view, the German reserves and Panzer divisions "were to be brought up only so close to the coast so as to enable them to take part in the first day's combat, remaining out of reach of the long-range artillery and the first heavy firing and bombing. The

---

[18]Hart, <u>Rommel Papers</u>, pg. 459.
[19]Ruge, "Atlantic Wall," A-982, pg. 16.
[20]Ibid., pg. 9.
[21]Hans Speidel, "Ideas and Views of Generalfeldmarschall Rommel on Defense and Operations in the West in 1944," MS B-270, pg. 12. Hereafter cited as "Rommel on Defense in the West," B-270.
[22]Zimmermann, "OB West," pg. 50.

(above) Gerd von Rundstedt
(left) Geyr von Schweppenburg

possibility of shifting or withdrawing reserves, particularly Panzer units, was always to be kept open."[23]

Rommel argued his concept vehemently, reminding them that the "enemy air supremacy and the supple use that he made of his aircraft made it impossible to throw a massed Panzer reinforcement into the battle. The Panzer divisions would be broken up before they could reach the Normandy front."[24] Von Schweppenburg was not convinced. He argued that he could bring his tanks forward during the night, or by day by spacing them 100 yards apart. But Rommel had an answer for that too. In Africa, he reminded von Schweppenburg, the Allied air force had used flares that lit the night as bright as day, and, besides, the enemy had so many fighters that any tanks moving during daylight would be destroyed. Despite the validity of Rommel's arguments, the meeting ended in a deadlock; no firm decisions were taken regarding the location of the German armored reserves.

Rommel's creative genius was undoubtedly the German's most potent weapon in France. A further example of this was the simple but effective stratagem he employed to divert Allied bombing attacks from his few precious coastal batteries. He ordered the construction of dummy positions *("Scheinbatterien")* along the entire coast. "Special orders were given for the realistic and clever construction of these installations and for the improvement of those already existing."[25] In the

[23]*Ruge, "Atlantic Wall," pg. 9.*
[24]*Ibid.*
[25]*Dihm, "Rommel's Views on Problems of the Defense," B-259, pg. 34.*

245

following months the dummy batteries were bombed repeatedly by enemy aircraft, and thus contributed greatly to the fact that German losses in coastal artillery before the invasion remained small.[26]

The overwhelming Allied air superiority, in fact, largely determined Rommel's plans for the defense of the Atlantic Wall. He was convinced that the Allies would only consider invading areas within the reach of their fighters based in southern England - that is, the coast somewhere between the southern part of Holland and the easternmost part of Brittany. The three chief possibilities seemed to be the Schelde, the Somme and the western part of the bay of the Seine (where the invasion actually occurred).[27] But again there was dissonance in the German High Command, for they were unable to reach a consensus over the probable location of the invasion. Hitler viewed the Cotentin Peninsula or the western tip of Brittany as the two most probable invasion sites. The Allies, he calculated, would need a major port to sustain a landing; the two west coast peninsulas, with their ports of Cherbourg and Brest respectively, offered the best possibilities for forming a bridgehead. OKW, in contrast, considered the narrows between Pas-de-Calais and Kent as the only logical invasion zone. In 1940 German plans for the invasion of England had envisaged a crossing at the Channel's narrowest point; OKW concluded that the Allies would attempt a similar maneuver. At OB West von Rundstedt and his staff believed the invasion would come on both sides of the Somme estuary. Rommel concurred.[28] He considered the areas in which Hitler expected the invasion too remote and lacking in good beaches. But there were different opinions even within Rommel's own staff. Ruge believed the landings would take place on the eastern coast of the Cotentin Peninsula (the Utah beaches). This controversy would continue well beyond D-Day, June 6.

The free hand which Rommel had exercised in North Africa was a thing of the past; as is evident, many of his ideas and plans were now rudely rejected. His attempt to standardize plans for the construction of the Atlantic Wall ran up against the powerful "Organization Todt." This organization, responsible for the major construction projects of the Atlantic Wall, the gigantic submarine pens and other projects, "worked independently, on orders from the Reichminister for Armament and Ammunition and OKW." OB West, Rommel's immediate superior, could issue no orders to "O.T." With a view to simplifying the intricate

---

[26]Before D-Day, June 6, the Germans lost 8 guns in the Pas-de-Calais, 5 in the Seine-Somme area and only 3 in Normandy. "Rommel as I Saw Him." Address given by Friedrich Ruge before the U.S. Officers Club in Stuttgart, 16 March 1980. Attended by the author.

[27]Friedrich Ruge, Rommel in Normandy: Reminiscences by Friedrich Ruge (San Rafael, Ca.: Presidio Press, 1979) pp. 26-28. Hereafter cited as Rommel in Normandy.

[28]Later, when Allied bombers began to show a keen interest in Normandy, Rommel would guess correctly that the invasion would come in the Seine Bay. After D-Day, however, he would persist in his view that the Normandy operation was only a diversion.

and confusing chain of command, Rommel proposed to Hitler that all three *Wehrmacht* branches (Rommel had no authority over Naval Group West or *Luftflotte* 3) be subordinated to him for the defensive mission in his command area. The proposal was sharply rebuffed by the Führer. "Hitler wanted fluctuation in the chain of command, [and] did not want too much power concentrated in one hand, least of all Rommel's."[29] Hitler continued to establish personally the priorities for the construction of the defenses along the French coast. Top priority was the Pas-de-Calais, then the Channel Islands, Fortress Cherbourg and, finally, the east coast of the Cotentin Peninsula.

Rommel devoted considerable time to inspecting the formations defending the coastline from Belgium to southern France. The majority of these were static infantry divisions, lacking in firepower and mobility; in some of them the average soldier was 35 years of age or even older. To fill manpower shortages many of these units had little choice but to enlist battalions of prisoners of war from the eastern front - men of dubious fighting value at best. Heavy weapons were also in short supply, and many divisions relied heavily on captured enemy equipment. The result was a confusing lack of uniformity in the equipment tables of the divisions defending the West Wall. One division boasted 98 different weapon-types.

Rommel reviews, with a skeptical eye, eastern troops assigned to the defense of the Atlantic Wall.

[29]*Speidel, "Rommel on Defense in the West," B-270, pg. 11.*

The inspections in late December also revealed the lack of a coherent command structure along the Atlantic Wall. Although Hitler's "Führer Directive 40" had, theoretically, clearly delineated the areas of responsibility (the navy would fight the enemy while he was still at sea, the army after he had landed), there was still considerable confusion: when did the navy relinquish its authority to the army; who determined target priorities, etc? The naval chain of command, moreover, was in need of fundamental reorganization. Along the coast there was the "Naval Commander Pas-de-Calais," the "Naval Commander Seine-Somme" and "Naval Commander Normandy," all of whom were subordinate to the "Commander Channel Coast," who, in turn, took his orders from "Naval Group West in Paris." Rommel labored, albeit with little success, to untangle this confusing command apparatus.

On the 27th Rommel met with the officer in charge of the "V weapons" (Hitler's secret rocket weapons) to discuss the construction of the firing ramps. Later that afternoon he, Gause and Colonel von Tempelhoff (the Army Group Ia) drove to Paris to meet with von Rundstedt. Von Rundstedt and Rommel, however, still differed greatly on how best to thwart an enemy landing in France. The next morning Rommel and Gause drove to the headquarters of *Luftflotte* 3 and met with its commander, Field Marshal Hugo Sperrle. The *Luftwaffe* could only report that, despite the 320,000 men it had in ground services, the weakness of the organization in air power could not be expected to improve. When Rommel met with Admiral Krancke (the Commander in Chief of Navy Group West) he received more discouraging news: the Navy could do little to help repell a major enemy landing. That evening, the 28th, Rommel asked his staff to submit reports on the inspection trips. These reports would be combined and submitted to OKW as a "Report of the Defense Readiness of the Artois (Region)." In this report Rommel once again insisted that he be given full command of the forces defending the Atlantic Wall.

On New Year's Day, 1944, Rommel was in southern Holland and was scheduled to meet with Ruge on the 3rd at the headquarters of 89 Corps in Antwerp. After meeting with the Corps' commander, General Baron von Gilsa, Rommel and the inspection team headed towards the island of Walcheren, where they spent most of 4 January examining the defenses and the nearby naval batteries. The next day, as Ruge noted, Rommel finally paused to relax. He and the Admiral visited the Brügge Town Hall and the local cathedral, which boasted a marble madonna by Michelangelo. But the brief hiatus was soon over, and Rommel raced off to meet with General von Salmuth (C in C 15 Army) at Tourcoing. Driving was one way Rommel liked to relax. He often took the wheel himself, driving so fast that others in the party could only catch his Horch staff car in the hills.

General von Schweppenburg and Rommel conferred on 8 January 1944, but the differences between the two men remained pronounced.

(Left) Rommel and Rear Admiral Heinecke, commandant of Cherbourg, discussing the positioning of coastal artillery.

Upon Rommel's instructions, portions of the coastline are plowed up as the first step in constructing new defense positions.

(Left) Rommel and General Baron von Gilsa inspecting defenses on the island of Walcheren on 4 January 1944.

249

Inspecting coastal defenses.

Jim Jones

General Hans von Salmuth, C in C of 15 Army.

As for Hitler, he had seen Rommel's report on the Artois and had come around to the Field Marshal's view that the enemy must be defeated on the beaches. There was still considerable opposition to Rommel's plans, however; thus Rommel met with von Rundstedt on the 12th and Jodl the next day in an unsuccessful effort to bring about a clearly-defined defensive policy.

Rommel now felt that his headquarters in Fontainebleau, some 65 miles to the south of Paris, was too far in the rear, and although a request to relocate to a camp near Leon had been rejected on 7 January, his staff had kept an eye open for a more suitable location. Fontainebleau may have been too removed from the coast for Rommel's liking, but it did have advantages. The countryside was varied and there were many opportunities to hunt in the woods and ravines (there was even an open season on wild boar). At dinner the conversation was open and frank, partly due to the lack of a NSFO (National Socialist Political Officer). In these pleasant surroundings, the members of Rommel's staff got to know and to trust one another completely.

The coastal tours continued through January and not even an attack of lumbago kept Rommel from the long, strenuous trips. As he told Lucie in a letter on the 31st, he was "on the move a lot and raising plenty of dust" wherever he went.[30] By early February Rommel had covered the French coastline from north of the Somme to eastern Brittany. From these inspections it was all too evident that western Normandy and the Cotentin Peninsula were weakly fortified. Only one static division, the 716, defended the vital strip of excellent landing beach between the Orne and the Vire (some 70km). The distance between strongpoints often amounted to several kilometers; the few fortifications that did exist were lacking in concrete bunkers and shelters. The artillery was also weak; a handful of naval guns (12cm) formed the largest battery.

Rommel meets "Pips" Priller during an inspection of a Luftwaffe base in France.

In the months preceding the invasion, Rommel did much to buttress the defenses in Normandy and in the Cotentin. He inserted a good infantry division, the 352, into the western half of the Orne-Vire sector and transferred the 91 Air Landing Division into the center of the Cotentin Peninsula. But his repeated requests to position several excellent Panzer divisions directly behind the Normandy beaches were rejected by Hitler. Merely the 21 Panzer Division was brought forward a bit, into the Caen-Falaise area. The other two, 12 SS and Panzer Lehr armored divisions, remained well back. His appeal to move up a *Nebelwerfer* Brigade and Pickert's Flak Corps also floundered on the Führer's opposition.

[30]Hart, *Rommel Papers*, pg. 463.

General Max Pemsel, Chief of the German Staff, 7 Army, and Rommel during an inspection tour of the southern France Mediterranean beaches.

(Below) Lang, General Botsch (Chief of Staff of 19 Army), General Weise and Rommel during a review of Mediterranean defenses on 8 February 1944.

W.M. James, Jr./Ruge

Rommel enters his command car at La Roche-Guyon.

Rommel drove to Paris on 13 February and conferred with von Rundstedt over the problem of training the forces along the coast. Following the meeting Rommel visited the headquarters of 9 SS Panzer Division and inspected the coast between the Somme River and Dieppe on the 14th and 15th. On the return trip to his headquarters, Rommel stopped at La Roche-Guyon to look over the castle which had been selected as his new headquarters. The château, built between the 12th and 17th centuries, belonged to the La Rochefoucauld family and was located about 50 miles west of Paris and 10 miles northwest of Nantes, overlooking the Seine River.

Rommel, von Rundstedt and Gause during a conference in which defenses and personnel were discussed. Note whited out map for security purposes.

When a high-level conference between the commanders-in-chief in the West and Hitler was postponed indefinitely, Rommel went hunting with Ruge. Work resumed quickly, however, and on the 18th Rommel, Ruge and Meise left at 0700 hours to tour the Brittany coastline. On the way they stopped for General Blumentritt, chief-of-staff to von Rundstedt, and then drove into St. Nazaire where they began the inspections. The tour continued from there and the group inspected the area around Lorient, Port Louis, the bay of Douarnenez, Brest, and the northwestern coast of Brittany.

Beginning on 21 February, Rommel took ten days leave and drove to Herrlingen for rest and a change of scenery. Towards the end of the month, the anti-Hitler conspirators made their first move in an effort to

General Günther Blumentritt, von Rundstedt's chief-of-staff.

(Left) Rommel at St. Nazaire inspecting submarine bunkers. Blumentritt is in the background with glasses.
(Below) Rommel and his staff being briefed on Brittany's secondary defenses.

(Above and Right) Rommel listens with interest as the details of the mining of the Brest Harbor are explained.

enlist Rommel in their cause. Dr. Karl Strölin, the Mayor of Stuttgart, visited Rommel at his home. Ironically, Dr. Strölin claims to have renounced National Socialism on the occasion of Hitler's entry into Prague in March of 1939, an event which saw his friend Rommel in command of the *Führerbegleitbataillon*. The Mayor, who had served with Rommel during the First World War, had recently helped the Field Marshal when he moved his family from Wiener-Neustadt to Herrlingen and had become close to Lucie. He had, in fact, already indirectly approached Rommel through Lucie. In August of 1943 Strölin had drafted a document with Dr. Goerdeler in which they courageously demanded that "the persecution of the Jews and the churches be abandoned, that civil rights be restored and that the administration of justice be taken out of the hands of the Party."[31] They had submitted it to the Secretary of the Ministry of the Interior and were promptly warned that unless they kept quiet they would face prosecution for crimes against the state. Strölin then knew that legal methods were useless; Hitler would have to be removed from power through force.

In November 1943 Strölin provided Frau Rommel with a copy of the document and requested that she show it to her husband. When Rommel read the document "it made a profound impression on him, since his own mind had been working in the same direction."[32] Strölin's visit to the Rommel home in February 1944 was made secretly; he had been warned that he was under surveillance and his telephones were tapped. The two men talked for some five-six hours, discussing the political and military situation in Germany. When the meeting ended they found themselves in agreement on many points. Strölin also intimated to Rommel that "certain senior officers of the Army in the East proposed to make Hitler a prisoner and to force him to announce over the radio that he had abdicated."[33] At this Rommel demurred. He was not ready to support such a violent measure. But he assured Strölin that he would talk with Hitler again and try to open his eyes to the true situation. If talking with the Führer did not bring him to reason, Rommel planned to write Hitler a memorandum outlining the entire situation plainly and demand that he "accept the political consequences." Only if this final effort failed would Rommel consider a more drastic move. He did add, without indicating which course he would take, that he believed it was his duty to come to the rescue of his country.

Rommel flew back to Paris on 3 March and drove the rest of the way to Fontainebleau that afternoon. Major General Schmundt, Rommel's friend and still Hitler's Chief Adjutant, was waiting at Rommel's headquarters when Rommel, Meise and von Tempelhoff arrived. Schmundt

[31]Young, *Desert Fox*, pg. 196.
[32]*Ibid*.
[33]*Ibid*. The hesitation Rommel showed was reported to the other members of the conspiracy. When the O.S.S. received an agent's report on the matter it stated that Rommel could not be counted on for cooperation by members of the anti-Hitler movement.

had brought a "draft manifesto of allegiance to Hitler,"[34] which he asked Rommel to read and then sign. Schmundt had drafted the manifesto following reports that several German generals in Russian captivity had become "turncoats." Apparently they had appealed to some of Germany's highest ranking officers to abandon Hitler's regime. The document was intended to confirm the loyalty of the rest of Hitler's field marshals. Rommel added his name below that of von Rundstedt's. During dinner that evening Rommel feigned cheerfulness, concealing his deep concern over the implications of his act. His signature on the document, coupled with the sacred oath taken in 1934, deterred Rommel from joining the anti-Hitler movement, delaying his direct action for some time.

Despite his deepening responsibilities and burdens, Rommel still found time for relaxation and sport. One incident casts a revealing light on Rommel's character. On March 4th, while unsuccessfully trying to bag some wild boar, "a royal stag with 16 points (antlers)" moved into a wide glade in front of the Field Marshal. Ruge and Meise were watching from a spot nearby and noticed that Rommel had looked down at his watch. "The shooting time had passed. [Ruge and Meise] advised him to shoot. [Rommel] quietly said 'the closed season has started,' and the stag was left with his life."[35] Thus adhering to the rules of the game and obedience to the "laws" governing hunting prevailed that afternoon.

Starting on 6 March Rommel and his staff began another inspection trip of the Normandy and Brittany coastline. Rommel was pleased with the work that had been done in erecting the beach obstacles but was quite disturbed when he heard that some unauthorized testing had been done. In one sector a 120-ton British landing craft, captured at Dieppe, was steered onto the obstacles and had crushed them easily - they had not yet been mined as Rommel had instructed. A 10-ton craft, on the other hand, was unable to pass through the obstacles and reach the beach. Tests without mines on the obstacles were useless and Rommel issued orders that no more trial runs were to be made. The next day Rommel stopped for the night at General Straube's 74 Corps headquarters at the Villa Mond. General Gause showed Rommel some beautiful pieces of antique Sèvres china. Rommel commented that he wished the manufacturers of these pieces could also make mines for them. He was not joking. Porcelain was antimagnetic, thus undetectable, and was also waterproof.[36] Orders were soon given for all china (porcelain) factories in the occupied western territory to produce every kind of mine covering. An invasion of France would be Germany's most crucial battle; Rommel would use every weapon to win that battle.

Rommel and his staff occupied the La Rochefoucauld family château at La Roche-Guyon on 9 March. The owners were allowed to stay on,

---

[34]Irving, _The Trail_, pg. 330.
[35]Letter, _Dr. W. Meise to W.M. James, Jr._, 21 March 1964, personal copy.
[36]Ruge, _Rommel in Normandy_, pg. 94.

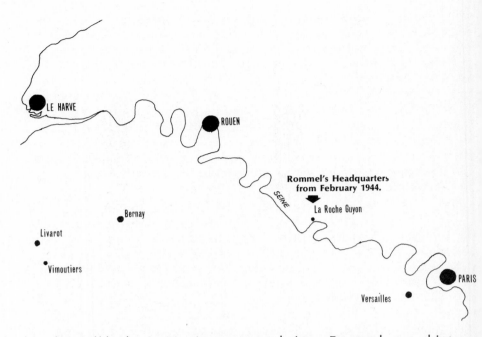

but the staff had priorities in accommodations. Rommel moved into a small ground floor room and occupied the study overlooking the garden. His new desk, on which Louis XIV's minister of war had signed the Edict of Nantes and other historic documents, now had Rommel's telephone on it but nothing else. "Rommel," writes Cornelius Ryan, could have walked out of that room without leaving a trace." The passages and caves underneath the chateau's tower (the oldest section) were occupied by the communications section. The daily routine for Rommel remained fundamentally the same: he still rose around 0500-0600 in the morning; went on his inspection trips until around 1800 and then had dinner, usually at 1930 with 10-12 members of his staff. Following the evening conferences, Rommel would walk through the grounds or woods nearby with either Ruge or Gause, under the watchful eyes of the *Feldgendarmerie* (the Army's Military Police).

After several unsuccessful attempts, Ruge finally convinced Rommel to take a break from his work and visit the Mont-St.-Michael Monastery. An inspection trip on 9 March took the team past the monastery and Rommel agreed to stop and visit it. He was impressed by the monastery and remarked to Ruge that it would make a good fortress!

Rommel's torrid pace continued through the month of March. A conference with von Schweppenburg on the 15th proved a disappointment, for the two men had failed to solve their differences over the employment of the Panzer units in France. Von Schweppenburg later commented that he considered Rommel to be "grossly overrated," but "brave and a good tactician."[37]

A lunch break during the visit to the Mont-St.-Michael Monastery.

---

[37]Letter, General der Panzertruppen (Ret.) Geyr von Schweppenburg to W.M. James, Jr., 11 February 1965, personal copy. Von Schweppenburg also wrote that Rommel was "a hopeless strategist. When it came to Normandy, it was he who bungled the outcome, in common with the Private First Class, and this against the advice of Guderian and myself, before the first shot was fired."

Allied agents reported that "commencing 19 March 1944, Hitler and Rommel inspected all headquarters in the island of Sjaelland, and, starting at Kjogl, from Denmark they proceeded on a similar inspection trip through Estonia. Field Marshal Rommel," the report continued, "devoted special attention to the availability and readiness of transportation means, both in Denmark and northern Estonia. This tour of inspection was surrounded with the deepest secrecy."[38] The report was grossly inaccurate, however, for Hitler was in conference at the Berghof with his leading field marshals, including Rommel. At the close of the conference, von Rundstedt read aloud to Hitler the contents of "the declaration of personal loyalty" which he and the other field marshals had signed. The next day, the 20th, the ranking officers from the western front assembled at the Berghof (Schloss-Klessheim), where they heard "an unusually uninspiring and pallid speech"[39] from Hitler. The Führer spoke confidently of the new wonder weapons - jet aircraft and the new submarines - and, after a warning to them about the danger of enemy parachutists, ended his speech in "a combination of rambling remarks and solecisms."[40] "We have the utmost confidence,"

The conference at Schloss-Klessheim, Rommel is second from left.

[38]*United States National Archives, Office of Strategic Services Report No. 69349:* "Secret Inspection Trip of Hitler and Rommel." *Hereafter cited as O.S.S. Report No.*
[39]*Irving, Hitler's War, pg. 614.*
[40]*Ibid.*

Rommel later wrote, "that we'll get by in the west."[41] But Hitler had still not decided between the operational views of the von Rundstedt-von Schweppenburg clique and those of Rommel. Hitler's indecision was contagious and it soon prevailed at OKW. Rommel's attempts to effect a lucid operational policy in the West were in vain.

Jim Jones

General Alexander von Falkenhausen, Governor General of Belgium and Northern France.

Beginning on 23 March, Rommel undertook a five-day inspection tour of the Netherlands. General Meise, Colonel Lattmann, Lieutenant Colonel von Tempelhoff, Admiral Ruge and the war correspondent, Hans H. Henne, accompanied him. The afternoon of the first day Rommel met with General von Falkenhausen, the Governor General of Belgium and Northern France. Early on the 24th he was off again, driving to the headquarters of Major General Reinhardt (commander, 89 Corps) in Utrecht. Reinhardt reported that the flooding operations were progressing, but that they had alienated the civilian population. Rommel reminded Reinhardt that military requirements took precedence over all else, but quickly suggested that he inform the civilians that if the countryside was protected against an invasion they would not suffer widespread damage to their towns, homes and farms. Rommel also proposed that Reinhardt offer the civilians work on the anti-invasion projects at the same wages the Germans were receiving.

[41]*Ibid.*

This method had proven successful in other areas and the military had actually recruited more labor than the Organization Todt.

Following the meeting with Reinhardt, Rommel drove to Holland on the 24th to meet with General Christiansen (the Military Governor in Holland) and to inspect the bases around Amsterdam. By the 26th Rommel was in Hoek van Holland, inspecting the fortress there. "From 8 o'clock in the morning until 1900 in the evening, the only break taken was the one for lunch," wrote Henne, and "the remainder of the time we were travelling by car, or by foot if necessary."[42] As they moved from base to base, Henne compiled his notes for an article he was

Rommel, Gause and General Christiansen (the Military Governor in Holland) discuss the defenses in Holland.

preparing, adding his own propagandized "truth" for color. "Soldiers in these countless bases are experienced fighters," noted Henne, "who have proven themselves in many a battle. Men with the EK 1 [Iron Cross First Class], 'Close Combat' and 'Assault Badges' outnumber all others. No one second rate is watching here!"[43] The truth was somewhat different. In one sector in Brittany the beaches were defended by 27 companies of fortress cadre troops, 7 eastern "Ost" battalions, 1 company of

[42]Hans H. Henne, "Die tödliche Landschaft. Skizzen von einer Besichtigungsfahrt mit Generalfeldmarschall Rommel," O. U. Den 9.4.44, pg. 1., personal copy. Henne was a lieutenant in "Berichtertrupp Ertel" and often accompanied Rommel on these trips. Hereafter cited as "Die tödliche Landschaft."
[43]Ibid., pg. 2.

Russian bicyclists, some Russian engineers and 1 Russian cavalry regiment. Other units identified as "first rate" included older men and convalescents. There were also a number of special "medical" units, such as 70 Infantry Division, which consisted of men with "stomach" problems.

By the 27th Rommel had reached a point near Calais, dead tired but far from disconcerted. During one tour of a fortified area, a "much talked about" incident took place. As Henne remembers the incident, a motorcycle messenger approached the group at a very high speed. In the sidecar "rode a beautiful girl, just as blonde and fresh-looking as the young soldier, who was giving her an unauthorized lift."[44] "In a cloud of dust," the messenger "swiftly screeched to a halt, handed the motorcycle to the apparently well-trained girl, saluted smartly and happily reported to the Field Marshal: 'Corporal Schmidt and the regiment's laundress on their way to work.' "[45] Rommel smiled but said nothing; the soldier saluted, hopped back on his bike, the "laundress" at his side, and sped off as quickly as he had arrived - before anyone could ask embarrassing questions.

When Rommel was pleased with the work that his troops were doing, he would present them with harmonicas or even accordians on a few occasions. As the small convoy neared the end of the tour, Rommel mentioned to Henne that he still had some 500 harmonicas at his headquarters which he intended to distribute to his men. To many of them, "that was just like a deserved medal."[46]

Rommel visits the factory making "Tetrahedron" beach obstacles.

---

[44]Ibid., pg. 5.
[45]Ruge, _Rommel in Normandy_, pg. 118.
[46]Henne, "Die tödliche Landschaft," pg. 5.

(Above and right) General
Marcks and Rommel during an
inspection tour of 84 Corps
defenses. General Marcks is
directly behind the unidentified general at right.

(Above) Rommel inspects a battalion of "tank hunters" (converted French Hotchkiss H-39 tanks).

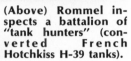

(Left and below) The inspection team visits a 28cm coastal artillery battery in Brittany.

As soon as he returned to La Roche-Guyon, Rommel conducted a series of conferences with his local commanders, his engineers and then with von Rundstedt. On 31 March Rommel met with Admiral Krancke and his chief-of-staff to discuss the laying of sea mines; he then talked with General Blumentritt. On the first day of April, Rommel drove to Paris to inspect the new revolving concrete turrets for the heavy artillery batteries. Following a series of conferences at La Roche-Guyon, he inspected the 348 Infantery Division at La Treport on the 3rd, and the 49 Infantry Division shortly thereafter. On 9 April Rommel met again with Blumentritt to discuss the Panzer units. A meeting with von Schweppenburg that afternoon again ended in failure. Rommel then returned to Brittany to inspect the construction projects, the major fortresses, factories making the "tetrahedron" obstacles and the railway gun batteries. After inspecting the divisions situated around Brest and Lorient, the Field Marshal drove to the Bay of Quiberon to inspect the 4./264 Railway Gun Battery. He returned to La Roche-Guyon on the afternoon of 16 April.

Meise, Gause and Rommel looking at a new family of sea mines.

Major General Dr. Hans Speidel reported for duty at La Roche-Guyon on the 16th, as a replacement for General Gause, who, due to a series of unfortunate incidents involving his wife and Frau Rommel, was being transferred. Rommel and Speidel had known each other since World War One when they both served in the Argonne in 1915; between the wars they had served together in 13 Infantry Regiment. General Speidel had been one of two officers recommended by the General Staff to

General Dr. Hans Speidel

replace Gause; he was six years younger than Rommel but a Knight's Cross holder for his part in the successful breakout from the Tscherkassy pocket in southern Russia.

Speidel had been a convert to the anti-Hitler movement for some time and planned to make this fact known to Rommel at the earliest possible moment. The perfect chance to reveal his involvement in the movement came after dinner that evening. Rommel informed Speidel that in "his opinion the war should be brought to an end as quickly as possible."[47] Speidel seized the opportunity to tell Rommel that he "had been for a long time in touch with forces and persons in the Army and homeland that were ready and determined to put an end to the [Hitler] regime and to bring peace in order to save the homeland in the last hour."[48] Speidel continued, revealing the terrible catastrophes that were occurring in the East, including the evacuation of the Crimea. When Ruge returned to La Roche-Guyon the next day he noticed that Rommel's demeanor had grown quite serious; he talked about the recall of Field Marshals von Manstein and von Kleist from Russia. The news that Speidel had brought from Russia was sobering indeed, but the fact that the anti-Hitler feelings were so widespread affected Rommel profoundly. As Ruge noted, Rommel was visibly changed.

Although Gause was still at La Roche-Guyon, Rommel put Speidel to work as **chief-of-staff** almost immediately. On the 17th Rommel, Speidel and Ruge left on a tour of the French coast between the Somme and the

---

[47]Hans Speidel, "Background for 20 July 1944," MS B-721, pg. 2. Hereafter cited as "20 July 1944," B-721.

[48]Ibid.

A farewell party for Gause at Val St. André on 11 April 1944.

Meise, Rommel, Ruge, General Hans-Kurt Höcker (commander of the 17 Luftwaffe Field Division) and Lieutenant Behr.

Rommel is saluted by the commander of an infantry company during one of the inspection tours. In the background is General Sinnhuber, commander of LXXXII. Army Corps, and Captain Lang.

W.M. James, Jr./Ruge

Rommel's staff gathers at Val. St. André (west of St. Malo). (right to left: Ruge, Behr, Rommel in the doorway, Dümmler, Lang and Ertel.

James Jones

Rommel and General Lieutenant Hermann Meyer-Rabingen, commander of the 159 Reserve Division, on the Atlantic coast in southwestern France.

Schelde. In order to make certain that the Allies knew of his inspection of the area's coastal defenses, Rommel continued to bring along the war correspondents; on this trip Lutz Koch (a friend from Africa), Ertel, Podewils and Baron von Esebeck (another friend from Africa) accompanied him. After inspecting the offshore obstacles in the sector defended by the 348 Infantry Division near Ault, the tour continued down the coast towards St. Valery (the scene of one of Rommel's victories during the 1940 French campaign). In a short time Rommel visited the 344, 331, 47 and the 18 Infantry Divisions (a *Luftwaffe* Field division). The tour ended on the evening of 20 April.

On the 21st Heinz Guderian (now Inspector General of Panzer Troops) arrived at La Roche-Guyon. The visit was the result of an earlier conference he had had with Hitler. After reviewing plans submitted to him by OKW, Guderian noted that the Panzer divisions - the principal reserves - were to be stationed in the front lines, along the coast. But Guderian believed that if the tanks were too far forward "they could not be withdrawn and committed elsewhere with sufficient rapidity should the enemy land at any other point than at which he was expected."[49] When Guderian expressed his views to Hitler, Hitler responded that the "present arrangement is the one suggested by Field Marshal

---

[49]Heinz Guderian, <u>Panzer Leader</u> (New York: E. P. Dutton & Co., Inc., 1960), pg. 329.

Rommel."[50] Somewhat out of character, Hitler continued, "I don't like to give contrary orders over the head of the responsible field marshal on the spot without having first heard his opinion. Go to France again and discuss the matter once more with Rommel."[51]

When Guderian met with Rommel he insisted that the Panzer units be held in the rear, out of range of the Allied naval guns and free to move immediately to any threatened sector. His view was supported by von Schweppenburg. This was incomprehensible to Rommel, and despite whatever lessons had been learned in Italy at the Allied landing sites there, he drew upon his experiences with the Allied air power in Africa. He explained that if the tanks were too far back when the Allies landed they would never get forward in time. Rommel pointed out "that as a man from the eastern front, [Guderian] lacked his experiences of Africa and Italy; that he knew, in fact, more about the matter in hand than [Guderian] did and that he was fully convinced that his system was right."[52] Faced with Rommel's intransigence, Guderian wisely avoided a confrontation, preferring to submit his report and contrary views to Hitler and von Rundstedt. Hitler later rejected the proposals submitted by Guderian and von Rundstedt "on the grounds that Rommel possessed more recent experiences of battle than did [Guderian and von Rundstedt]."[53] Von Schweppenburg, however, remained outside Rommel's authority and, as the commander of Panzergruppe West, persisted with his own views. Thus the controversy continued. OKW decreed on the 7th that Rommel would receive command of 2, 21, and 116 Panzer Divisions. The other four tank divisions were to remain inland under the command of Panzergruppe West, away from the coast as an OKW reserve - an ineffective compromise at best.

On the morning of the 15th, Hitler placed a call to La Roche-Guyon to discuss the question of locating *Nebelwerfer* Brigade 7. OB West (von Rundstedt) wanted to move the unit to an area about 80km behind the coast near Beauvais, while Rommel wanted to switch it to the Cotentin Peninsula. To cover himself in the case of a misinterpretation of the conversation by Hitler or OKW, Rommel asked Speidel to listen in on the extension. Ruge also listened in for a few moments and, following the conversation, left for a meeting with Admiral Krancke while Rommel and Speidel drove to Mareil-Marly to meet with General von Stülpnagel (the Military Governor of France). The Rommel-von Stülpnagel meeting was guarded by a unit of grenadiers from the newly reorganized 21 Panzer Division, which was officially on hand to protect the generals from French partisans. Actually it was there to prevent any unwanted interference. Rommel and Speidel conferred with von Stülpnagel, General Heinrich Baron von Lüttwitz (2 Panzer Division

---

[50]*Ibid.*
[51]*Ibid.*
[52]*Ibid.*, pg. 330.
[53]*Ibid.*

Rommel and General Carl-Heinrich von Stülpnagel at Mareil-Marly on 15 April 1944.

commander), General von Falkenhausen and General Gerhard Count von Schwerin (116 Panzer Division commander). The main topic was how best to "conclude a separate peace on the western front and overthrow the Nazi Regime."[54] Von Stülpnagel spoke for all present when he stated that Rommel "was the only one who would have the undisputed esteem among the [German] people and the armed forces, even among the Allies in case of a rebellion."[55] Rommel stood firm in his belief that if Hitler were assassinated "he would be turned into a martyr and that the public would therefore fail to realize his guilt and total responsibility."[56] Rommel preferred to have Hitler arrested and brought to trial before the German people. The more radical members of the movement's inner circle, however, pressed forward with their plans to assassinate the Nazi dictator.

Following his own commitment to the resistance, Rommel was able to influence Dr. Julius Dorpmuller (Minister of Transport) and Karl Kaufmann (Gauleiter of Hamburg) to join the movement. Rommel then turned to planning what he considered the necessary steps in the event of the actual removal of Hitler. He prepared a list of those persons he considered capable of negotiating with the Allies: von Schweppenburg,

[54]*Speidel, "20 July 1944," B-721, pg. 3.*
[55]*Ibid.*
[56]*Hoffmann, German Resistance, pg. 352. Post war charges that Rommel planned to withhold 2 and 116 Panzer Divisions during an Allied invasion in order to have a reliable strike force to quell any resistance by the SS after Hitler's arrest are completely untrue. In a statement issued on 23 February 1951, General Blumentritt asserted that "on the contrary Rommel and his Chief of Staff, in the same way as Rundstedt, did everything to transfer any possible reserves to the invasion front."*

von Stülpnagel, Speidel, von Schwerin, Ruge and Dr. Caesar von Hofacker. Negotiations with the Allies would be based on the following points: "A) evacuation of the occupied territory in the west; B) withdrawal of the Western Army behind the West Wall; C) transfer of administration of the occupied Western area to the Allies; D) shortening of the East front and holding it for the protection of the west; E) cessation of the enemy bomb war on Germany; F) imprisonment of Hitler [and the removal of Himmler] so that he could be brought before a German tribunal; G) elimination of all internal resistance (Gestapo) in the west; H) proclamation to the German people from all broadcasting stations of the occupied territory: outspoken information on the true political and military situation and the crimes of the Hitler government; I) assumption of governmental power in Germany by the resistance forces of all classes and ranks under the leadership of Dr. Goerdeler and Colonel General Beck."[57] No one, including Rommel, expected all of the terms to be accepted by the Allies, but they represented a good starting point.

Bundesarchiv

On 8 May 1944, a major conference was held in Paris to discuss the expected Allied invasion and how to repell it. (Above) Von Schweppenburg, Blaskowitz, Sperrle, von Rundstedt, Rommel and Krancke. (Right) Blaskowitz, Rommel and von Rundstedt.

National Archives

<hr>

[57]*Speidel, "20 July 1944," B-721, pg. 3.*

When von Rundstedt visited Rommel at La Roche-Guyon on 20 May, the anti-Hitler movement and Rommel's involvement were not mentioned. After discussing a wide range of "service matters," the conversation turned to von Rundstedt's favorite pasttime - Karl May detective stories. Shortly after the conference, Speidel brought two captured British commandos into Rommel's study, ignoring standing orders from OKW that prisoners of this sort were to be handed over to the SD (*Sicherheitsdienst* - the Security Service Branch of the SS). Rommel agreed with Speidel's intention to surrender them to the Army and, after a lengthy discussion with the "commando gangsters" sent them off to a military prisoner-of-war camp.

On 20 May 1944 von Rundstedt (OB West) and his chief-of-staff, Blumentritt, visited Rommel at his headquarters in La Roche-Guyon. (Above left) Blumentritt, Speidel, Rommel and von Rundstedt.

By late may 1944, despite intricate security, the Allied preparations for the invasion of France were obvious; the invasion itself certainly close at hand. On 22 May Rommel took his friend, Lutz Koch, on an inspection of Heeresgruppe B's alternate command post at Le Vernon. Rommel hoped that Koch's report would receive widespread coverage and thus divert some of the Allies' attention away from La Roche-Guyon. Although the numerous daily bombings were directed mainly at bridges, radar stations, and other similar sites, Rommel felt that his headquarters would not be spared much longer.

When Speidel departed for his home in Freundstadt to meet with former Foreign Minister, Konstantin von Neurath, he was acting on Rommel's behalf. It was not considered safe for Rommel to make the trip

Von Rundstedt pets one of Rommel's dogs on the castle terrace.

After the conference the group moved to the terrace. The dog is the one given Rommel by the Organization Todt (see "The Rommel Papers," pg. 464).

Rommel bids farewell to his immediate superior, von Rundstedt as he and Blumentritt sit in their command car.

himself, thus Speidel was empowered to carry on the discussions with von Neurath and Dr. Strölin. Strölin had requested this meeting; he wanted to strengthen connections with the resistance forces in Germany, especially with Dr. Goerdeler. During the meeting Strölin emphasized that after Hitler's arrest the people would have to be enlightened if a civil war was to be avoided. Von Neurath agreed but mentioned one more fact: Himmler would also have to be removed if there was to be any salvation for Germany. Rommel was now very careful in what he wrote Lucie and, on the 29th, told her that "the Anglo-Americans did not let up in their round-the-clock bombing yesterday."[58] He went on to say that the French had suffered heavy civilian casualties from the bombings but that most of the bombs had dropped on dummy positions and the Atlantic Wall had suffered little damage.

On 1 June the radio interception crew at the headquarters of 15 Army overheard the first part of the first verse from a poem by Paul Verlaine

In the field once more, Rommel inspects an American B-17 which was downed during a bombing raid on German defenses in France.

(Chason d'Automne). Unlike most of the hundreds of messages and codewords broadcast by the BBC to the French underground, this particular message was far from meaningless. A paid informant for the *Abwehr* (the Wehrmacht's military intelligence branch) had told Admiral Canaris, its head, that this broadcast would alert the French underground that the invasion would take place within two weeks. When *Feldwebel* Walter Reichling heard the BBC announcer say "Les sanglots longs des violons de l'automne"[59] - the long sobs of the violins of

[58]*Rommel Collection*, T-84, 274, #001142.
[59]*Cornelius Ryan, The Longest Day* (New York: Simon and Schuster, Inc., 1959), pg. 33.

autumn - he dropped his earphones and scurried from the bunkers heading towards the office of the intelligence officer, Lieutenant Colonel Meyer. After listening to a recording of the message, Meyer informed Major General Rudolf Hofmann, the 15 Army chief-of-staff, who in turn alerted the whole of 15 Army. At the same time Meyer teletyped OKW and then telephoned von Rundstedt at OB West and finally Rommel's headquarters at Heeresgruppe B. At OKW the message was delivered to Colonel General Jodl, Chief of Operations. It remained on Jodl's desk. "He did not order an alert. He assumed that von Rundstedt had done so, but von Rundstedt thought Rommel's headquarters had issued the order."[60] 7 Army, which was defending the coast of Normandy, was not notified and did not order alert status. The radio interception crews were alert, however, and were determined to catch all the messages broadcasted - the only way to insure the monitoring of the second half of the verse by Verlaine which would signal an impending invasion.

When von Falkenhausen visited Rommel at La Roche-Guyon on 2 June, Rommel found the general's views very close to those of von Stülpnagel. Von Falkenhausen's "arguments in the field of world politics impressed Rommel especially."[61] Rommel planned to drive to Paris on the 3rd to clear a trip (through OB West) to meet with Hitler. The meeting with von Falkenhausen certainly influenced the points Rommel was prepared to discuss with the Führer. He intended to "expound [to Hitler] the military and political facts of the situation and demand a change in top-level organization and bringing up of the reserves of all three arms of the *Wehrmacht*."[62] The only way that Rommel could persuade Hitler was through a personal interview. "The last man who sees Hitler wins the game," he had often told his personal aide, Hellmuth Lang.[63]

Captain Lang picked up the morning report for 4 June at around 0600 hours. A quick glance at the report revealed that, with the exception of the nightly bombings in the Pas-de-Calais, everything was "all quiet." With a 20-30 miles an hour gale blowing in the English Channel, and promises of only more bad weather predicted by Professor Walter Ströbe (the Chief Meterologist in Paris), there seemed to be little cause for Rommel to cancel his trip to Germany. Lang brought Rommel the morning report. Rommel read it quickly and went to breakfast with Lang. When the two walked out to the car they met von Tempelhoff, who was also driving back to Germany that morning. Rommel invited him to ride with them. Von Tempelhoff's driver was to follow behind Rommel's car, but there were no escort vehicles. By the time Rommel left La Roche-Guyon that morning, waves in the English Channel were

[60]*Ibid.*
[61]*Speidel, "20 July 1944," B-721, pg. 3.*
[62]*Zimmermann, "OB West," B-308, pg. 77.*
[63]*Ryan, The Longest Day, pg. 30.*

Rommel and Lang during one of the numerous inspection tours in the spring of 1944.

reported to be between five and eight feet high. Even the staff at OKW considered the seas too rough for the Allies to attempt a landing.

The inclement weather brought a false sense of security that would have disasterous consequences for the Germans. Hitler had allowed Admiral Dönitz to go on leave for the first time since the war had begun; Hitler himself was at his Bercthesgaden retreat. General Marcks (84 Korps), Lieutenant General Hellmich (243 Infantry Division), Lieutenant General von Schlieben (709 Infantry Division) and Major General Falley (91 Air Landing Division) were all preparing to attend a *"Kriegsspiel"* ((map exercise) at Rennes. At La Roche-Guyon Ruge had departed for some official business elsewhere; Speidel had invited guests for dinner on the evening of the 5th: Ernst Jünger, the author; Consul General Pfeiffer; Colonel List; Ritter von Schramm, the war correspondent; and Dr. Horst, Speidel's brother-in-law, had all accepted the invitation.

5 June remained stormy, so rough in fact that Admiral Krancke's patrol boats could not leave their bases. Across the Channel, however, General Eisenhower, Supreme Commander of the Allied Forces, had already given the order to his forces that Tuesday, 6 June, would be D-Day - the invasion of Europe.

The Invasion

The radio interception team at 15 Army monitored the second half of the BBC "Verlaine" message, broadcast to the French underground, at 2115 hours on 5 June: "Blessent mon coeur d'une langeur monotone - wound my heart with a monotonous langour."[1] Once again Meyer was on hand; he rushed the spectacular intercept into von Salmuth's dining room, where the general was playing bridge. Informed of its contents, von Salmuth (15 Army commander) routinely placed his army on full alert. "I'm too old a bunny to get too excited about this," he calmly declared.

But von Salmuth's zealous intelligence officer soon had the 15 Army teleprinters chattering: "Urgent to 67, 82, 89 Corps; Military Governor Belgium and Northern France; Heeresgruppe B; 16 Flak Division; Admiral Channel Coast; Luftwaffe Belgium and Northern France. Message of BBC, 2115, June 5 has been processed. According to our available records it means 'Expect invasion within 48 hours, starting 0000, June 6.'"[2] Meyer then notified OB West, which, in turn, informed OKW. The 7 Army headquarters in Le Mans was not alerted.

Around 2200 hours numerous unusually large waves of Allied aircraft swept over the east coast of the Cotentin Peninsula. Alarmed by the sudden surge of enemy activity, General Erich Marcks limped into his command bunker in St. Lô. His 84 Army Corps was responsible for the defense of the Normandy coastline.

As the Cathedral clock struck midnight, several officers of the 84 Corps staff entered the main cell of the command bunker. June 6 was General Marcks' birthday. Lieutenant Colonel von Criegern, Major Viebig and Major Hayn had planned a modest celebration, Surprised, Marcks spied his well-wishers. His artificial leg creaked as he stood to greet them.[3] Each man drank a glass of Chablis. But the festivities found

---

[1] Paul Carell, Invasion- -They're Coming (New York: E.P. Dutton and Co., Inc., 1963), pg. 19. Hereafter cited as Invasion.

[2] Ryan, The Longest Day, pp. 96-97. Teleprinter message No. 2117/26.

[3] Marcks had lost a leg in Russia, and suffered eye and head injuries as well. Friedrich Hayn, Die Invasion. Von Cotentin bis Falaise. Wehrmacht im Kampf Series, Bd. II. (Heidelberg: Kurt Vowinckel Verlag, 1954), pg. 20. Hereafter cited as Die Invasion.

**General
Erich Marcks**

their conclusion only minutes after they had begun, for there were pressing tasks at hand.

The General bent his slender frame over the situation maps. He had last-minute preparation to do for the scheduled conference in Rennes. One map showed the distribution of the Allied forces in southern England. His eyes scoured the little colored flags, the red and blue lines and curves that represented the more than 30 English, American and Canadian divisions discovered by German intelligence. The five enemy airborne divisions were specially marked.

Suddenly, at exactly 0111 hours, the shrill tone of the bunker's field telephone pierced the early morning air. It was Major General Wilhelm Richter, the commander of 716 Infantry Division. "Enemy paratroopers have landed east of the Orne," he blurted into the receiver. "The area," Richter continued, "seems to be around Bréville and Ranville, and along the northern fringe of the Bavent Forest."[4] The news, remembers Major Friedrich Hayn, the chief intelligence officer at 84 Corps, struck them "like lightning."[5] Some fifteen minutes later Marcks' chief-of-staff telephoned 7 Army headquarters and spoke with his counterpart, Major General Max Pemsel. Shortly thereafter, 0135 hours, Pemsel briefed Speidel; he then placed 7 Army on full alert.[6]

Speidel notified OB West in Paris, but refused to take the enemy airborne landings in Normandy seriously. He had also received reports of paratroop drops farther east, in the 15 Army sector.[7] In addition, he

[4]*Ibid*. pp. 13-14. *These were the lead elements of the British 6 Airborne Division, under Major General Richard Gale.*

[5]*Ibid.*, *pg. 14.*

[6]*Armies. 7 Army Telephone Log, 6 June 1944. T-312, 1568, #000938. Hereafter cited as Armies, name of army, T-312, 1568, frame no.*

[7]*At 0130 hours von Rundstedt's staff also received a report (from Naval Group West) that several airborne landings had occured in the 716 and 711 Infantry Division sectors. KTB OB West, 6.6.44. BAMA. RH 19IV/43.*

learned that straw dummies had been discovered in Normandy. These "revelations" reinforced Speidel's own conviction that the real invasion could only come at Pas-de-Calais.[8] Pemsel was not so sanguine. At 0215 he called Rommel's château again. "It's a major operation," he protested. But Speidel was not convinced. "It's only a local matter," he assured the 7 Army chief of staff.[9] At 0300 he went so far as to inform OB West that "the possibility exists that bailed-out airplane crews are being mistaken for paratroopers."[10]

Between 0130 and 0400 von Rundstedt's headquarters was barraged with reports from the invasion front. At 0325 Naval Group West reported landing craft off the Calvados coast - at Port Bessin and Grandcamp. Swarms of Allied aircraft, towing gliders, had also been sighted drifting slowly southward above the Channel islands.[11] These and other reports pointed to a major operation. Thus, by 0350 General Blumentritt, von Rundstedt's chief of staff, had also shifted to Pemsel's view.[12]

Von Rundstedt, in fact, in partial defiance of his standing orders from OKW, had already dispatched elements of 12 SS Panzer Division towards the coast - to undertake reconnaissance in 711 Infantry Division sector. At 0425 hours he ordered the powerful Panzer Lehr Division up to its emergency assembly areas. Von Rundstedt followed these moves with a formal request (0445 hours) to OKW for the release of the strategic Panzer reserves. He argued that if the tanks moved forward quickly, they could reach the invasion front the same day.[13]

Jodl, however, was asleep, and his staff was not convinced the situation was serious enough to disturb him. At 0500 Jodl's staff awakened Captain Karl von Puttkamer, Hitler's naval aide, and informed him in vague terms that the Allies had undertaken an operation in France. Von Puttkamer, aware that Hitler had not retired until 0400 that morning, elected not to rouse the Führer. There "wasn't much to tell him anyway," he reasoned; and he wanted to spare the staff one of Hitler's "endless nervous scenes which often led to the wildest decisions. Von

[8]Irving, The Trail. pp. 366-367.
[9]Armies, 7 Army, T-312, 1568, #000938.
[10]Telefonkladde Meyer-Detring. Ic OB West. BAMA. RH 19IV/134.
[11]KTB OB West. BAMA. RH 19IV/43.
[12]Irving, The Trail, pg. 367.
[13]KTB OB West. BAMA. RH 19IV/43. In April 1944 OKW transferred 12 SS "Hitler Jugend" Panzer Division from Belgium into the area southeast of Caen. The division, which fought with exemplary courage and skill throughout the Normandy campaign. was comprised of 177 tanks and 28 assault guns. See Hubert Meyer, "12.SS Panzer Division 'Hitler Jugend,' Juni bis September 1944," MS P-164.
The Panzer Lehr Division (Fritz Bayerlein) was stationed south and west of Chartres. On 6 June 1944 it boasted a compliment of 190 tanks plus a handful of assault guns. BAMA. RH 19IX/3, fol. 31. OKW, however, had ordered the Lehr's Panther tank battalion (I./6 Panzer Regiment) to the Russian front. On 5 June the first transport trains were rolling through Germany. The next day the battalion was ordered back to France but would not reach the invasion front until 10 June. Helmut Ritgen. Die Geschichte der Panzer-Lehr-Division im Westen. (Stuttgart: Motorbuch Verlag, 1979), pp. 102;134. Hereafter cited as Panzer Lehr.

Puttkamer decided that the morning would be time enough to give Hitler the news. He switched off the light and went back to sleep,"[14] in a situation similar to the El Alamein crisis.

The agitated Pemsel, meanwhile, again telephoned La Roche-Guyon (0515 hours). Enemy ships, he informed Speidel, were concentrating between the mouths of the Vire and the Orne. Once more he insisted that a major enemy operation was underway.[15] But Rommel's chief was not to be swayed. He was still mesmerized by the reports from von Salmuth's 15 Army.[16] And, after all, no Allied forces had yet landed from the sea. A quarter of an hour later, however, enemy naval units began a terrific bombardment along the entire Calvados front, smothering the German heavy gun batteries and coastal fortifications with shell-fire. From 0600 hours on followed the landings from the sea. Wave after wave of Allied assault craft plowed through the dark green water and touched down along the Normandy coastline. As the war diary of the German 7 Army dolefully recorded, the landings began at low tide;[17] not at high tide, as the German naval experts had anticipated. In this manner the lion's share of Rommel's beach obstacles, so assiduously installed in the months preceeding the invasion, were rendered useless.

At 0600 Blumentritt contacted Warlimont in Berchtesgaden. "In all probability," he asserted, "this [is] the invasion ... Normandy [is] apparently the area."[18] Warlimont had first learned of the Allied movements several hours earlier. As deputy chief of the OKW Operations Staff, he had alerted its members at once. Blumentritt urged OKW to release the Panzer reserves. Warlimont was well aware that "this was the first and most important decision which [OKW] had to take and [he] therefore got onto Jodl by telephone."[19] But Jodl maintained that the real Allied invasion had not yet begun; the moment had not come to commit the armored reserves. OB West must "first try to clear up the situation with the forces of Heeresgruppe B."[20]

In any case, Jodl's decision was not binding; only Hitler could release these units, but he still slept. Jodl refused to wake him. When Blumentritt relayed this information to von Rundstedt, the aristocratic Field

[14]Ryan, The Longest Day, pg. 185.

[15]Armies, 7 Army, T-312, 1568, #000941.

[16]Speidel was not alone in this belief. Many other high-ranking German officers refused to believe that the Normandy operation was anything but a secondary or diversionary move. Von Rundstedt, Sperrle, Admiral Krancke and even Rommel still expected the major Allied landing to come in the Pas-de-Calais sector.

[17]Armies, KTB 7 Army, T-312, 1569, #000005.

[18]Warlimont, Hitler's Headquarters, pg. 424. At 0642 hours Naval Group West reported the appearance of six Allied battleships and some 20 destroyers west of Le Havre, as well as 50-80 enemy warships in the vicinity of Barfleur. "This report," concluded OB West, "confirms that the invasion has actually begun." KTB OB West. BAMA. RH 19IV/43.

[19]Warlimont, Hitler's Headquarters, pg. 425.

[20]Ibid., pg. 425. Jodl vetoed the release of the tank divisions at 1000 hours. KTB OB West. BAMA. RH 19IV/43.

Marshal fumed with rage. He became "red in the face, and his anger made his speech unintelligible."[21] Had Rommel been present he would have telephoned Hitler directly and insisted that he be wakened. But Rommel was still in Herrlingen and unaware of the Allied landings. Von Rundstedt, "who openly referred to his Führer as 'that Bohemian corporal' would not stoop to petition."[22]

Thus as the final hours of darkness slipped irretrievably away, the OKW tank reserves had yet to launch a counterattack. The one tank unit closest to the invasion front, Feuchtinger's 21 Panzer Division (located between Caen and Falaise), had also not received its operational orders. This division, with its 146 tanks (Panzer IV's), 51 assault guns and 300 personnel carriers, represented a significant striking force;[23] it also belonged to the three tank divisions which comprised Rommel's tactical reserve.

Shortly after 0100 Feuchtinger had learned of airborne landings in the Troarn area. He had relayed this news at once to Rommel's headquarters. In accordance with his standing orders, he had committed his foremost infantry battalions to engage the enemy parachutists both east and west of the Orne. Before daylight, he had dispatched his reconnaissance unit to comb the area south and west of Caen, where further airborne drops had been reported.[24] But "during the hours of darkness when his tanks might have been moving unimpeded from Falaise to Caen, they were immobilized because he had no orders from Army Group B regarding their employment."[25] With Rommel absent, Speidel was reluctant to commit 21 Panzer until he had determined the *Schwerpunkt* of the enemy seaborne landings. Throughout the morning Feuchtinger repeatedly petitioned 7 Army for permission to advance against the invasion front.[26] But Dollmann (7 Army commander),

---

[21]John Toland, <u>Adolf Hitler</u> (New York: Doubleday, 1976), pg. 367. Hereafter cited as <u>Hitler</u>.

[22]<u>Ibid</u>.

[23]Rommel's old 21 Panzer Division, destroyed during the fighting in Africa and Tunisia, had been reformed in May 1943. Despite its impressive number of armored fighting vehicles, the division suffered from numerous shortcomings. Except for its weapons, it was heavily dependent upon French and English vehicles captured in 1940. Replacement personnel was often poor, including numerous Volksdeutsch (ethnic Germans), many of whom could not understand the German language. "Despite all its troubles," wrote Feuchtinger, "the standard of training of 21 Panzer Division was sufficiently high at the time of the invasion. Edgar Feuchtinger, "History of the 21st Panzer Division from the time of its formation until the beginning of the Invasion," pg. 17. MS B-441. Hereafter cited as "21 Panzer Division." After the war Feuchtinger emigrated to East Germany, having undertaken espionage activities for the East Germans and the Soviets. (letter from Curt Ehle, director of the Traditionsverband 21 Panzer Division, to author, dated 21 February, 1979).

[24]These reports proved false, however. Feuchtinger, "21 Panzer Division," B-441, pp. 18-19. Chester Wilmont, <u>The Struggle for Europe</u>, (New York: Harper and Row, 1952), pg. 282. Hereafter cited as <u>Struggle for Europe</u>.

[25]<u>Ibid</u>.

[26]"Kurzschilderung des Gegenangriffes der 21. Pz. Div. am 6.6.44," (Bearbeitet von Oberstl. i.G. Frhr. v. Berlichingen) In: Bodo Zimmermann, "Geschichte des OB West." MS 308, pg. 1033. Hereafter cited as "Gegenangriff der 21. Pz. Div."

286

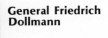
General Friedrich Dollmann

Jim Jones

J.R. Angolia

General Edgar Feuchtinger

without instructions from Army Group B, could do nothing. Finally, at 0645 hours, perhaps after speaking with Rommel in Herrlingen, Speidel authorized Dollmann to employ 21 Panzer in the Caen area. Fifteen minutes later, Pemsel subordinated the division to Marcks (84 Corps), with orders to destroy the enemy bridgehead east of the Orne.[27] Due to a breakdown in communications, another two hours were lost before Feuchtinger received his operational orders from 84 Corps. In the meantime, on his own initiative, he had sent his tanks rumbling northward to attack the British airborne division.[28]

---

[27]Wilmont, *Struggle for Europe*, pg. 282. Armies, *7 Army*, T-312, 1568, #000942.
[28]Wilmont, *Struggle for Europe*, pg. 282. Feuchtinger, "21 Panzer Division," B-441, pg. 20.

This was the situation when, at 0900, Schmundt awakened the Führer. Hitler was scheduled to meet with the leaders of Hungary, Slovakia and Romania (Horthy, Tiso and Antonescu). After his staff had briefed him on the reports from Normandy, Hitler sent for Keitel and Jodl. "Well, is it or isn't it the invasion?" he inquired in near hysterical fashion. As Warlimont recalled, Hitler soon collected himself and "decided to put on an act." The midday briefing conference was conducted at Klessheim Castle, in honor of the visiting potentates. As Hitler approached the maps "he chuckled in a carefree manner and behaved as if this was the opportunity he had been awaiting so long to settle accounts with his enemy. In unusually broad Austrian he merely said 'so, we're off.' "[29]

By midday Rommel, too, was off - racing on into France with his aide Lang. It cannot be stated with certainty when Speidel first telephoned the Field Marshal. What is certain, however, is that Rommel departed Herrlingen no earlier than 1030. Overcome with anxiety, he avoided conversation, speaking only when he urged Daniel to "drive faster." [30]

As Rommel sped back to his headquarters, Blumentritt called Speidel at 1540 hours and informed him that "OKW has released the 12 SS and Panzer Lehr Divisions."[31] But the order had come too late to permit their rapid deployment. Allied air superiority would render it impossible to move large units before dusk. Thus 12 SS Panzer Division would not reach the front before the 7th; Panzer Lehr would not be there before the 8th. The units Rommel had begged for were, as he had warned, too far inland.

When Daniel drove into Rheims (some 85 miles northeast of La Roche-Guyon), Rommel ordered him to stop at the garrison commander's headquarters. Once there, Rommel placed a priority call to Speidel. A short time later Rommel returned to the car. His soured expression left little doubt that he had received unpleasant news. The enemy, Speidel had informed him, had punched a large hole in the Atlantic Wall; thousands of men, supported by prodigious quantities of heavy weapons, had poured into the bridgehead. Feuchtinger's counterthrust had been delayed - he was still awaiting reinforcements. Rommel demanded that 21 Panzer attack immediately, and began the last stretch of his long journey to La Roche-Guyon. [32] "My friendly enemy, Montgomery," he muttered to himself.[33] Later he exclaimed to Lang,

[29]Warlimont, Hitler's Headquarters, pg. 427.
[30]In both editions of his book, We Defended Normandy (London: Herbert Jenkins, 1951) and Invasion 1944 (Chicago: Henry Regnery Co., 1950), Speidel places the time of his call to Rommel at 0600. The records of Heeresgruppe B indicate 1015 as the time; Warlimont in his book Hitler's Headquarters says that it was 1030.
[31]OKW released the Panzer reserves at 1430, some ten hours after OB West had lodged its first request. KTB OB West. BAMA. RH 19IV/43.
[32]By midday the invasion forces had formed a bridgehead with a five kilometer depth along a twenty-five kilometer front from the mouth of the Orne to Ryes. Armies, 7 Army, T-312, 1569, #000005-6.
[33]Montgomery had command of the Allied ground forces in Normandy.

"My God! If 21 Panzer can make it, we might just be able to drive them back in three days."[34]

By 1200 Feuchtinger's tanks had occupied their assembly areas in the woods southeast of Caen.[35] But just as they were ready to move against the English paratroopers (east of the Orne), Feuchtinger received new instructions. Recognizing the greater danger now posed by the advance inland of the British and Canadian forces towards Caen, Marcks ordered 21 Panzer to switch its attack to the west bank of the Orne.[36] In compliance with the new directive, Feuchtinger's armor (22 Panzer Regiment under Colonel von Oppeln-Bronikowski) reached Caen without much delay, but found the city a shambles. Allied bombers had piled the streets high with debris, and, as Bronikowski observed, "everyone in the city was on the move trying to get out."[37] Since his tanks could not get through the battered city they were forced to go around it - a loss of precious time. Enemy aircraft and naval guns constantly blasted the marching columns; the division suffered heavily before it reached its new staging area north of Caen.[38]

As Bronikowski assembled his tanks for the assault against the high ground at Périers and Bieville (both north of Caen), Marcks and Feuchtinger arrived. Awed by the drama of the moment, Marcks took the Panzer commander aside and intimated, "Oppeln, the future of Germany may well rest on your shoulders. If you don't push the British back into the sea, we've lost the war."[39] It was now 1700 hours. Marcks gave the signal to attack.[40]

The tanks rattled forward in two columns. Bronikowski struck towards Bieville with 25 Panzer IV's; Captain von Gottberg (a battalion commander) advanced on Périers - just four miles from the coast. Both attacks were stopped short. Bronikowski was out-gunned and lost six tanks in fifteen minutes. Von Gottberg's battalion encountered a well-entrenched adversary on the Périers heights. He lost ten Panzers. With its spearhead blunted, the Panzer regiment pulled back and dug in, to await the inevitable Allied counterthrust.

At the same time, elements of 192 Panzer Grenadier Regiment (of 21 Panzer Division), personally led by General Marcks, found the gap between the British and Canadian beachheads and sliced through to the coast at Luc-sur-Mer. Here, for a two-mile stretch, the German defenses were still intact. If they could be quickly reinforced, "a wedge could be maintained between the two beachheads and it might be possible to wipe out the British forces which had landed in the Orne Valley."[41] But

[34]Ryan, The Longest Day, pg. 296.
[35]Von Berlichingen, "Gegenangriff der 21. Pz. Div." In: Zimmermann, "Geschichte des OB West," MS 308, pp. 1038-39.
[36]Armies, 7 Army, T-312, 1568, #000945.
[37]Ryan, The Longest Day, pg. 295.
[38]Feuchtinger, "21 Panzer Division," B-441, pg. 21.
[39]Ryan, The Longest Day, pg. 297.
[40]Hayn, Die Invasion, pg. 28.
[41]Wilmont, Struggle for Europe, pg. 286.

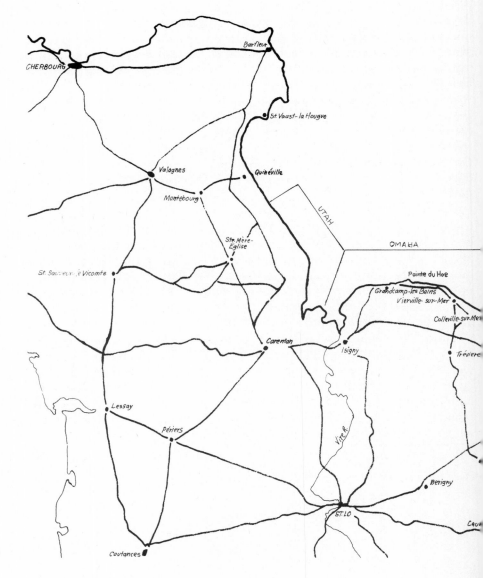

CHERBOURG

Barfleur

St.Vaast-la-Hougue

Valognes

Quinéville

Montebourg

UTAH

Ste.Mère-
Eglise

OMAHA

St.Sauveur-le-Vicomte

Pointe du Hoe

Grandcamp-les Bains
Vierville-sur-Mer

Colleville-sur-Mer

Carentan

Isigny

Trévieres

Lessay

Périers

V.r.e R.

Berigny

ST.LO

Cau

Coutances

the British had rebuffed the German armor, and, around 2100 hours, hundreds of Allied aircraft buzzed in low over the battlefield. The sky was soon filled with swarms of gliders and parachutes descending directly behind the Panzer division. Unnerved by the awesome display of enemy airpower, Feuchtinger called off his attack. He did not know that the parachutes carried supply canisters - not men.

Rommel arrived at La Roche-Guyon at 2000 - at almost the same time the *Panzergrenadiers* from 192 Regiment had linked up with the remnants of Richter's 716 Infantry Division on the coast. The news that greeted him was that Feuchtinger's counterstroke had failed. Lang queried if they could still hurl the invaders back into the sea. "I hope we can," Rommel replied. "I've nearly always succeeded up to now."[42] It would be no easy task, for Montgomery's invasion forces had established footholds on five separate beachheads. By the evening of 6 June, over 130,000 Allied troops were defending these footholds: 23,250 at Utah; 34,250 at Omaha; 24,970 at Gold; 21,400 at Juno; and 28,845 at Sword.[43] In addition, there were 23,000 airborne troops in widely scattered pockets, creating confusion for the German defenders.

Rommel spent the night trying to contact his units and to gather information. Most of his efforts were useless, for the Allied bombing had badly disrupted his communications network. He did speak with Dollmann (2240 hours) at 7 Army[44] and issued orders to 21 and 12 SS Panzer Divisions to attack the enemy bridgehead at 0800 the next morning.

---

[42]Ryan, *The Longest Day*, pg. 301.
[43]L. F. Ellis, *The Battle for Normandy*, Vol. I of *Victory in the West* (London: Her Majesty's Stationary Office, 1962), pg. 223. Hereafter cited as *Battle for Normandy*.
[44]Armies, *7 Army*, T-312, 1568, #000951.

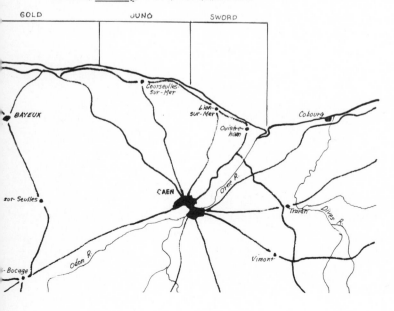

Chain of Command: 6 June 1944

Supreme Commander of the Armed Forces (OKW) and
Commander-in-Chief of the Army (OKH)
Adolf Hitler

OKL   OKM
Reich-Marshal Göring   Admiral Dönitz

OB West (HQ in Paris)
Field Marshal von Rundstedt[1]

Heeresgruppe B (HQ at La Roche-Guyon)
Field Marshal Rommel[2]
7 Army (HQ at Le Mans)
Colonel General Dollmann[3]
15 Army (HQ at Tourcoing)
Colonel General von Salmuth

Panzergruppe West (HQ at Thury-Harcourt)
General Geyr von Schweppenburg[4]

Militärbefehlshaber (Governor Generals)
France: General Karl Heinrich von Stülpnagel[5]
Belgium/Northern France: General Alexander
von Falkenhausen
Netherlands: General Christiansen

---

[1]*Relieved of command 2 July 1944; replaced by Field Marshal von Kluge, who took his own life on 18 August 1944.*
[2]*Severely wounded on 17 July 1944; replaced by Field Marshal von Kluge, who also retained command of OB West.*
[3]*Committed suicide; replaced by SS-Obergruppenführer Paul Hauser.*
[4]*Relieved of command on 3 July; replaced by General Eberbach.*
[5]*Relieved of command on 15 July; replaced by Gauleiter Grohe.*

Normandy - The Invasion Battle

Allied intentions for 7 June (D-Day + 1) were to secure their beachheads and to build up a crushing superiority on the ground to match that in the air.[1] The German ground forces in Normandy still enjoyed a numerical advantage over those of the Allies. Rommel's divisions, however, with the exception of the tank units and the elite SS formations, were greatly inferior in quality and mobility. Many of them relied on bicycles and horses for limited mobility. Fully motorized units began to lose vehicles at an alarming rate to the Allied fighters and bombers; all units suffered heavily under the rain of shells from the enemy warships anchored off the Calvados coastline. The German defenders were further handicapped by the almost non-existent *Luftwaffe*.[2] Despite the *Wehrmacht's* shortcomings, German intentions for 7 June were, as Rommel told Pemsel, "to stop the enemy from getting a foothold, whatever happens."[3]

During the morning Rommel visited the commander of 1 SS Panzer Corps, *Oberstgruppenführer* Sepp Dietrich. Dietrich's task was to launch Rommel's counterstroke against the Allied beachhead, but he was reluctant to move forward. The lead elements of 12 SS Panzer Division were only just arriving at the invasion front. The division had been badly bombed from the air during its 75 mile approach march;[4] it was now so strung out and disorganized that the counterattack (originally set for 0800) was rescheduled for 1200 hours. The enemy, Dietrich informed the Field Marshal, "has total command of the air over the battle area up to a point some 60 miles behind the front." The result of this, as Rommel noted later in a report to OKW, was that "during the day, practically our entire traffic - on roads, tracks and in open country - is pinned down by powerful fighter-bomber and bomber formations, [thus]

---

[1]By the evening of 7 June, German intelligence was estimating Allied strength in Normandy at 10-12 divisions. Schramm, KTB des OKW, IV, pg. 312.

[2]On D-Day the Allied air forces flew over 10,000 sorties. The German 3 Air Fleet, in contrast, managed only 319 sorties. O. Jaggi. "Normandie 1944. Auswirkungen der alliierten Luftüberlegenheit auf die deutsche Abwehr." pg. 335. In: Allgemeine Schweizerische Militärzeitschrift. Jg. 124, H. 5, 1958. Hereafter cited as "Auswirkungen der alliierten Luftüberlegenheit.

[3]Irving, The Trail, pp. 372-73.

[4]Betrachtungen der Oberbefehlshaber der Heeresgruppe B. 3.7.44 1a Nr. 4257/44 g. Kdos. Chefs. Bundesarchiv Militärarchiv (BAMA). RH 19IX/4. See also Tagebuch der Divisions-Begleit-Kompanie der 12. SS-Pz.Div. "H.J." 1943-1945. BAMA. RS 3-12/1.

the movement of our troops on the battlefield is almost completely paralyzed, while the enemy can maneuver freely."[5] The counterattack had to be postponed - to 8 June. At midday, Rommel telephoned Jodl at the Berghof and lodged a formal complaint about the total lack of *Luftwaffe* support in Normandy.

At 0640 hours the next morning (8 June), Heeresgruppe B received an urgent signal from the 7 Army chief of staff. An enemy operational order, Pemsel insisted, "has been recovered from the water. Contents will be transmitted by telegraph."[6]

The captured document, salvaged from the wreckage of an Allied landing boat that had drifted ashore near the mouth of the Vire River, was nothing less than the complete operation plan for the American 7 Army Corps. It clearly delineated the U.S. strategy in the Cotentin Peninsula: breakthrough to the west coast and the capture of Cherbourg from the land side.[7]

Cherbourg was of vital importance to the Allies. It was a major deep water port, and, if captured, would greatly facilitate the landing of men and material in Normandy. Hitler recognized the tremendous value of the port to the German defense. He issued instructions to prepare the fortress city for a protracted siege.[8]

That evening, Rommel again telephoned Jodl. His most pressing task, he instructed the OKW operations chief, was to prevent the two major enemy bridgeheads from linking up. When Jodl declared that there would be no second Allied landing, Rommel emphatically disagreed. Montgomery, he stated confidently, still had an army group in England, under Patton; it would soon undertake a major operation in the Pas-de-Calais.

For the next five weeks, Rommel's fear of a second landing on the Channel Coast would undermine his conduct of the invasion battle. What Rommel did not know was that his anxiety was the product of enemy deception and of duplicity among his own intelligence experts. To distort the strategy of the German High Command, the enemy had concocted an entire army group - the 1 U.S., under the fiery General Patton. This "army group" existed only on paper, but Rommel's intelligence staff was only too eager to swallow the bait. Colonel von Roenne, the chief of German intelligence in the West, had consistently exaggerated the strength of the Allied forces massing in England; now he tacked on Patton's ghost army group to his estimates, complete with 25 battle-worthy divisions. These divisions, he maintained, were being held back for a second invasion. Von Roenne was a member of the anit-Hitler resistance. He was later executed by the Nazis.[9]

[5]Hart, <u>Rommel Papers</u>, pp. 476-77. See also Rommel's Betrachtungen 3.7.44. BAMA. RH 19IX/4.
[6]Milton Schulman, <u>Defeat in the West</u>. (New York: E.P. Dutton and Co., Inc., 1948), pg. 106. Hereafter cited as <u>Defeat</u>.
[7]Hayn, <u>Die Invasion</u>, pg. 48.
[8]see Schramm, <u>KTB des OKW</u>, IV, pg. 313.

To meet Patton's blow, Rommel "was determined to keep 15 Army intact north of the Seine to guard the V-weapon sites and the short road to the Ruhr. One of its divisions (346 Infantry, summoned from Le Havre to the Orne valley) had already begun to cross the Seine on D-Day, but nothing else was to be moved, except a battalion of Tiger tanks and a flak brigade. The [15 Army] tactical reserves, five infantry and two Panzer divisions with 300 tanks, were to stay where they were, idle and useless. 7 Army must deal with the landings in western Normandy from its own resources, strengthened by the five divisions in von Rundstedt's strategic reserve of armor."[10]

During the 8th Bayerlein's Panzer Lehr Division limped into Tilly-sur-Seulles (south of Bayeux), after a harrowing 110 mile approach march from Chartres. The division had begun to move up on the afternoon of the 6th; enemy aircraft had immediately pounced on it. By nightfall Bayerlein had lost 20 to 30 vehicles. After moving all night with only three hour's rest, the division was again blasted from the air. "Around noon," reported Bayerlein, "the situation was terrible. My men were

Destroyed German vehicles on a road leading to the invasion front.

[9]Iving, _The Trail_, pp. 363; 373. As late as 26 June 1944, under the influence of von Roenne's spurious data, Heeresgruppe B was estimating the number of enemy divisions in England at 67, of which 57 were considered fit for action in France. Wochenmeldung Heeresgruppe B. 19.-26.6.44. 1a Nr. 4043/44 g. Kdos. BAMA. RH 19IX/8. See also Anton Staubwasser, "Das Feindbild beim O.dHg.B. 6.6.-24.7.44," B-782. In fact, there were only fifteen divisions in England at the time awaiting transport to Normandy.

[10]Wilmont, _Struggle for Europe_, pp. 294; 296.

calling the main road from Vire to Beny-Bocage a fighter-bomber racecourse. Every vehicle was camouflaged with branches of trees and moved along hedgerows and the fringes of woods.... But by the end of the day I had lost 40 petrol wagons and 90 other vehicles. Five of my tanks were knocked out, as well as 84 half-tracks, prime-movers and self-propelled guns. These were serious losses for a division not yet in action."[11] "The enemy's air superiority," Rommel lamented to Lucie two days later, "has a very grave effect on our movements. There's simply no answer to it."[12]

By June 9 the invasion battle had turned badly against Rommel. In the Caen sector, Dempsey's 2 (British) Army had established a solid bridgehead - at least 22 miles wide and five to ten miles deep.[13] Farther west the Americans had forced the Aure River and expanded their foothold in the Cotentin Peninsula. Rommel had only been able to form a thin defensive screen by committing all his tank units in the front line. His hopes of launching a powerful counterattack to hurl the invaders into the sea had, so far, been dashed.

Rommel surveyed the deteriorating situation with grim resolve. He was determined to prevent the fall of Cherbourg. Early that afternoon he motored to Le Mans to meet with the staff of 7 Army. At 1730 hours the Field Marshal issued the following directive: "The enemy must be prevented at all costs from a) getting the fortress of Cherbourg, and harbor, in his hands. b) establishing the connection between both bridgeheads: that west of the Orne and west of the Vire."[14]

Pemsel's view was that the determined German resistance south of Montebourg would compel the Allies to use airborne forces to effect a quick capture of Cherbourg. Rommel disagreed. OKW had warned the Field Marshal that an enemy landing in Belgium was imminent; thus it had cancelled the transfer of the crack 1 SS Panzer Division from Belgium to Normandy.[15] The High Command, Rommel told the 7 Army Chief, "expects a large landing on the Channel Coast within the next few days, and therefore the enemy will not have more airborne troops available."[16]

The next morning (10 June) Rommel drove to the front to meet again with Dietrich. The skies teemed with enemy aircraft searching for ground targets. Forced to dive for cover nearly 30 times, Rommel drove to the headquarters of Panzer Group West instead. Von Schweppen-

---

[11]Jaggi, "Auswirkungen der alliierten Luftüberlegenheit." pg. 344. Bayerlein himself had had his vehicle shot out from under him, but escaped with only minor injuries. Ritgen, Geschichte der Panzer Lehr Division, pg. 109.

[12]Hart, Rommel Papers, pg. 491.

[13]Wilmont, Struggle for Europe, pg. 297. Schramm, KTB des OKW, IV, pg. 313.

[14]Schulman, Milton, Defeat in the West (New York: E.P. Dutton Co., Inc., 1948), pg. 107.

[15]Schramm, KTB des OKW, IV, pg. 313.

296   [16]Schulman, Defeat in the West, pg. 108.

conversation in November 1942."[32] Rommel was referring to the discussion he had had with Lucie following the collapse of the Afrikakorps at El Alamein. The war was lost is what he had told her then, and he had concluded that "an attempt would have to be made as soon as possible to arrive at a compromise peace."[33]

The next day, 16 June, Rommel met with General Fahrnbacher (84 Corps commander, replacing General Marcks) and General Meindl (commander, 2 Parachute Corps). He then stopped briefly at Marcks' grave site and visited Dollmann in Le Mans. When Rommel returned to La Roche-Guyon that afternoon, he received an unexpected call from the High Command. Hitler had finally consented to the requests of Rommel and von Rundstedt for a meeting. The field marshals, along with their chiefs of staff, were to meet the Führer at his "Wolfsschlucht 2" command post at Margival (north of Soissons) at 0900 on the 17th.[34]

Hitler and his staff departed for Margival late on the 16th, flying to Metz in four Focke Wulf Condor aircraft.[35] Security precautions for the Führer were elaborate. To prevent a mishap, Luftwaffe fighter units were grounded while Hitler was in the air. Flak units along the route were ordered to stand down. But the Luftwaffe was out in force the next morning, to provide air cover as Hitler covered the last stretch of the way by car. When Rommel and von Rundstedt arrived at the hermetically-sealed complex, Hitler was nervous and still tired from his trip. As the conference began he crouched on his stool and fumbled impatiently with his glasses and colored pencils. The Führer was in a bad mood. He was displeased that the enemy invasion had succeeded and accused the field marshals of incompetence. He then turned to the problem of Cherbourg, insisting that the fortress be held "at all cost."[36]

Von Rundstedt spoke only briefly, then yielded to Rommel. Rommel declared that the one-sided struggle in Normandy was hopeless. The troops were fighting "to the last breath" but were being decimated by the crushing enemy superiority in the air, on land and in the sea. He pointed out the senselessness of holding fortresses to the last man and

---

[32]Ibid., pp. 491-92.
[33]Ibid., pg. 492.
[34]The "FHQU Wolfschlucht 2" had been built in 1940 to serve as Hitler's command post for the planned invasion of England. 17 June 1944, however, was the first and only time Hitler would ever set foot in the complex, which included many well-camouflaged bunkers. The site had been chosen primarily because the nearby railroad tunnel northeast of Soissons could easily conceal Hitler's special train. Hans Speidel, "Die Besprechung bei Adolf Hitler in Margival am 17.6. pg. 73. In: "Die Schlacht in der Normandie 1944. Führung Gedanken Feldmarschall Rommels." C-017 Hereafter cited as "Besprechung bei Hitler."
[35]According to Speidel, Hitler was accompanied by Jodl, Buhle, Schmundt, Scherff, Voss, von Puttkammer and von Below. Speidel, "Besprechung bei Hitler," pp. 73-74, C-017.
[36]At 1000 hours Speidel telephoned the château and informed von Tempelhoff that "the fortress Cherbourg must be held at all cost." KTB Heeresgruppe B. BAMA. RH 19IX/84.

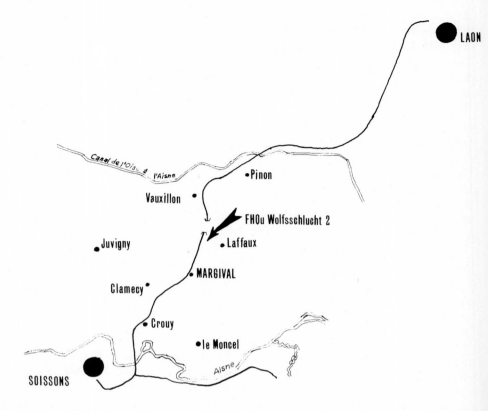

LAON

Canal de l'Ois... à l'Aisne

Pinon

Vauxillon

FHQu Wolfsschlucht 2

Juvigny • Laffaux

MARGIVAL

Clamecy

Crouy

le Moncel

Aisne

SOISSONS

repeated his demand for freedom of manouver in the West. First class reinforcements - troops, tanks, air cover and naval support - were desperately needed, as was a Führer directive to deal with the imminent German collapse of the Cotentin Peninsula.

Von Rundstedt seconded Rommel's demands, but it was all in vain. Once again Hitler fell back on his wonder weapons - the flying bombs and the new jet fighters. Then he began to ramble. "The conference upon which the two field marshals had set so much hope seemed to be tailing away in an irrelevent monologue."[37] Rommel and von Rundstedt requested that the V-weapons be employed against the Allied beachheads. Hitler refused. Heinemann supported Hitler's decision: the V-1 guidance system was too inaccurate, thus the weapon would pose a threat to the German troops in Normandy.

When air raid sirens signalled the approach of enemy aircraft, the conference was suspended. Hitler, Schmundt, the two field marshals and their chiefs of staff gathered in the air raid shelter. Rommel "seized the opportunity to pass from the military to the political situation." He predicted the Wehrmacht's collapse on all fronts and emphasized Germany's complete political isolation. The time had come, he told Hitler,

---

[37]Speidel, "Besprechung bei Hitler," pp. 73-74, C-017. See also Speidel, _We Defended Normandy_, pg. 108.

to bring the war to an end. Rommel's words elicited a sharp rebuke from his Führer: "That has nothing to do with you," Hitler snapped back, "your business is to resist the invasion."[38]

The Margival conference increased Rommel's alienation from Hitler.[39] The chasm between the two men was now so wide that Rommel would never again trust the Nazi dictator.

Before Rommel and Speidel began the drive back to La Roche-Guyon, they learned that Hitler was planning a visit to their headquarters in the next few days - to hear first-hand reports from the invasion front. The next day Speidel spoke with Blumentritt but was told that Hitler had cancelled the visit. A few hours after the Margival Conference a flying bomb with a defective steering mechanism had crashed directly above Hitler's bunker. Badly shaken, the Führer had departed at once for Berchtesgaden.

Back at the château, Rommel strolled the grounds with Ruge. He was in a contemplative mood. German losses since 6 June had mounted steadily; 26,000 men were killed, wounded or missing, including a corps and five division commanders. Material losses were enormous. Rommel's troops had destroyed over 500 enemy tanks and 1,000 enemy planes,[40] but the Allies could easily replace these losses. And although Montgomery had made little progress at Caen or St. Lô, and had even been pushed back at Caumont, the Americans had been able to sever the Cotentin Peninsula and to isolate Cherbourg.[41] Anticipating the enemy breakthrough, Rommel had already issued secret instructions to General Stegman to begin extricating his 77 Infantry Division southward from the peninsula. There was no point, Rommel thought, in needlessly sacrificing the division in a forlorn battle. In this manner he disobeyed Hitler's explicit order to defend Cherbourg with all available means to the bitter end. OKW would launch an investigation when it learned of the incident.

In the peninsula itself, Rommel had chosen General von Schlieben as the Cherbourg fortress commander, with orders to begin a fighting withdrawal into the fortified landfront defending the port, retiring only under enemy pressure and taking care not to be outflanked. Hitler demanded that von Schlieben "defend the fortress like Gneisenau had once defended Kolberg" (against Napoleon).[42] But to conduct his defense, Hitler's "Gneisenau" had only the battered remains of three divisions; he was expected to hold out until mid-July.

---

[38]Ibid., pg. 78, C-017.

[39]Ibid., pg. 79.

[40]Wochenmeldung Heeresgruppe B. 12.-19.6.44. 1a Nr. 3723/44 g. K. BAMA. RH 19IX/8.

[41]On 18 June the Americans reached the west coast of the Cotentin at Barneville. KTB Heeresgruppe B. BAMA. RH 19IX/84.

[42]Fernschreiben vom 21.6., 18.30 Uhr an Heeresgruppe B. O.B. West, 1a Nr. 437/44 g. Kdos.Chefs. BAMA. RH 19IX/7.

The American offensive in the Cotentin, led by the brilliant, quick-hitting General "Joe" Collins, quickly disrupted German planning. To the south Stegman's 77 Infantry Division was plastered by Allied aircraft and artillery. Only 1,400 men escaped encirclement, having lost most of their heavy weapons.[43] Stegman himself was killed by an enemy fighter-bomber. Farther north Collins sliced through the brittle German defenses; by the evening of 21 June, his troops had "drawn up right against the Cherbourg fortress" and were poised for a final assault.

The next day, the 22nd, Rommel inspected the front of 15 Army. He observed the V-1 launchings and was "thrilled by the spectacle of the little stubby aircraft streaking low across the sky, trailing a jet of flame behind them." The V-1 sites, Rommel thought, were reason enough for the enemy to make a second landing here. "Patton's 'army group,' according to the new reports from Colonel von Roenne, was evidently as large as Montgomery's. Rommel was waiting for Patton - waiting, waiting, totally disoriented by "Fortitude" [code name for the Allied deception]), so obsessed by a potential threat from a purely theoretical army group that he underestimated the very real and present threat to France in Normandy."[44]

But the flying bombs could hardly bring relief to Rommel's hard-pressed invasion front. "Militarily things aren't at all good," he wrote Lucie on the 23rd. "Even Cherbourg will not be able to hold out for long in these circumstances. We must be prepared for grave events."[45]

A terrific storm had rocked the Channel on the 19th. It had destroyed the American artificial harbor and pier facilities at the invasion beaches beyond repair. Thus the speedy capture of Cherbourg became more important than ever for the Allies. Enemy air attacks intensified over the fortress, spraying the defenders with bombs. By 23 June the Americans had pierced von Schlieben's landfront and were battling it out among the German artillery positions.[46] Two days before, a nervous Hitler had lectured the unfortunate von Schlieben that "even if worst comes to worst, it is your duty to defend the last bunker and leave to the enemy not a harbor but a field of ruins. . . . The German people and the entire world are watching your fight; on it depends the conduct and success of the operations to smash the beachheads, and the honor of the German Wehrmacht and of your own name."[47]

But von Schlieben was in desperate need of reinforcements. His troops, mostly overage, untrained and showing signs of "bunker paralysis" (verbunkert), were exhausted in "body and spirit."[48] Cher-

---

[43]KTB Heeresgruppe B. BAMA. RH 19IX/84.

[44]Irving, The Trail, pp. 389-90.

[45]Hart, Rommel Papers, pg. 492.

[46]KTB Heeresgruppe B. BAMA. RH 19IX/84. Schramm, KTB des OKW, IV, pp. 318-19.

[47]Fernschreiben vom 21.6., 18.30 Uhr an Heeresgruppe B. O.B. West, 1a Nr. 437/44 g. Kdos. Chefs. BAMA. RH 19IX/7.

[48]KTB Heeresgruppe B. BAMA. RH 19IX/84.

bourg, Rommel wrote Lucie on the 24th, "can hardly hold out for long despite the heroic struggle of its defenders. Given a sufficient weight of bombs and heavy shells, the enemy can make any place ripe for assault. The tragedy is that we can't reply in the same terms."[49]

Von Schlieben, meanwhile, attempted to bolster flagging morale by handing out Iron Crosses flown into the embattled fortress at his request. But that afternoon he signalled Rommel that further sacrifice was useless. Rommel shot back a carefully worded reply: "You will continued to fight to the last cartridge in accordance with the Führer's order."[50] Rommel and von Rundstedt both avoided any "fight to the last man" cliche.

Allied naval forces joined the siege on 25 June, sailing within range of the port to let loose their salvos, but still beyond the reach of the fortress artillery. On the land side, Collins began the assault on Fort du Roule, "a massive stronghold on the crest of the precipitous bluff which towers above the city."[51] The fort fell quickly. Its final signal was a brief one: "Documents burned, codes destroyed." By the evening of the 26th, all organized resistance in Cherbourg had flickered out. When von Schlieben surrendered he refused to make a general surrender of the fortress. Thus isolated pockets of defenders would fight on for days, including a group of some 6,000 men on the Cap de la Hague.

General Karl-Wilhelm von Schlieben at the time of his surrender.

George Petersen

---

[49]Hart, _Rommel Papers_, pg. 493.
[50]_KTB Heeresgruppe B_. BAMA. RH 19IX/84. KTB O.B. West. BAMA. RH 19IV/43.
[51]Wilmont, _Struggle for Europe_, pg. 330.

On 20 June Hitler had ordered Rommel to prepare a powerful offensive between Caumont and St.Lô. The SS Panzer divisions enroute from Poland to the invasion front - 9 and 10 SS divisions of 2 SS Panzer Corps - were to form the spearhead of the attack; their goal was "to cleave a corridor to Bayeau and the coast, isolate the British and 'Dunkirk' them."[52] Montgomery, however, frustrated the Führer's plan by attacking first. Early on 25 June British tanks and infantry struck southwest of Caen, at the inner flanks of Panzer Lehr and 12 SS Panzer Divisions. By 0700 the fog had lifted and the enemy air forces were swarming over the battlefield, bombing and strafing anything that moved and making any reinforcement of the creaking German front impossible during the daylight hours.

Rommel spent the day at his headquarters, trying to keep control of the surging battle. The reports from the front were not encouraging. Enemy tanks had broken through on both sides of Tilly sur Seulles, to a depth of one to two miles.[53] Sepp Dietrich, whose 1 SS Panzer Corps was defending Caen, reported that his already burned-out divisions could no longer seal off the enemy breakthrough. He cried for reinforcements.[54] Rommel ordered elements of 1 SS Panzer Division to be hurled into the gap.

Under constant threat of attack from the air, Tigers from the 1 SS Panzer Division move towards the invasion front.

[52]*Ibid.*, pg. 334. Schramm, *KTB des OKW*, IV, pp. 317-18.
[53]*KTB Heeresgruppe B*. BAMA. RH 19IX/84. KTB O.B. West. BAMA. RH 19IV/43.

As the fighting raged Rommel received visits from numerous high-ranking officers, including Field Marshal Sperrle of the *Luftwaffe*. A Colonel Eberhard Finckh, who had just taken over as von Rundstedt's new quartermaster general, reported to Heeresgruppe B. Finckh was a member of the anti-Hitler group; Speidel got him an interview with Rommel at once. The Colonel declared that an assassination attempt against Hitler was in the wings. Visibly shaken by the news, Rommel refused to play any part in the affair. The battles in Normandy, moreover, had reached a critical stage and demanded the Field Marshal's undivided attention.

The British 8 Corps began its big offensive the next day - 26 June. It smashed head on into the 12 SS Panzer Division (Hitler Jugend). The boys of the Hitler Jugend Division (average age 18) had turned the sleepy French hamlets west of Caen into death traps for the enemy; they fought like tigers even when surrounded or cut off.[55] The division

Young members of the 12 SS Panzer Division in the outskirts of Caen.

---

[54]*The day before Dietrich had reported the casualities of his tank divisions to Heeresgruppe B: 21 Panzer, 84 officers, 2,513 men; 12 SS Panzer, 76 officers, 2,474 men; Panzer Lehr, 78 officers, 2,286 men. "The divisions," he concluded, "are in desperate need of infantry. The Panzer Lehr has practically burnt itself out." BAMA. RH 19IX/3. fol. 27.*

[55]*Gefechtsbericht zum 26. Juni 1944, SS Pz.Pi.Btl. 12. In: Records 12 SS Panzer Division. Microcopy T-354, 154, #3797709-714.*

The 12 SS Panzer Division near Caen. (below) The officer in the lower left portion of the photo is SS-Obersturmbannführer Bernhard Krause, commander of SS-Pz.Gren.Rgt.26.

suffered indescribable losses but brought the British thrust to a temporary halt.[56] Dietrich and Dollmann (7 Army commander) screamed for reinforcements. They enjoined Rommel to throw the just-arriving 2 SS Panzer Corps (Paul Hausser) into the breech. At first Rommel resisted their pleas; he still hoped to use Hausser's corps for the big offensive to Bayeux. But the increasing enemy pressure west of Caen forced him to relent. "Everything that Hausser can scrape together," he instructed Dollmann, "must be thrown into the fight." At that moment, however, only one of Hausser's two high-grade tank divisions had reached the battlefront; the other (10 SS Panzer) was still far back - delayed by enemy air attacks. Thus any counterattack, as Rommel noted the next day, could not begin before the 29th.[57] In the meantime General Dollmann, already shaken by Hitler's wrath over the loss of Cherbourg, committed suicide.[58]

Montgomery continued his hammer blows on the 27th and 28th. His troops seized intact one of the Odon River crossings; elements of the 11 (British) Tank Division quickly established a foothold south of the river, threatening Caen with envelopment. Von Rundstedt acted later that day, signalling the High Command that "if the German troops [facing the British between the Orne and the Vire] were not soon to be encircled, commanders should 'now' be given freedom to withdraw to a more favorable line. In conjunction with Field Marshal Rommel," he continued, "I therefore ask for a free hand to order extensive adjustments of the front . . . and for a corresponding directive."[59] Hitler reacted swiftly - he called a meeting with the two field marshals.

On the evening of 28 June, Rommel received a call from Blumentritt. Hitler, he said, had summoned von Rundstedt and Rommel to Berchtesgaden for a conference to take place the next day. Both men left for the conference on the 28th. For von Rundstedt, the drive from Paris to Hitler's mountain retreat was a gruelling one. He needed 18 hours to get there. Forbidden to fly, Rommel also made the trip by car, but stopped at Ulm that night to see his family. Von Rundstedt arrived at Berchtesgaden an exhausted man, but was compelled to wait another six hours before he could see the Führer. He told Keitel "that they need not be surprised up 'above' if he too, and old and sick man, fell dead one day, like Colonel General Dollmann."[60]

---

[56]The 12 SS Panzer Division, commanded by Kurt Meyer, had begun the 26th with 94 "runners" (tanks ready for action). BAMA. RH 19IX/3. fol. 34. By the next day, the division had been reduced to 56 runners. BAMA. RH 10/321. On 26 June only 53 of the Panzer Lehr's original 190 tanks were ready for action. BAMA. RH 19IX/3. fol. 40.

[57]KTB Heeresgruppe B. BAMA. RH 19IX/84.

[58]See Irving, The Trail, pp. 394-95. Paul Hausser took over as 7 Army commander in chief.

[59]Ellis, Battle for Normandy, pg. 296. Also KTB O.B. West. BAMA. RH 19IV/43.

[60]Zimmermann, "O.B.West," B-308, pg. 116. Von Rundstedt was unaware that Dollmann had committed suicide.

Finally, around 1800 hours, Hitler received his generals. Rommel opened the conference. "Mein Führer," he proceeded bluntly, "I am here as commander of Heeresgruppe B. I think it is high time that I - on behalf of the German people to whom I am also answerable - tell you the situation in the West. I should like to begin with our political situation. The entire world is arrayed now against Germany, and this balance of strength . . ."[61] Hitler interrupted and admonished the brave Field Marshal to remain within the realm of military matters. Then Hitler began one of his endless monologues. He demanded that the front line in the West remain where it was. There could be no question of withdrawals. "New weapons," he exclaimed, "are coming, new fighter planes, more troops."[62] Rommel and von Rundstedt tried to present their views on the Normandy battle, which was rapidly nearing collapse. Finding this impossible, Rommel asked Hitler how he imagined the war could still be won. The question stung Hitler. He dismissed Rommel from the room and finished the conference without him, announcing for the record that, "the enemy's overpowering air superiority and his very effective naval artillery limit the possibilities of a large scale attack on our part. . . . We must not allow mobile warfare to develop, since the enemy surpasses us by far in mobility due to his air superiority and his superabundance of motor vehicles and fuel. Therefore, everything depends on containing him in his bridgehead by building up a front to block it off, and then on fighting a war of attrition to wear him down and force him back, employing every method of guerrilla warfare."[63]

Bundesarchiv

This supply train, carrying "Panther" tanks begins its dangerous trip towards the Normandy front.

---

[61]Irving, <u>The Trail</u>, pg. 398.
[62]Zimmermann, "O.B.West," B-308, pg. 116.
[63]Lagevorträge des Oberbefehlshabers der Kriegsmarine vor Hitler 1939-1945. Herausgegeben von Gerhard Wagner. (München: J.F. Lehmanns Verlag, 1972), pg. 592.

Rommel departed Berchtesgaden at 2115 hours on the 29th, but would not arrive at La Roche-Guyon until almost midnight the next day. During his absence the British had struck again. Supported by naval gun fire, generous amounts of artillery and the ubiquitous air forces, Montgomery's armored spearheads had captured the strategically located Hill 112,[64] which permitted an unobstructed view of the entire area west of Caen. That afternoon (29 June) von Schweppenburg, back in command of Panzergruppe West, ordered the long-delayed armored counterattack to get underway. "This is our one big chance," Geyr exclaimed later that night.[65] But von Rundstedt was not so optimistic. He warned OKW that the British successes pointed to the imminent collapse of the Normandy front. Keitel telephoned him later and queried, "What shall we do? 'Make peace, you fools,' exploded Rundstedt. 'What else can you do?' "[66]

Von Schweppenburg's tank attack recaptured Hill 112 but died in the ferocious fire of the Allied naval guns.[67] Geyr now submitted a candid report to his superiors at 7 Army. In it, he recommended the immediate withdrawal from the Caen bridgehead, and the occupation of a new line outside of the range of the enemy's devastating naval gun fire.[68] His memorandum was forwarded to Heeresgruppe B and O.B. West for consideration. Late that evening (30 June) Speidel approved Geyr's recommendations and authorized him to begin the evacuation. But when Rommel returned to the château, he quickly countermanded Speidel's order. Ever since the El Alamein debacle, Rommel's faith in his Führer had steadily declined. But Hitler's personal magnetism could still compel Rommel to toe the line: the Field Marshal returned to France determined to keep Caen in his grip at all costs - as the Führer had insisted. The next day he drove out to Geyr's headquarters. The tank divisions, he told von Schweppenburg, were to remain where they were - in the main battle line. He repeated Hitler's own argument that Caen was the pivot (Angelpunkt) of an enemy advance on Paris. "It is essential," Rommel concluded, "that we push more and more forces up to the city."[69]

Von Rundstedt, however, had passed on Geyr's memorandum to OKW with his own covering letter, requesting a free hand to pull his

[64]Meyer, "12. SS Panzer Division," P-164, pg. 44.

[65]The attack began at 1430 hours. KTB Panzergruppe West. BAMA. Pz. AOK 5/63181/1.

[66]Toland, Hitler, pg. 789.

[67]KTB Panzergruppe West. BAMA. Pz. AOK 5/63181/1. According to German accounts, the unprecedented Allied artillery and naval fire resembled the terrific bombardments of the First World War. Lagebericht der 9. SS-Pz.Div. "Hohenstaufen" für die Zeit vom 29.6.1944 12.00 Uhr bis 2.7.1944 19.00 Uhr. BAMA. RS 3-9/2.

[68]A copy of Geyr's memorandum exists among the records of 7 Army. BAMA. AOK 7/57350/2.

[69]Geheim Aktennotiz! Besprechung zwischen Oberbefehlshaber H.G.B. Generalfeldmarschall Rommel und Oberbefehlshaber Panzergruppe West am 1.7.44. BAMA. Pz.AOK 5/63181/4.

divisions from the Caen pocket. Hitler fumed. "The present positions," the Führer decreed, "are to be held. Any further breakthrough by the enemy will be prevented by tenacious defense or by local counterattacks." Von Rundstedt immediately cancelled the planned withdrawal.

Hitler had had a belly full of his generals' complaints. He ordered von Rundstedt's dismissal. Thus on "2 July Hitler's adjutant [Lieutenant Colonel Borgman] entered the O.B. West command post, and, in the Führer's name, presented von Rundstedt with the Oak Leaves to the Knight's Cross together with a polite hand-written note from Hitler relieving the Field Marshal of his command on grounds of age and health."[70] The next day the enraged dictator sent von Schweppenburg packing as well. As for Rommel, he had never waivered in his resolve to keep hold of Caen, thus he was spared Hitler's fury.

By the beginning of July, Montgomery's offensive had ground to a halt. Rommel had kept his front intact, but only by yielding ground and throwing in his last tank reserves. The enemy, moreover, now possessed a bulging bridgehead west and south of Caen, out of which he could threaten Rommel's line with envelopment.

**General Field Marshal
Günther von Kluge**

[70]Zimmermann, "O.B.West," B-308, pg. 116.

On 2 July Rommel was in Paris, attending Dollmann's funeral, then he returned to La Roche-Guyon. He was shocked and disappointed to learn that Field Marshal von Kluge had replaced von Rundstedt; he had expected the posting himself.

Von Kluge drove out to La Roche-Guyon on the 3rd. His meeting with Rommel was less than cordial. A tough, capable veteran of the Russian front, von Kluge informed Rommel that he no longer had Hitler's complete confidence, and accused him of not obeying orders. "Rommel, you must obey unconditionally from now on," he warned. "It is good advice that I am giving you."[71] An angry Rommel riposted that von Kluge should have a good look at the situation before making such statements. The meeting became so heated that Speidel and von Tempelhoff were ordered from the room. The following day Rommel dispatched a terse note to von Kluge, along with a copy of the memorandum he had already submitted to Hitler laying out in some detail the reasons for the success of the Allied invasion:

> H.Q. 5 July 1944
> To C. in C. West
> Herr Generalfeldmarschall von Kluge
> I send you enclosed my comments on military events
> in Normandy to date.
> The rebuke which you leveled at me at the beginning
> of your visit, in the presence of my Chief of Staff and
> 1a, to the effect that I, too, 'will now have to get ac-
> customed to carrying out orders,' has deeply woun-
> ded me. I request you to notify me what grounds you
> have for making such an accusation.
> (signed) Rommel
Generalfeldmarschall[72]

Von Kluge took Rommel's advice and conducted a two-day tour of the tottering German front. When he returned to Rommel's château a few days later, he "took back all his reproaches, excusing his behavior on grounds of false information that Hitler and Keitel had given him."[73] He would refrain, he said, from meddling in the internal affairs of Heeresgruppe B.

The haughty von Schweppenburg had also had a change of heart. Shortly after his removal from the command of Panzergruppe West, he had written to Rommel:

> Sir,
> Allow me to add some words to my official reporting-
> off. The recent fighting, more difficult than I have

---

[71]Speidel, <u>We Defended Normandy</u>, pg. 121.
[72]Hart, <u>Rommel Papers</u>, pg. 481. Rommel's memorandum can be found among the records of Heeresgruppe B. BAMA. RH 19IX/4.
[73]Speidel, <u>We Defended Normandy</u>, pg. 122.

ever experienced, wrought an inner change in me. . . . Your soldierly qualities and experience transformed my forced obedience to a different and better one. I feel I may ask you, Herr Field Marshal, to accept my thanks for the confidence you placed in me and my men in the brief, difficult days of battle we experienced together. As I regard my military activities as finished, I think I can say this without the danger of misinterpretation.

Your obedient servant
Sir
Baron von Geyr[74]

With the relief of von Schweppenburg, Rommel was the sole survivor among the original Normandy commanders. His job was again complicated by the fear of an Allied landing on the Channel Coast. His intelligence experts warned him that Patton's army group could burst

These Panzer reinforcements are held in reserve in anticipation of a second invasion front.

314

[74]*Letter, F. Ruge to W.M. James, Jr., April 1951, personal copy.*

ashore at any moment. As the records of Heeresgruppe B indicate, Rommel still took these warnings seriously.[75] Even though the invasion front was starving for reinforcements, he ordered Eberbach (Geyr's replacement) to keep two tank divisions on stand-by - ready to move into any new beachhead and smash Patton's divisions the moment they landed.

The serious nature of the Normandy battles is evident in the faces of Rommel and his staff. To his right is paratroop General Meindl.

[75]Wochenmeldung Heeresgruppe B vom 3.7.-9.7.44. 1a Nr. 4595/44 g. Kdos. BAMA. RH 19IX/8.

Late on 7 July the British unleashed another savage stroke against Caen. Montgomery's field artillery and naval guns pummeled the German defenders on the fringe of the city with some 80,000 shells. Then the R.A.F. bombers came, hundreds of them; they rained over 2,500 tons of bombs into the dying city.[76] At 0420 the next morning, the British armor thundered forward, cutting through the 16 *Luftwaffe* Field Division like butter. The survivors of Meyer's Hitler Jugend Division (12 SS Panzer) again put up a terrific struggle, destroying 103 enemy tanks.[77] But soon Montgomery's tanks had climbed atop the important patch of

German infantrymen retreat from the destroyed city of Caen.

high ground directly north of Caen; by the next morning they were rumbling into the city itself.[78] To avoid encirclement, Rommel's troops withdrew to the east bank of the Orne (the river which runs through the city). The hotly-contested Caen was finally in British hands.

Speidel, meanwhile, had slipped away to Paris to confer with von Stülpnagel. The meeting skirted topics far removed from the fighting in Normandy. As a result of the conference, Dr. Caesar von Hofacker

---

[76]*KTB O.B.West. BAMA. RH 19IV/44.* See also E. Wehrli, "Tactische Bombenteppiche," pp. 445-46. In: *Allgemeine Schweizerische Militärzeitschrift. Jg. 130. 1964. Nr. 7.*

[77]*Wochenmeldung, Heeresgruppe B. 1a Nr. 4595/44 g. Kdos. BAMA. RH 19IX/8.*
[78]*Tagebuch der Divisions-Begleit-Kompanie der 12.SS-Pz.Div. "H.J." 1943-1945. BAMA. RS 3-12/1.*

visited Rommel at his headquarters on the 9th, accompanied by Dr. Max Horst. Von Hofacker was a cousin of Stauffenburg's (the man entrusted with the task of killing Hitler) and a member of von Stülpnagel's staff. The two emissaries had brought a secret memorandum. It outlined von Stülpnagel's views on the military and political situation and ended "with an appeal to [Rommel] to take independent action at once to end the war."[79] After Rommel had read the document, von Hofacker asked him how long the Wehrmacht could hold out in the West. "At the most fourteen days to three weeks," the Field Marshal replied, "then the breakthrough may be expected. We have nothing more to throw in."[80]

Von Kluge paid a visit to La Roche-Guyon on the 12th. The Prussian Field Marshal had long since wavered in his loyalty to the Führer. He asked Rommel to issue a statement making clear "how much longer, in view of the decreasing fighting power and the complete lack of reserves, the invasion front could be held."[81] Rommel said that he would contact his army commanders and put the question to them. He then suggested that their views be compiled into a report and presented to Hitler, along with an ultimatum.

Rommel spent the next few days touring the battlefield and talking to his generals. Though the British offensive had tapered off, the Americans had resumed their push southward from the Cotentin Peninsula. For the most part Rommel's troops still fought magnificently. A handful of gritty German paratroopers clung desperately to the important St.Lô crossroads. West of St.Lô the exhausted grenadiers of Bayerlein's Panzer Lehr Division (recently transferred from Tilly sur Seulles) dug in around their few remaining tanks and successfully smashed every enemy attack.[82] But the defenders were taking terrific punishment - some divisions, in fact, had been reduced to a fighting strength of two weak battalions. After five weeks of bitter combat, Rommel's formations were literally melting away. Post invasion losses had risen to well over 80,000 men, but less than 6,000 replacements had reached the front.[83] So far, the Panzer divisions had received practically no replacement armor. A catastrophe of immense proportions loomed over the battlefront. Many German soldiers had begun to ask when the war would end.

By the morning of the 15th, Speidel had prepared a dramatic document on the crisis in Normandy for Rommel to sign. It predicted the complete collapse of the front in a short time. Rommel attached his signature to the report and sent it to von Kluge, who was to relay it on to the Führer. Thus Rommel had taken the final, desperate step: he had issued his ultimatum to Hitler. To Speidel he stated bluntly, "I have

[79]Speidel, We Defended Normandy, pg. 123.
[80]Ibid.
[81]Hans Speidel, "The Battle for Normandy 1944," MS C-017, pg. 94.
[82]See Ritgen, Geschichte der Panzer Lehr Division, pp. 155-61.
[83]KTB O.B.West. BAMA. RH 19IV/44.

Rommel visits a rear portion of the front where he is greeted by General Meindl, commander of 2 Parachute Corps, and General d. W-SS Paul Hausser, commander of 2 SS-Panzer Corps who would shortly assume command of 7 Army upon the death of General Dollmann.

Hausser, Rommel and Parachute General Meindl.

Bundesarchiv

Bundesarchiv

319

WH

given [Hitler his] last chance. If he does not take it, we will act."[84] What Rommel had in mind can be gleaned from a conversation he had with the chief operations officer of 17 *Luftwaffe* Field Division (in 15 Army sector) the next day. If the Führer did not see reason, Rommel was ready to surrender the western front to Montgomery. "Only one thing matters now," he admitted openly, "the British and Americans must get to Berlin before the Russians do!"[85]

Rommel visited the front once again on the 15th, stopping at the headquarters of 346 Infantry Division. Lang recorded most of the comments that day, and noted that on this division's sector it had been quiet the last few days. Huge convoys of enemy trucks, however, had been observed rolling south from Riva Bella. The division commander informed Rommel that weapons and ammunition were running short. One thousand men had already arrived as replacements, but 800 more were needed. Rommel then drove out to the 16 *Luftwaffe* Field Division. It was still licking its wounds from the battle for Caen and had suffered an alarming increase in deserters. All its antitank guns had been destroyed. Before returning to La Roche-Guyon, Rommel looked up Feuchtinger's 21 Panzer Division. The division, he learned, was down to 47 tanks. The 16th was a quieter day, with fewer inspection trips. An important meeting with Dietrich was scheduled for the next day; it would be the last act of Rommel's military career.[86]

[84]Speidel, <u>We Defended Normandy</u>, pg. 127. See Appendix VI for the text of Rommel's "ultimatum."

[85]Irving, <u>The Trail</u>, pp. 413-14.

[86]United States National Archives, Report: Trip of the O.B. H.Gr. B to 346 Inf. Div., 16 LW F.D. and 21 Pz.Div., 15 July 1944, pg. 1.

The Strafing Incident - 17 July 1944

It took Rommel some six hours to reach the combat positions of 277 Infantry Division, which were located in the 1 SS Panzer Corps sector. He confered with the division commander and then motored to the headquarters of 276 Infantry Division (47 Panzer Corps). Shortly thereafter he visited with Dietrich (commander 1 SS Panzer Corps) in St. Pierre-sur-Dives.

As Rommel prepared to return to La Roche-Guyon, Dietrich warned him of the threat from the Allied air forces. The dusty roads were making it easy for enemy aircraft to detect traffic; Dietrich recommended

Rommel and Dietrich shortly before the strafing incident.

321

that Rommel make the journey in "a more manoeuverable [sic] Volkswagen jeep because of the fighter bombers."[1] Though Rommel was fully cognizant of the dangers (Bayerlein had already had six cars shot out from under him in Normandy), he elected to use his own Horch staff car. Rommel, Lang, Major Neuhaus, the driver Daniel and Holke (acting as aircraft lookout) started back to the château around 1600 hours. Allied air activity had increased significantly since midday. Rommel and his party could see twisted, burned-out vehicles along the roads; several times they were forced to detour onto "second-class roads" to avoid the fighter bombers. Around 1730 they reached the outskirts of Livarot. Swarms of Jabos blanketed the town, thus Rommel chose to by-pass it. He ordered Daniel to turn onto a covered secondary road (now D155) which led to the main highway between Livarot and Vimoutiers (N179). When they reached N179 they "saw eight enemy Jabos over Livarot, which, as was determined later, had been watching and strafing traffic on the roads leading to Livarot for about four hours. Since we believed that we had not been spotted by the enemy planes," Lang reported later, "the trip was continued on the direct route from Livarot to Vimoutiers."[2]

As the car approached the top of a small rise halfway between the secondary road to Lisores and the Usine Laniel access road, Holke "reported that two planes had turned in the direction of the road." Rommel instructed Daniel to "drive at highest speed to reach a park road turning to the right approximately 300 meters away" (the Usine Laniel driveway). Before they could reach cover, however, the lead plane had closed the gap to 500 meters and started firing. "At this moment Field Marshal Rommel looked back. The strafing plane unloosed [a burst of] high-explosive shells. Rommel was hit in the face by glass splinters and received a blow against the left temple and cheek bone, which resulted in a triple fracture of the skull and immediate un-

---

[1]Carell, Invasion, pg. 299. In Brown, Bodyguard of Lies, Rommel's staff car is incorrectly identified as a six-wheeled Mercedes.

[2]The story of the accident is based almost entirely on Captain Lang's report found in the Rommel Collection, T-84, 277, #000067, entitled "Bericht über die Verwundung des Oberbefehlshabers der Heeresgruppe B, Generalfeldmarschall Rommel, durch Tieffliegerangriff am 17.7"

Irony played its part in the accident; the nearest farm was named Foy-de-Montgomery.

The O.S.S. received its first report on the accident in April 1945 when an account was given to them by PW KP/221861 Kreitmeier, HQ Grenadier Regiment 1052, who had been captured at Lackhausen-Wesel on 24 March 1945. According to this report, Office of Strategic Services Reports, No. CID 128345; "Rommel's Accident," (hereafter cited as O.S.S. Report on Rommel's Accident), "the PW heard that Rommel took over the Weichs Armeegruppe in Austria in June '43 and went with it to Garda on Lake Garda (Italy). In December 1943 Rommel went by special train on a tour of inspection to Denmark, and from there to Fontainbleau where the PW joined Rommel's staff as a driver. The PW stated that he drove Rommel on a few occasions. On the occasion of Rommel's fatal accident , PW, who was a driver in one of the escort cars, was one of the first on the scene. PW is a Catholic, intelligent and willing talker. The information

consciousness. One shell exploded on Major Neuhaus' holster, which was on his back, resulting in a fracture of the pelvic bone."

Daniel received severe injuries to his left arm and shoulder and immediately lost control of the car (he was probably unconscious). The Horch plunged down the hill, "hit a tree stump on the right side of the road and then bounded at a sharp angle to the left side of the road and into a ditch." Rommel, still unconscious, was hurled from the car and into the road (some 20 meters behind the car)."Lang and Holke jumped out of the car and sought cover on the right side of the road. At this moment the second plane flew over the site of the accident and showered us with another round of shellfire."[3]

Lang and Holke carried Rommel to cover near the Usine Laniel gatekeeper's lodge - just a few meters away. Alain Roudeix, a Frenchman who had been working closeby repairing fences, had witnessed the attack. As he reached the entrance to the Usine Laniel he was asked for the location of the nearest hospital. He told Lang that "the nearest town, Vimoutiers, only two kilometers away did not have a hospital and suggested a pharmacy at Livarot, eight kilometers in the opposite direction."[4] Rommel was still unconscious and "covered with blood. He was bleeding from many wounds in the face and especially from the eye and mouth. The left temple, which seemed to be smashed, was facing upwards." It took Lang and Holke nearly 45 minutes to find another vehicle to take the wounded to Vimoutiers; the Allied fighters had slowed German vehicular traffic to a snail's pace.

Rommel and the other wounded were brought to the Vimoutiers pharmacy. Marcel Lescene, a local pharmacist, treated the Field Marshal. He administered two injections of etherated camphor, which probably saved Rommel's life.

When Lang learned that there was a Luftwaffe hospital at Bernay, 40 kilometers away, he arranged for Rommel and Daniel to be transferred

---

is considered reliable. On 16 or 17 July 1944, Rommel intended to pay a visit to General Eberbach (PW). He started off in a Kuble car (his own was under repairs), attended by a Major and driven by O/Fw Daniel. The escort consisted of three other cars carrying his ordnance officers. PW was the driver of the second car. The escort cars, however, could not keep up with Rommel's car, which was going too fast: Rommel always insisted on being driven at great speed (80-100 km per hour). PW states that Rommel's car was attacked by aircraft. The driver's left arm was torn off and he immediately lost consciousness. The car, out of control, dashed straight into a tree. The Major who was sitting in the rear of the car was hit on the revolver pocket and wounded. Rommel received splinters in the back from the Major's revolver, and was thrown clear of the car through the windscreen; he suffered concussion and leg wounds. Both Rommel and the driver were immediately taken to the Luftwaffe hospital in Lisieux. PW heard that Rommel's first thought in hospital, after gaining consciousness, was for his driver, who had, however, died soon after arriving at the hospital."

[3]Rommel struck his head on the pillar of the windscreen and was not injured by the cannon shells or fragments from Major Neuhaus' pistol.

[4]See After the Battle Number 8: It happened Here - Rommel's Accident, [n. d.], pg. 44.

This wing camera film is purported to be of the strafing of Rommel's staff car some 20 miles behind the front lines. Air Force records show that only one staff car was strafed on the day in question on the Normandy front. Photo (3) shows flame and smoke enveloping the car after the gas tank was punctured. Photo (4) shows the vehicle swerving into the ditch.

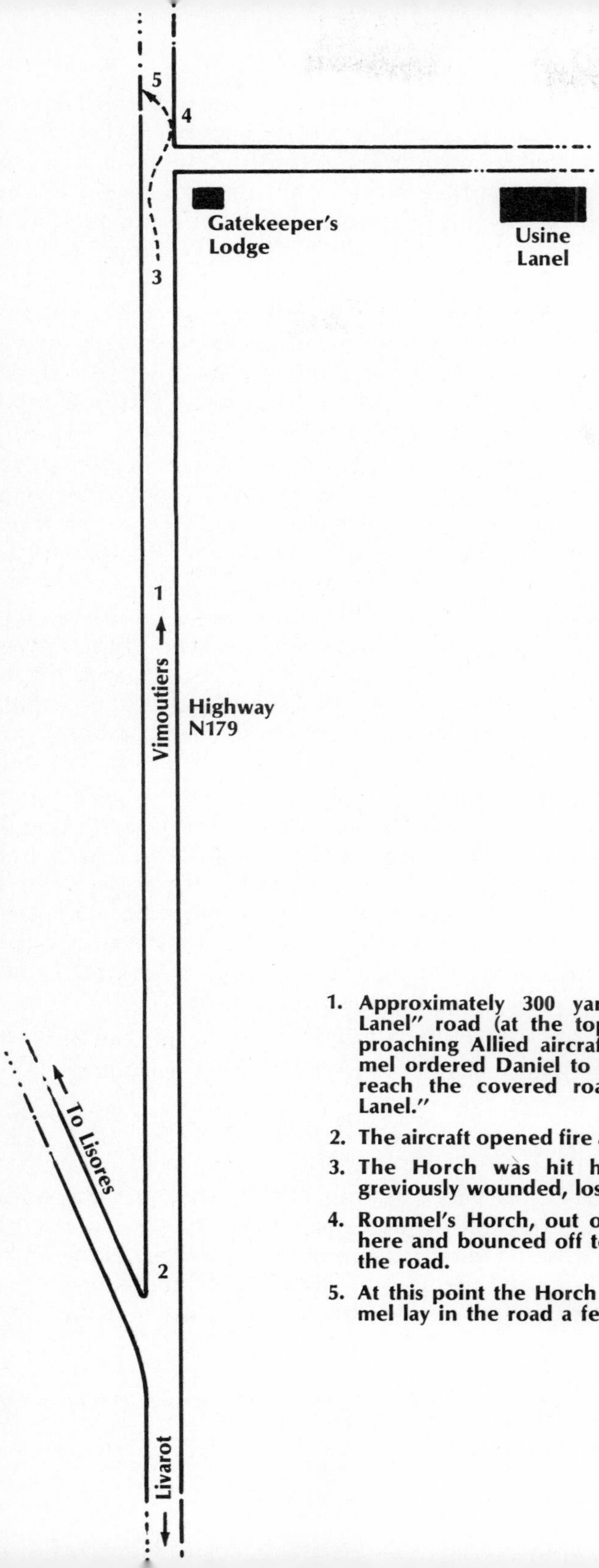

5

4

Gatekeeper's
Lodge

Usine
Lanel

3

1

↑
Vimoutiers

Highway
N179

↑
To Lisores

2

Livarot
↓

1. Approximately 300 yards from the "Usine Lanel" road (at the top of a small hill), approaching Allied aircraft were spotted. Rommel ordered Daniel to drive faster and try to reach the covered road leading to "Usine Lanel."

2. The aircraft opened fire at a range of 500 yards.

3. The Horch was hit here and Daniel was greviously wounded, losing control of the car.

4. Rommel's Horch, out of control, hit a stump here and bounced off towards the left side of the road.

5. At this point the Horch finally stopped. Rommel lay in the road a few yards behind.

there as soon as possible. Still unconscious, Rommel was transferred to the hospital at Bernay and quartered in Room Number 9. The doctors diagnosed "a severe skull fracture (fracture of the skull base, two fractures at the temple and a smashed cheek bone), an injury to the left eye and splinter injuries of the head as well as a concussion. In spite of blood transfusions, Daniel died during the night as a result of his severe injuries."

Plans were made to move Rommel to Le Vesinet (east of St. Germain), where he could be placed under the care of Dr. Esch; because of his severe skull fracture, a later transfer to Tübingen for treatment by Dr. Albrecht and Dr. Stock was also considered necessary. This final move was only to be made after three weeks of rest.

As soon as Speidel learned of the accident, he informed his staff and ordered Major Behr and Dr. Schuenig, the staff physician, to leave immediately for Bernay. When Behr entered Rommel's room, he found the Field Marshal conscious. As weak as he was, Rommel told Behr that he wanted to return to work at Heeresgruppe B.

Ruge and Speidel took advantage of the hazy weather and low cloud cover on the 22nd to visit Rommel in Bernay. They found him still very weak. Rommel ignored his doctor's orders and sat up to greet his guests. He was visibly shaken by the news that Count Stauffenberg, one-time Ia of 10 Panzer Division in Africa, had carried a bomb into Hitler's briefing bunker at Rastenburg.[5] The violent explosion had failed to kill the Dictator; his revenge was swift and brutal.

Sunday, 23 July, was generally quiet. At 0500 hours Rommel's doctors moved him to Le Vesinet. That afternoon Ruge and Baron von Esebeck called on Rommel. They learned from Dr. Esch that the drive had tired Rommel, but his complete examination that morning had been favorable. After Ruge and Rommel had talked, the Admiral read to him. By Ruge's next visit Rommel had regained enough strength to shave himself.

A "get well" telegram from Hitler arrived on the morning of the 24th:

Accept, Herr Field Marshal, my best wishes for your continued speedy recovery.

Yours,
Adolf Hitler[6]

Ruge and Speidel returned to visit the Field Marshal that afternoon; this time Rommel was in better spirits and, in defiance of his doctor's orders, was moving about. He talked about his World War I adventures and then "reflected on the Russian campaign." Later that afternoon he dictated his first letter to Lucie since the accident (but was unable to sign it himself):

---

[5]Stauffenberg was seriously injured during the last days of the fighting in Africa and was evacuated, thus escaping capture.
[6]Hart, Rommel Papers, pg. 493.

24 July 1944

I'm now in hospital and being very well looked after. Of course I must keep quiet until I can be moved, which will be a fortnight yet. My left eye is still closed and swollen, but the doctors say it will get better. My head is still giving me a lot of trouble at night, though I feel very much better in the daytime. The attempt on the Führer, coming on top of my accident, has left me very badly shattered. We must thank God that it passed off as well as it did. I sent my views on the situation shortly before it happened.

I'm terribly grieved about Daniel, he was an excellent driver and a loyal soldier.

All my love and best wishes to you and Manfred.[7]

Captain Hellmuth Franz, one of Rommel's aides, began to write to Lucie on Rommel's behalf:

26 July 1944

Dear Madam,

It seems that the Field Marshal's health is improving every day. His headaches, however, were rather severe last night, which can be attributed to the hot, humid air. So far the press has published nothing about the injuries to the Field Marshal. Perhaps this is a good thing. The flood of visitors would never cease. On the other hand all of Paris is informed, and already the most beautiful rumors are floating around. I myself am happy that I am permitted to be close to your husband; even before the accident I had taken great pride in being the escort of the Field Marshal. It is a pity, however, that Mr. ...,[8] who reads to him daily, will be leaving us. Also General Dihm will soon no longer be a member of the staff, while Captain Aldinger has returned from his trip and has visited with the Field Marshal already.

You will probably have read with pleasure that the last major offensive of the British has failed, hopefully the front will withstand further pressure.

Yours very respectfully,
Hellmuth Franz[9]

---

[7]*Ibid.* Rommel was unaware that the conspirators were actually going to follow through with their plan to kill Hitler.

[8]*The name of this gentleman is not included in the quoted version of the letter and may have been omitted from the original to save him from any reprisals later on. Ruge was not present to read to Rommel every day.*

[9]*United States National Archives, Record Group 242: EAP-21-X-14/9B, pg. 188.*

27 July 1944

Dear Madam,

The doctors have decided that the Field Marshal should not be moved to Herrlingen after all, until eight-ten more days. The head fracture must first heal sufficiently that, according to human judgment, nothing can go wrong during the move. For this purpose our best car will be rebuilt in such a manner that a quiet ride will be guaranteed. It will, of course, be difficult to find a replacement who will be up to Daniel's standards. The staff is presently making a selection. There is much regret amongst the staff that, even though temporarily, the Field Marshal is not in their midst. In spite of the respect for the new commander-in-chief, everyone has been affected by the change of command. The whole staff would have already come to the hospital to show their reverence and love, but the doctors were not willing to agree to so many visitors. By the way, Guenther is also here, doing his handy work in his usual manner.

I am sending my regards to you, dear Madam,

Yours very respectfully,

Hellmuth Franz[10]

Ruge visited Rommel that afternoon and found him visibly better. His reflexes had improved, and he displayed his determination to ignore his doctor's orders by killing a troublesome fly with his slipper. Their conversation skirted topics from Africa to Goebbels to Hitler. Rommel's interest in the war had revived considerably, as is evident from Franz's letter to Frau Rommel the following day:

28 July 1944

Dear Madam,

It is getting to be a pleasant habit for me to give you a daily report on the well being of the Field Marshal. I spend little time with the Field Marshal himself, though I enjoy doing so, for he has orders to rest. The demands of the doctors, however, cannot always be met. These people are often too meticulous and do not understand the restlessness of the mind that can result from being secluded. The Field Marshal wishes to be informed about daily events. As far as the attacks of the Americans at St. Lô are concerned, which were mentioned in the *"Wehrmachtsbericht"* [Military Report], General Speidel seems to be confident; also in the East a position seems to be built up; General

[10]*Ibid.*, pg. 189.

Mein Führer,   1 Oct 1944

Unfortunately my health is not yet as I could have wished. The quadruple fracture of the skull, the unfavorable development of the situation in the west since I was wounded, and not the least the removal from his post and arrest of my former Chief-of-Staff Lieutenant General Speidel - of which I learnt only by chance - have made demands on my nerves far beyond endurance. I no longer feel myself equal to further trials.

Lieutenant General Speidel was assigned to me as Chief-of-Staff in the middle of April 1944, in succession to Lieutenant General Gause. He was very well reported on by Colonel General Zeitzler and by his former Army Commander, General Wöhler. Shortly before taking up office with the Army Group he had been awarded the Knight's Cross by you, and had been promoted to Lieutenant General. In his first weeks in the west, Speidel showed himself to be an outstandingly efficient and diligent Chief-of-Staff.[3] He took firm control of the staff, showed great understanding for the troops and helped me loyally to complete the defenses of the Atlantic Wall as quickly as possible with the available means. When I went up to the front, which was almost every day, I could rely on Speidel to transmit my orders - as discussed beforehand - to the Armies, and to carry on all talks with superior and equivalent formations along the lines I required.

When the battle in Normandy began, Speidel did not spare himself to bring success in the struggle with the enemy, who set us a heavy task, above all with his air superiority, his heavy naval guns and his other material superiority. Up to the day when I was wounded, Speidel stood loyally at my side. Field Marshal von Kluge also seems to have been satisfied with him. I cannot imagine what can have lead to Lieutenant General Speidel's removal and arrest. Oberstgruppenführer Sepp Dietrich and Speidel were good friends and met frequently.

Unfortunately it proved impossible to fight the Normandy battle in such a manner that the enemy could be destroyed while still in the water, or at the latest at the moment of landing. The reasons for this I gave in

---

[3]Ulrich von Hassel wrote in his diaries (Von Hassel Diaries), pg. 318, that "in Speidel Rommel had an excellent, clear-headed Chief of Staff."

the attached report, which General Schmundt no doubt placed before you while he was still with you.[4] When Field Marshal von Kluge assumed command in the west, an acrimonious scene took place at Army Group B in the presence of my Chief-of-Staff and Ia. I did not take silently the charges leveled against me, but spoke my mind in private to Field Marshal von Kluge, and asked him, moreover, on the following day, to let me know what grounds he had for making them. The charges were withdrawn verbally in the course of a conversation in which I pressed Field Marshal von Kluge, with all urgency, always to report the situation at the front to you quite openly and not to conceal unpleasant facts; for only by such service could you, mein Führer, be enabled to see clearly and arrive at the right decisions. My last situation report went to C-in-C West the day before I was wounded and was - as von Kluge later told me - sent on to you with a supplementary note by him.

You, mein Führer, know how I have exerted my whole strength and capacity, be it in the Western campaign 1940 or in Africa 1941-43 or in Italy 1943 or again in the west 1944.

One thought only possesses me constantly, to fight and win for your new Germany.

Heil, mein Führer,

E. Rommel[5]

On 7 October Rommel received a phone call from General Wilhelm Burgdorf of the Army Personnel Branch. This call, placed on Hitler's direct orders, summoned Rommel to Berlin on the 9th for an important interview with the Führer. Rommel's doctors strongly advised him not to make the trip due to his still fragile health. Rommel, heeding his doctors' advice, and, perhaps, his own intuition, decided not to travel to Berlin. Instead he ordered Aldinger to telephone Keitel for him. But when the call was placed, Burgdorf was reached. Rommel agreed to speak to him and informed the general "that the doctors would not allow him to travel in his present state of health."[6] There was no immediate reaction to Rommel's statement and "l'affair Rommel" was temporarily dropped.

On 11 October, after finishing his business in Stuttgart, Ruge drove to Rommel's home in Herrlingen. The Admiral was a welcome guest at the Rommel home and Frau Rommel prepared a "festive meal" for him.

---

[4]General Schmundt died as a result of wounds received in the 20 July explosion at Hitler's headquarters.

[5]Hart, Rommel Papers, pp. 500-501.

[6]Young, Desert Fox, pg. 207.

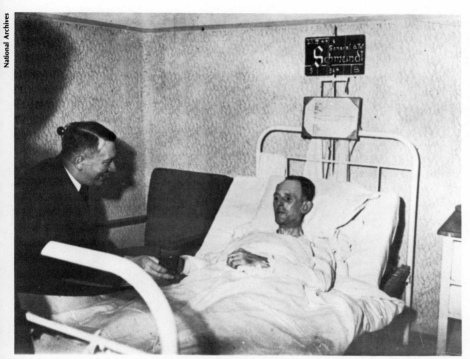

On 1 October 1944, the day that Rommel's letter at left was written, General Schmundt died at a Ratzeburg hospital. Above he is shown receiving the special 20 July Wound Badge personally from Hitler.

Later, Rommel and Ruge withdrew into the study and talked until after midnight.[7] Rommel had only minor complaints about his health (headaches and lack of energy) and was in a good humor. He jokingly mentioned that on the 15th he would no longer be entitled to a car, and, as an inactive field marshal, guards would no longer be stationed around his home. When the conversation turned to Speidel's arrest, Rommel mentioned the summons he had received from the OKW and that he had declined to go because of his health. "I shall not go to Berlin," Rommel insisted. "I would never get there alive."[8]

After a brief walk and breakfast, Rommel and Ruge drove to Augsburg. The outing was a pleasure for both men.[9] It would be their last meeting.

"L'affair Rommel" surfaced again on 12 October. Hitler ordered Generals Burgdorf and Maisel to visit Rommel in Herrlingen. They were instructed to bring along an incriminating protocol[10] and a letter which Hitler had personally dictated to Keitel. "In this letter it was submitted

[7]*Ibid.*
[8]*Ibid.*
[9]*Ruge, Rommel in Normandy, pg. 246.*
[10]*Rommel was heavily incriminated in the protocol by the testimony of one of the main conspirators of 20 July 1944, a Lieutenant Colonel on von Stülpnagel's staff. He was also on a list prepared by Burgermeister Goerdeler as "Ministerpraesident."*

335

to Rommel that he should report to the Führer if he believed himself innocent; if he could not, then his arrest was inevitable, and he would be obliged to answer for his actions before a court *(Volksgericht).* He might like to consider what the consequences would be;[11] on the other hand there was another way out for him to take."[12] "Keitel also gave to Burgdorf a box of poison ampules and charged him to give Rommel verbal assurance that, should he elect to use them, the Führer would promise him a state funeral with full military honors, and that no reprisals would be taken on his family."[13] Burgdorf and Maisel, accompanied by Major Ehrnsperger, left Berlin that afternoon, with plans to arrive in Herrlingen on the 14th.

**General Wilhelm
Burgdorf**

A call was placed to the Rommel home from the headquarters of War District 5 at Stuttgart on the 13th. A soldier-servant, Loistl (a badly wounded war veteran), was the only one present to receive the call. Loistl was instructed to inform Rommel of the arrival of two officers from Berlin on the next day around noon. Rommel and Lucie, meanwhile, were visiting two of their old friends, Lieutenant Colonel of Reserves Oskar Farny and his wife. While at his friend's home, Rommel intimated that he was in grave danger, and suspected that Hitler wanted him out of the way. Rommel went on to confide that he was to be

---

[11]*Regarding the conspirators, and anyone closely connected with them, Hitler had reiterated a "steady scream of demands for the extermination, root and branch, of all those even remotely inculpated in the Putsch. They and their families were to be liquidated; they were to perish as though they had never been born, and their children after them." See Wheeler-Bennett, Nemesis, pg. 676.*

[12]*Wilhelm Keitel, The Memoirs of Field Marshal Keitel (New York: Stein and Day, 1966), pg. 194. Hereafter cited as Memoirs. Keitel, with full knowledge of the true story of Rommel's death from the very start, casually furthered the false version in a letter to his wife dated 24 October when he wrote "Rommel has died after all from the multiple skull injuries he received on a car journey, through a blood-clot; it is a heavy blow to us, loss of a commander well favored by the gods."*

[13]*Wheeler-Bennett, Nemesis, pg. 686.*

eliminated because of his "ultimatum to [Hitler] on 15 July, his open and honest opinions, the events of 20 July and the reports of the Party and the Security Service."[14] As he and Lucie departed the Farny home, Rommel told Frau Farny that "if anything should happen to me, do not believe that I raised my hand against myself."[15]

Rommel returned home and received the message about the arrival of the two officers. He told Aldinger "that the two generals were doubtless coming to talk to him about the invasion or a new job."[16]

Manfred Rommel arrived on the train at 0600 on 14 October. He and his father had breakfast and then "went walking together until 11 o'clock." Rommel told his son that "he was expecting two generals of the Army today, that is General Maisel and General Burgdorf, both of the Personnel Division of the Army. He remarked that he did not entirely trust this matter, and that he did not know whether the reason given, to discuss further use of his services, was not only to be a cover-up maneuver in order to do away with him."[17] One possibility was that Rommel would be offered a command in the east; when Manfred asked if he would accept such a command Rommel replied that he would.

At precisely noon on 14 October, the visitors from Berlin arrived at Rommel's home in a dark green staff car with Berlin license plates. While Aldinger remained outside talking with Major Ehrnsperger, the others followed Rommel inside and into the downstairs study. When the men were alone, Rommel was told the true reason for the visit. Rommel was handed the protocol, and, after reading it, inquired if Hitler were aware of it. He then asked for time to think. General "Burgdorf had personal orders from Hitler to prevent Rommel from committing suicide by shooting himself; he was to offer him poison in order that the cause of death be attributed to the brain damage he had suffered in the motor accident, that would be an honorable demise and would preserve his national reputation."[18] A gunshot wound was to be prevented at all costs.

A few minutes later Rommel emerged from the study and went upstairs to tell Lucie what would happen shortly. Soon thereafter Manfred followed and found his father "standing in the middle of the room, his face pale." Rommel took his son into another room and said I "shall be dead in a quarter of an hour."[19] Rommel told Manfred that he had been

[14]Speidel, _We Defended Normandy_, pg. 157. There were a number of instances of strange characters being spotted in and around the grounds of the Rommel home. Rommel, who hardly ever wore a pistol, reportedly began to carry one during his walks with his son in the woods nearby.

[15]_Ibid._, pg. 158.

[16]Young, _Desert Fox_, pg. 208.

[17]Manfred Rommel's April Statement.

[18]Keitel, _Memoirs_, pg. 194. Far more important than helping Rommel "preserve his national reputation," Rommel's suicide would prove more embarrassing than any prior to, or after, the 20 July bomb plot.

[19]Hart, _Rommel Papers_, pg. 503.

offered a choice between taking poison or going before a *Volksgericht*, and had elected to take the poison and thus escape death "by the hand of one's own people." He told Manfred that he needed to have his and Lucie's promise of "strictest silence," or Hitler would no longer feel bound to keep his promise. When Aldinger suggested defending themselves or attempting to escape, Rommel replied that it was hopeless - the roads were blocked and the house surrounded by armed SS men. As Manfred Rommel later stated, they had "noticed that the house was surrounded by at least four or five automobiles. The cars apparently had armed civilians in them [an indication that the Gestapo was present], so the eight-man guard stationed in [the] house, being in possession of two machine guns only, would have been powerless."[20] Rommel then said, "There's no point. It's better for one to die than for all of us to be killed in a shooting affray."[21] He went on to explain that after he had left, a call would be placed from the Wagnerschule Reserve Hospital in Ulm; the caller would simply state that Rommel had suffered a brain seizure on the way to a conference and was dead.

After glancing at his watch, Rommel told Manfred and Aldinger that he must go, for the two generals had only given him ten minutes. The three of them walked downstairs together and went outside, heading slowly down the graveled driveway. When they approached the waiting car, Hitler's generals gave the Nazi salute with a "Heil Hitler." The driver, SS-Hauptscharführer Heinrich Doose, opened the door for Rommel, who tucked his baton under his right arm and climbed into the back seat. The car left quickly and headed down the road in the direction of Blaubeuren. Manfred and Aldinger walked back to the house when the car was out of sight, and began the long wait for the telephone call.

Doose drove around a bend in the road after leaving the Rommel villa, which was soon out of sight. After continuing a few hundred yards, Doose pulled the car to the side at a predesignated spot. The SS had stationed more men in the woods nearby to stop any last minute attempt at escape. When the car stopped Maisel and the driver got out and walked down the road, leaving Rommel and Burgdorf alone in the car. "When the driver was permitted to return ten minutes or so later, he saw [Rommel] sunk forward with his cap off and the marshal's baton fallen from his hand."[22] Rommel was dead: the poison had only taken seconds to kill him.

Doose climbed back into the car and drove to the Army Reserve Hospital, where Rommel's body was removed. "General Burgdorf forbade Dr. Meyer, the chief doctor of the hospital, to make an autopsy, explaining that all arrangements had already been made, from Berlin."[23] Dr. Meyer later told the Rommel family that, on orders from

[20] *Manfred Rommel's April Statement.*
[21] Hart, *Rommel Papers*, pg. 503.
[22] *Ibid.*, pg. 505.
[23] Speidel, *We Defended Normandy*, pg. 158.

the two generals, he had "given [Rommel] an injection to stimulate the heart. There was no reaction."[24] The two generals then drove to the Ulm army headquarters to make their report to Hitler.

Twenty minutes after Rommel had said his final farewell, his family received the telephone call, exactly as they had been told. "It was Major Ehrnsperger speaking from Ulm. 'Aldinger, a terrible thing has happened. The Field Marshal has had a hemorrhage, a brain storm, in the car. He is dead.' "[25] Aldinger hung up the phone and told Lucie and Manfred what they already knew.

That evening the Rommel family drove to the hospital. They noticed the uneasiness of the hospital staff, who now suspected something irregular. In a small room, lying on a camp bed, they found Rommel's body, still dressed in the uniform he had chosen to wear on that last day - the brown uniform of the Afrikakorps. There was an expression of "immense disdain" on his face, which his sister later described as contempt.

According to Dr. Reynitz, a former member of the Stenographer Service in the Führerhauptquartier, "the Führer was only informed that Field Marshal Rommel had passed away. No details concerning his death were reported." Hitler, well aware of the truth of the matter,

---

[24]Young, _Desert Fox_, pg. 211. _This took place at 1325 hours. It could have been an attempt to provide further evidence that Rommel had indeed died from natural causes._

On 27 March 1945, the O.S.S. received Report No. 122313: "Consolidated Interrogation report - Medical Intelligence" in which section III-E mentioned Rommel's death. This report was based upon the interrogation of Dr. Alois Esch, of Military Hospital 2/680, and contained information on Rommel's death as Prof. Esch knew it. "Esch treated Rommel from 5 days after his wound until approx. 10 Aug 44. Rommel received a skull fracture after the driver of his staff car was killed by a bullet from a strafing plane, and the car had turned over. The skull fracture was not particularly dangerous. After having been for approximately 4 weeks in the hospital at Le Vesinet, Rommel was so far recovered that he could walk, and only needed occasional check-up. On about 10 Aug 44, Esch brought him to his estate at Herrlingen near Ulm, leaving him in the care of Prof. Dr. Albrecht, chief surgeon of the reserve hospital at Tübingen. After Rommel's death in Oct. 44, Esch wrote a letter to Professor Albrecht, asking him the details of the cause. He received an answer, in which he was told that Rommel's skull fracture had nothing to do with the cause of his death. Though the Marshal had preferred to stay at his estate, he had been able personally to drive 60 kms every week to the hospital at Tübingen and in the view of his doctor he had been ready to take up his duties again. The cause of his death was Coronary Sclerosis, which may have been caused originally by the severe attack of infectious jaundice which the Marshal had had in Africa early in 1943. The death occurred at Rommel's estate, and Professor Albrecht had not been able to reach Herrlingen in time." This opinion was in direct contrast to the cause of death which was announced in the newspapers and in the eulogy. Although Albrecht may have suspected some other cause, it is surprising that he offered an opinion without having performed an autopsy or even examining the body.

[25]_Ibid. It is not known whether Major Ehrnsperger was speaking for the benefit of persons at his end of the line, or if he was merely following orders and giving Aldinger the "prepared" version of Rommel's death, unaware that Aldinger had been told by Rommel of what would happen. Manfred Rommel's Statement of 24 May 1945 mentions the cause of death as a "cerebral apoplexy."_

feigned surprise and exclaimed, "again one of the old ones!" He ordered that the news of Rommel's death be withheld from the press for a few days. The Führer had already remarked several times that he did not believe that Rommel had belonged directly to the conspiracy. Rommel, however, had let seditious thoughts and plans grow amongst his staff and had taken no steps to intervene. When the Führer briefed Lieutenant General Krebs, the new chief-of-staff Heeresgruppe B, he ordered him to thoroughly purge this staff which was 'totally contaminated,' and gave him the necessary authority to do so."[26]

The Rommel home in Herrlingen

Rommel's body was returned to his home on 15 October, to the same room in which his fateful interview with Hitler's generals had taken place. His marshal's baton was not among the personal effects. When Aldinger realized this he demanded that Burgdorf return it. The coffin

[26]*Rommel Collection,* T-84, 277, #000115.

was placed before a large tapestry from Africa. The Afrikakorps' symbol was woven into the pattern in several places. After the family had been alone in the room for a while, an honor guard of two officers was placed at the foot of the coffin with orders to stand guard throughout the night.

Clint Hackney

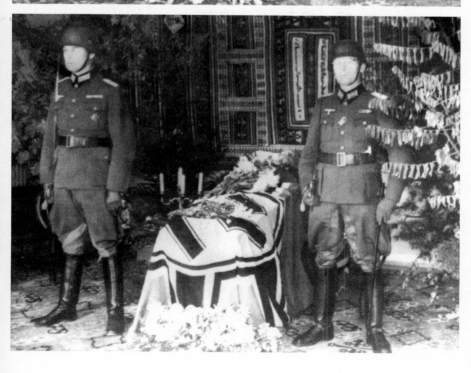

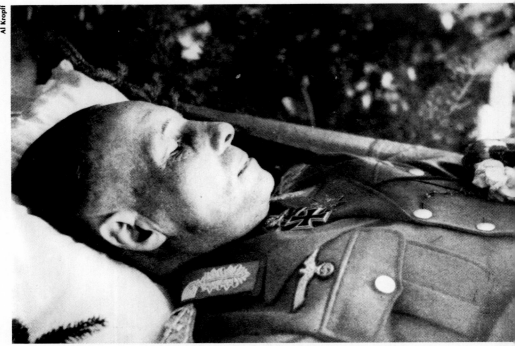

Rommel lying in state in the family home at Herrlingen.

At 2000 hours, and then again at 2200 hours, a simple message to the German people was broadcasted over the radio:

> Field Marshal Rommel has died as a result of his severe head injury which he, as Chief Commander of a Heeresgruppe in the West, received in a motor vehicle accident. The Führer has ordered a state funeral.

The next day, the 16th, Frau Rommel received a short note with Hitler's condolences:

> In the Field   45/44a   16.10.44   15.34 Hrs.
>
> Telegram from the Führer to Frau Lucie Rommel
>   Herrlingen at Ulm Donau
>
> Accept my sincerest sympathy for the heavy loss you have suffered with the death of your husband. The name of Field Marshal Rommel will be forever linked with the heroic battles in North Africa.
>
> Adolf Hitler[27]

On the morning of October 18, a state funeral was held for the Field Marshal. After passing an honor guard, Rommel's coffin was placed on a gun carriage drawn by a half-tracked personnel carrier. A large war flag was draped over it. From the Rommel home the procession inched

---

342   [27]See also Hart, _Rommel Papers_, pg. 505.

its way solemnly through the streets of Herrlingen and up to the town hall of Ulm, where the official program began.

A special train had been ordered to take many of the military representatives to Ulm for the funeral. Ruge was selected to represent the navy; after his arrival at the train station in Ulm, he met Gause, von Tempelhoff andAldinger on the street.

Al Kropff

Rommel's flag-draped coffin is carried from the family home to a waiting half-tracked personnel carrier.

"Minute by Minute Program"[28]
For the State Funeral Ceremonies for Field Marshal Rommel

12.53 hours	Departure of the Field Marshal [von Rundstedt] from the hotel (Lotse Rittmeister Freiherr von Gultingen)
12.58 hours	Arrival of the Field Marshal in front of the Town Hall. There reporting of the funeral parade with passing in review. Commander: Lieutenant Colonel Stickel. The Funeral Parade consists of: a) two army companies b) one mixed company navy, *Luftwaffe* and Waffen SS. Also assembled in front of the Town Hall are: a) a delegation of the Party with formations b) followers of the *Hitlerjugend*.
13.00 hours	The Field Marshal enters the Town Hall, salutes the deceased, and to the right, the family.

(right) The funeral procession arrives at the town hall in Ulm. (below) Former members of the Afrikakorps form the Honor Guard.

Following that he takes a seat in the front row at the right. Next to him sits the widow of the deceased.

Beginning of the State Funeral

13.00 hours	Funeral March from the 'Eroica' by Ludwin von Beethoven.
Afterwards	Commemorative speech of the Field Marshal.[29]
Afterwards	The Field Marshal puts down the wreath of the Führer. While the wreath is being laid down:

        a) song 'Ich hatt einen Kameraden' one stanza (57 seconds)

        b) 19 gun funeral salute by the salute battery

Afterwards	the Field Marshal returns to his seat.
Subsequent	National Anthem.
Afterwards	The Field Marshal turns to the bereaved sitting to the right of him and expresses the condolence of the Führer as well as his condolence.

The surviving family sits in the following order:

    Mrs. Lucie-Maria Rommel as widow

    Manfred Rommel, 16 years old, son

    Helene Rommel, sister

    Dr. Karl Rommel, brother

    Gerhard Rommel, brother

Afterwards	the Field Marshal salutes the deceased and leaves the hall of the State Funeral ceremonies.

A car is waiting in front of the exit.[30]

Following the funeral program at the town hall, the coffin was carried to the gun carriage and the procession started towards the crematorium at the outskirts of the city. Large crowds from Ulm and Herrlingen lined the streets; the *Hitlerjugend* was also out in numbers.

When the procession reached the crematorium, Ruge was able to talk privately with Aldinger. The Admiral had suspected that all was not well; with tears in his eyes, Aldinger said, "On Saturday they came." Ruge guessed the rest.[31]

When the mourners reached the gravesite, there were several speeches. Afterwards the salute battery fired three salvos and the band played "Ich hatte einen Kameraden" as the wreaths were placed on Rommel's coffin.

Rommel's ashes were brought home the next day, 19 October. The newspaper *Rheinische Landeszeitung* ran an article on the 20th reporting on the funeral:

---

[28]This program had been prepared a few days earlier by Lieutenant Colonel Fressen.

[29]A teletyped "eulogy" was sent out by the OKW signals section to the Supreme Commander West sometime later.

[30]*Rommel Collection*, T-84, 277, #000094.

[31]Ruge, *Rommel in Normandy*, pg. 248.

(above) The Führer's funeral wreath and (below) Rommel's coffin are removed from the Ulm town hall after the official program.

(above) Rommel's casket is flanked by four army generals as it is carried to the crematorium. (below) The Honor Company at the crematorium.

(above) The urn, containing Rommel's ashes, is carried to the grave site. (below) The army bids farewell to its Field Marshal.

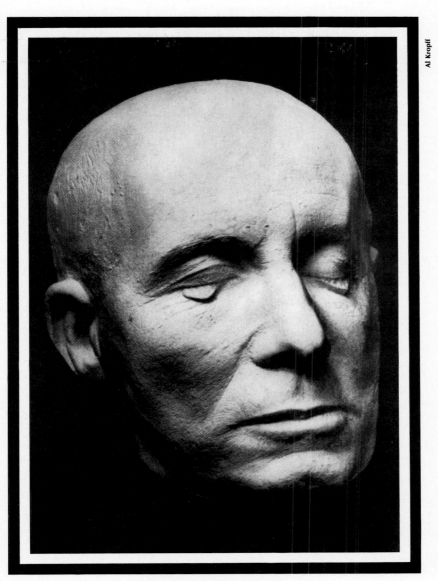

The Rommel death mask.

Order of the day by the Führer
On the death of Field Marshal Rommel

From the Führer Headquarters, 19 October. On the death of Field Marshal Rommel, the Führer has issued the following order of the day:

On October 14, 1944 Field Marshal Rommel passed away as a result of his severe injuries which he received in a car accident while on a patrol to the front in the west as the Supreme Commander of an army group. With him one of the best leaders of the Army has gone. In the present fight of destiny of the German people his name has become the symbol for extraordinary bravery. The heroic two-year battle of the Afrikakorps under his agile and inspirational command against manifold superior forces had found recognition in awarding to him, as the first soldier of the Army, the *Eichenlaub mit Schwertern und Brillanten zum Ritterkreuz des Eisernen Kreuzes* (The Knight's Cross of the Iron Cross with Swords, Oakleaves and Diamonds).

As Supreme Commander of a Heeresgruppe, until his severe injuries, he again gained decisive results in our defensive battle in the west.

Before this great soldier the Army is lowering the Reich's War Flag in proud mourning. His name has been entered into the history of the German People.

signed Adolf Hitler[32]

During the final days of the war, Frau Rommel received a letter which provided further evidence of the chaos which convulsed Hitler's crumbling empire:

The Architect in Chief
for German Warriors
Cemetaries

Berlin-Grunewald
Lassenstrasse 32/31
13b Castel Leutstetten
Near Starnberg/Upper Bavaria
Tel: Starnberg 2388

Frau Rommel
Herrlingen at Ulm

Dear Frau Rommel,

The Führer has instructed me to erect the memorial to your late husband, Field Marshal Erwin Rommel. I have requested several architects to work with me in accordance with his wishes in producing several

[32]*Rommel Collection, T-84, 277, #000113.*

designs for this memorial. The enclosed illustrations show these designs.

As it is not possible at the present moment either to build it to full size or to transport a fullsize memorial when built, it will be produced first on the scale of a model. But it is appropriate to place a simpler token on the grave now in the shape of a large tablet in stone with the name and emblems inscribed. This slab will be three feet broad and six feet long. The highest decoraction awarded to the Field Marshal will be engraved over the inscription.

I thought it right to commemorate the heroism and stature of the Field Marshal in the form of a lion. Professor Thorak has modeled a dying lion, Professor Breker a roaring lion and sculptor Lohner a lion rampant. I have chosen the third design for the medallion on the slab, as it will show by far the best. But if you wish it, the dying lion can also figure on the stone, as modeled by Professor Thorak and displayed on one of these reproductions.

The gravestone can be immediately put in hand, as I have obtained special permission from Reichsminister Speer, although at the moment monuments in stone are not permitted for anyone, including soldiers and even Knights of the Iron Cross. I have a special permit giving me freedom to work on and erect these stones in exceptional cases, and will, if you allow me, make my first gravestone that of the hero Rommel, which will be ready shortly to be placed on the grave.

Heil Hitler!

(signed) Dr. Kreis,
Architect General[33]

Frau Rommel had her own plans for honoring Rommel's gravesite and did not honor this letter with a reply.

Some time after the occupation of Herrlingen by the Americans, but before the war ended, Captain Marschall and Tec. 3 Greiner from 6 Headquarters Corps visited Frau Rommel at her home and interviewed her about "the life and death of her husband, about Germany and about the war." Frau Rommel refused to talk about the leaders of the NSDAP or the military, informing the two Americans that she had a "16 year old son in the Labor Service." The military police and SS squads were executing civilians and soldiers alike for offenses far less than unkind words about the leaders of the Party and military. Frau Rommel, moreover, was well aware that Hitler had promised them safety only so

---

[33]Speidel, _We Defended Normandy_, pg. 158.

long as she remained silent about her husband's death. Frau Rommel did say that Rommel "was only briefly associated with Göring and Himmler."[34] The rumors of Rommel's murder, however, were beginning to surface; the two Americans, "in order to clarify the question of how her husband really died," questioned Frau Rommel on the subject. "He was a man who drove himself, his friends and his staff mercilessly," she began. "During the entire war he never listened to a concert, never took time out for any kind of relaxation. He did nothing but work and worry about the troubles of war."[35] Finally, Frau Rommel talked about the death of her husband, but, still mindful of the squads conducting the "Flying Court Martials," told the Americans that "on October 14, apparently on the way to final recovery, his heart weakened and the Field Marshal died in bed at home."[36] It would be some time before the true story was revealed to the world.

Rommel's final resting place.

[34]Lucie Rommel, Statement to Capt. Charles Marschall and Tec. 3 Thomas Greiner (unpublished document, personal copy).
[35]Ibid.
[36]Ibid.

APPENDICES

Appendix I

General von Rintelen's report on the meeting between General Guzzoni and General Rommel on 11 February 1941:

"This morning (11th February) General Rommel was received by General Guzzoni. General Gandin and I were also present. General Guzzoni spoke as follows:

'By order of the Duce I welcome the commander of the German troops provided for Libya. The Duce's instructions regarding the conduct of operations in Tripolitania comply with the Führer's opinion that the defense must be advanced far enough to the East to leave sufficient room for the operations of a strong Air Force, and also to keep the British in the desert. The first line of defense lies at Sirte; the main defense will be carried out at Misurata. An infantry division will be dispatched to the east tomorrow. Graziani, who is now relinquishing command to Gariboldi, was of the opinion that there are more favorable tactical positions between Misurata and Homs. His objection to advancing defense further to the east was, however, not recognized. On 12th February I will send General Roatta to Tripoli to supervise the carrying out of the Duce's instructions. The next few weeks will bring about a serious crisis until we succeed in building up an effective defense and in forming a mobile motorized group. During this period the Air Force will bear the brunt of defensive operations. Today I instructed the Chief of the Air Force General Staff, General Pricolo, to carry out the following three tasks with the Italian Air Force in cooperation with Fliegerkorps X: air attacks against Malta and Benghazi, and against concentrations and advances of armored forces on the coastal road.

'General Rommel is requested to acquaint himself with the situation and as a proven leader of Panzer units to make his advice available to the Commander-in-Chief, General Gariboldi. As soon as active units of the German defense force arrive, a mobile group will be formed under the command of General Rommel. Italian mobile formations (hitherto only the Ariete Armored Division, to which the I Medium Tank Battalion is now being sent) - will be subordinated to this group.

'The Duce wishes to speak to General Rommel personally after he has acquainted himself with the situation.

'If it becomes clear in the course of the next few days that Tripolitania cannot be held, I will be the first to admit that it is not worth sending German units to Libya only to be captured by the enemy. The prestige of the German Army forbids this and it is also not in keeping with the Italian conduct of the war. On this point my opinion coincides with that of the Duce. However, I am absolutely confident that the crisis will be successfully overcome.' "[1]

---

[1]*AHBT*: VII/80-81.

Appendix II

Kriegsrangliste Deutsches Afrikakorps[1]

Befehlshaber:	Generalleutnant Rommel
Chef des Generalstabes:	Oberstleutnant von dem Borne

Führungsabteilung (Ia)

Ia:	Major i.G. Wu Stefeldt
01:	Hptm. Heuduck
05:	Obltn. von Hosslein
06:	Obltn. d.R. Dr. Wagner
Ia/Mess:	Hptm. (Ing.) Hintze
Ia/Verk:	Major Tootz
Ia/Pi:	Hptm. Goetzelmann
Ia/Gabo:	Hptm. d.L. Tschirner
ABT IC:	Hptm. i.G. Roestel
03:	Obltn. d.R. Behrendt
04:	Ltn. d.R. Siegfried
Ic/Prop:	Ltn. d.R. Berndt
Dolm:	Sdfr. Frh. von Neurath
	Obltn. d.R. Will
	Sdfr. Dr. Franz
	Dr. Hagemann
Nachr Führer:	Major Reimer
Stoluft:	Major Heymer

Ober-Quartiermeisterabteilung (O.Qu.)

Leitung:	Major i.G. Schleusener
Abt. Qu. 1:	Major i.G. Otto
02:	Obltn. d.R. Kloppmann
07:	Obltn. d.R. Lichtwald
08:	Ltn. d.R. Ziemke
Munition:	Hptm. (W) Strohbehn
Waff u Gerat:	Obltn. (W) Palme
Abt. HMot:	Major (E) Kohmen (Sachbearb f.d. Kraftfahrwesen)
Mitarbeiter:	Tech O.Insp. Neugebauer
Abt V:Korpsingenieur:	Major (Ing.) Hofweber
Mitarbeiter:	Tech Insp. Rubner
Abt IVA:	Korpsintendent Intend Rat Dr. Alves
Mitarbeiter:	St.Zm. Rohmer
	Ob. Zm. Froehlich
	Zm. Schneider
Abt IVB:	Korpsarzt Oberstarzt Dr. Stahm
Adjutant:	Stabsarzt Dr. Lehmann
Apotheker:	Stabsapotheker Dr. Daudert
Armeenachschule Führer:	Major Luebbsike
Adjutant:	Obltn. d.R. Stahl
Offz. z.b.V.:	Rittm. Mommers
	Hptm. d.R. Frhr. von Wechmar

Adjutantur (IIa)
Leiter: Major Schraepler
Abt. IIa: Adjutant Major Schraepler
Abt. IIb: Major Schultze Brocksien

Hauptbüro
Leiter: Sekr. Weihrauch
Ass: Kraemer

Gericht (Abt III)
Richter: Ob.Kr. Ger. Rat Stark
     Feld-Kr. Ger. Rat Dr. Schoenberg
Ukundsbeamter: Inst. Insp. Himmler

Hauptquartier (H.Qu.) Kommandant: Major Zimmermann
Führer der Feg. Staffel: Ltn. d.R. Saumer

---

¹T-313, Roll #458, frame #8754810

Appendix III

Order of Battle for Panzerarmee Afrika (15 August 1942)

Stab der Armee (Armeeoberkommando)
Brigade Stab z.b.V. (mot) 15
Kampfstaffel (mot)
Armee-Kartenstelle (mot) 575
Stab Koluft Libyen (Kommandeur der Luftwaffe)
Sonderverband (mot) 288
Aufklärungsstab 2 (Heer)/14.Panzer
Panzerjäger-Abteilung (mot) 605
Artilleriekommando 104 (Arko 104)
   Stab Artillerie-Regiment (mot) 221
   Stab Schwerste Artillerie-Abteilung (mot) 408
     2.u. 3. Batterie/408
     5./Artillerie-Regiment 115
   Artillerie-Abteilung (mot) 364
   Stab Schwerste Artillerie-Abteilung (mot) 528
     2. u 3. Batterie/528
   Artillerie-Batterie 528
   Artillerie-Batterie 533
   Artillerie-Batterie 902
   Stab I./Artillerie-Regiment (mot) 115
     4./Artillerie-Regiment (mot) 115
     6./Artillerie-Regiment (mot) 115
     4./Armee Küstenartillerie-Batterie 149
Artillerie-Vermessungs-Trupp (mot) 721-722-723-724-725-726-727-728-729-730
   Beobachtungs-Abteilung (mot) 11
   Stabs Batterie

Schallmess-Batterie
Lichtmess-Batterie
Flak-Abteilung (mot) 606
Flak-Abteilung (mot) 612
Flak-Abteilung (mot) 617
Flak-Regiment (mot) 135
Heeres-Bau-Dienst (mot) 73
Bau-Bataillon 85
1./Landesschützen-Bataillon 278
Nachrichten-Regiment (mot) 10
Kurierstaffel
V. Heeres-Funkstelle
VI. Heeres-Funkstelle
XIII Heeres-Funkstelle
"Tripolis" Heeres-Funkstelle
Funk-Truppe z.b.V. "Afrika"
Nachrichten-Zug 937
Nachschub-Regiment (mot) 585
Stab Nachschub-Bataillon (mot) 619
Entlade-Stab z.b.V. (mot) 681
Stab Nachschub-Bataillon z.b.V. (mot) 792
Stab Nachschub-Bataillon z.b.V. (mot) 798
Nachschub-Bataillon (mot) 148 - Italian
Nachschub-Bataillon (mot) 149 - Italian
Nachschub-Bataillon (mot) 529
Nachschub-Bataillon (mot) 532
Nachschub-Bataillon (mot) 533
Nachschub-Bataillon (mot) 902
Nachschub-Bataillon (mot) 909
Kraftfahrzeuginstandsetzungs-Abteilung (mot) 548
    Panzer-Berge-Zug (mot)
    Reifenstaffel (mot) 13
    Reifen und Ersatzteillager (mot) 548
    Reifeninstandsetzungsstaffel (mot) 573
    Kraftwagenwerkstatt-Zug (mot) 534
    "Volkswagen Kraftwagenwerkstatt-Zug (mot)
    "Bosch Kraftwagenwerkstatt-Zug (mot)
Munitionsverwaltung-Zug (mot) 542-543-544-545-546-547
Betriebsstoffuntersuchungs-Trupp (mot) 12
Heeres-Betriebsstoffverwaltungs-Zug (mot) 5
Betriebsstoffverwaltungs-Zug (mot) 979-980-981
Geräte-Verwaltungsdienste (mot)
Heeres-Kraftfahr-Park (mot) 560
Heeres-Kraftfahr-Park (mot) 566
Feldzeugdienst-Zug (mot) 1-2-3
1./Bäckerei-Kompanie (mot) 554
Schlächterei-Kompanie (mot) 445
Verpflegungsamt (mot) 317

Verpflegungsamt (mot) 445
Verpflegungsamt "Afrika" (mot)
Stab Kdt. V.A. 556
2./Sanitäts-Kompanie (mot) 592
1./Krankentransport-Kompanie (mot) 705
"Tripolis"-Kriegslazarett (mot)
5./Kriegslazarett (mot) 542
Kriegslazarett (mot) 667
Leichtkrankenkriegslazarett (mot)
Sanitätspark (mot) 531
Geheime Feldpolizei (mot)
Haupt-Streifendienste (mot)
Feldgendarmerie-Trupp (mot)
Wach-Bataillon "Afrika"
Ortskommandant "Misurata" 615
Ortskommandant "Barce" 619
Ortskommandant "Tripolis" 958
Ortskommandant "Benghazi" 959
Ortskommandant "Derna"
Tripolis-Lager Kdr. (km 5)
Kriegsgefangen-Durchgangslager 782
13./Lehr-Regiment "Brandenburg" 800
Transport Standarte "Speer"
Feldpostamt z.b.V. (mot) 659
Feldpostamt z.b.V. (mot) 762
Feldpostamt z.b.V. (für die Luftwaffe) (mot)
Feldpostamt z.b.V. anstelle Armee-Briefstelle (mot)

Deutsches Afrikakorps
  15. Panzer-Division
  21. Panzer Division

90. Leichte "Afrika" Division

164. Leichte "Afrika" Division

Fallschirmjäger-Brigade "Ramcke"

X. Korps
  Infanterie-Division "Brescia"
  Infanterie-Division "Pavia"

XX. Korps
  Panzer-Division "Ariete"
  Panzer-Division "Littorio"
  Motorisierte Division "Trieste"
  Fallschirmjäger-Division "Folgore"

XXI. Korps
  Infanterie-Division "Trento"
  Infanterie-Division "Bologna"

Appendix IV

On 15 May 1944, the Adjutant of Rommel's headquarters prepared the following list which named all the members of Heeresgruppe B: "Offizierstellenbesetzung des Oberkommandos der Heeresgr. B

Dienststellung	Dienstgrad	Name	LebAlter	Ziv.Ber.b. Offz.d.Res.
Oberbefehls-haber	Gen.Feld-Marschall	Rommel	52	
Chef GenSt.	Gen.Lt.	Speidel	46	
Ord.Offz.O.B.	Hptm.d.R.	Lang,Hellmuth	36	Kaufm.
Ord.Offz.Chef	Lt.d.R.	Scheer, Max	34	BankKaufm.

Führungsabteilung

Dienststellung	Dienstgrad	Name	LebAlter	Ziv.Ber.b. Offz.d.Res.
I a/H	Obstlt.i.G.	von Tempelhoff	37	
I d	Major (Kdt. zum GenSt.)	Behr	26	
0 1	Oblt.	Maisch	25	
0 4	Oblt.d.R.	Dummler,Hans	42	Vorst.Mitgl.der Allianz A.G.
I a/Mess	Major	Wagner (Karl)	31	
I c	Obstlt.i.G.	Staubwasser	35	
0 3	Hptm.d.R.	Aldinger, Hermann	48	Gartengestalter
0 5	Oblt.d.R.	Utermann,Kurt	40	Rechtsanw.u.Nota
Dolmetscher	Oblt.d.R.	Etter,Gustav	38	Betr.Leiter (Ing.)
Dolmetscher	Lt.d.R.	Mackenroth, Gerhard	40	Univ.Prof.
Dolmetscher	durchSdf.	besetzt		

(Z) Stoart

Dienststellung	Dienstgrad	Name	LebAlter	Ziv.Ber.b. Offz.d.Res.
Stoart	Oberst	Lattmann	49	
Adjutant	Hptm.d.R.	Kracht, Hugo	46	Kaufm.Angest.

Gen.d.Pi.

Dienststellung	Dienstgrad	Name	LebAlter	Ziv.Ber.b. Offz.d.Res.
Gen.d.Pi.	Gen.Lt.	Meise	52	
Pi.Offz.	Major	Johanns	39	
Adj.,zugl. Ord.Offz.	Oblt.d.R.	Borzikowsky, Reinhold	30	Reg.Rat

H.Gr.Nachr.-Führer

Dienststellung	Dienstgrad	Name	LebAlter	Ziv.Ber.b. Offz.d.Res.
Nachr.Führer	Gen.Lt.	Gerke	53	
Adjutant	Hptm.d.R.	Kaboth,Walter	43	
Bearb.f. Fspr.Wes.	Major	Baumann	34	
Bearb.f. Funkwesen	Major	Osterroth	33	
Bearb.f. Schl.Dienst	Hptm.	Hartl (noch nicht eingetroffen)		

Adjutantur

Dienststellung	Dienstgrad	Name	LebAlter	Ziv.Ber.b. Offz.d.Res.
II a	Oberst	Freyberg	44	

Hilfsoffz. bei IIa	Lt.d.R.	Weinert, Cristoph	25	Student
Kommandant H.Qu.	Major d.R.	Jamin,Alfred	45	Staatsbankdir.
Truppenarzt	Oberstabs- arzt d.R.	Dr.Scheunig, Friedrich	48	Arzt
Verpfl.Offz.	Rittm.d.R.	Schumacher,Egon	28	Dipl.Landw.
Fhr.Kft.- Staffel	Oblt.d.R.	Schon,Heinz	38	Dipl.Volksw.

Oberquartiermeister - Abteilung

O.Qu.	Oberst i.G.	Heckel	41	
2 GenSt.Offz. (Qu.1)	Major i.G.	von Ekesparre	31	
Ord.Offz.f.	Hptm.d.R.	Fleiner, Wilhelm	31	Kaufm.
Ord.Offz.	Lt.d.R.	Furtner,Johann	35	Zahlmeister
Sachbearb.NT	Hptm.d.R.	Wels,Georg	47	Kaufm.
Fachbearb.f. Betr.Stoff	Major	Heynold, (Johannes)	47	
Fachb.f.Mun	Major (W)	Rohner	40	
Fachb.f.Inf., Art.,allg.H. u.Gasgerät(W)	nicht besetzt			
San.Offz.	Oberstabs- arzt	Dr.Merkle	33	
San.Offz. (Mitarb.)	Stabsarzt	Breitfeld	29	
Vet.Offz.	Oberstabs- veterinar	Dr.Hofmann (Kurt)	31	
Fachb.f.Kfz. Insts.u.Ers. Teile,Kdr. Kf.Parktr.	Obstlt.	Gehrels	49	
Mitarbeiter	Hptm.	Simon(Karl)	33	
Kdt.St.Qu.	Major d.R.	Gschwendtner, Carl Max	49	Kunstmaler
Dolmetscher	Oblt.dRzV.	Priebisch, Leopold	49	Stud.Rat

Admiral bei H.Gru.B

Admiral	Vizeadmiral	Ruge	49	
Asto	Kpt.z.S.	Peters (Werner)	51	
Adjutant	Kpt.Lt.(V)	Frauendorff	30	

I a / Luftwaffe

I a/L	Obstlt.i.G.	Queisner (Wolfgang)	38	
I c/L	Oblt.(K.O.)	Stehnken,Hans	36	Sparkassendir.

Kp.Führer	Oblt.	Faiss (Anton)	26	
Gren.Zgf.	Lt.d.R.	John,Josef	29	Installateur
Pz.Spähzgf.	Lt.d.R.	Wehlau,Edgar	27	Kaufm.
General zur bes.Verfg. des O.B.	Gen.Lt.	Dihm	64	
Verb.Offz.) in West zur) H.Gru.B/Gen) d.Pi.)	Obstlt.	Loos	45	
Hilfsoffz.)	Lt.Dr.	von Stryk, Harry	38	Landw.

Oberst u.1.Adjutant''

Appendix V

Rommel's Ultimatum to Hitler, 15 July 1944

Oberbefehlshaber Heeresgruppe B   H.Q. 15 July

The situation on the Normandy front is growing worse every day and is now approaching a grave crisis.

Due to the severity of the fighting, the enemy's enormous use of material - above all, artillery and tanks - and the effect of his unrestricted command of the air over the battle area, our casualties are so high that the fighting power of our divisions is rapidly diminishing. Replacements from home are few in number and, with the difficult transport situation, take weeks to get to the front. Up against 97,000 casualties (including 2,360 officers) - i.e. an average of 2,500 to 3,000 a day - replacements to date number 10,000 of whom about 6,000 have actually arrived at the front.

Material losses are also huge and have so far been replaced on a very small scale; in tanks, for example, only 17 replacements have arrived to date as compared with 225 losses.

The newly arrived infantry divisions are raw and, with their small establishment of artillery, antitank guns, and close-combat antitank weapons, are in no state to make a lengthy stand against major enemy attacks coming after hours of drum-fire and heavy bombing. The fighting has shown that with this use of material by the enemy, even the bravest army will be smashed piece by piece, losing men, arms and territory in the process.

Due to the destruction of the railway system and the threat of the enemy air force to roads and tracks up to 90 miles behind the front, supply conditions are so bad that only the barest essentials can be brought to the front. It is consequently now necessary to exercise the greatest economy in all fields, and especially in artillery and mortar ammunition. These conditions are unlikely to improve, as enemy action is steadily reducing the transport capacity available. Moreover, this activity in the air is likely to become even more effective as the numerous air-strips in the bridgehead are taken into use.

No new forces of any consequence can be brought up to the Normandy front except by weakening Fifteenth Army's front on the Channel,[1] or on the Mediterranean front in southern France. Yet Seventh Army's front, taken over all, urgently requires two fresh divisions, as the troops in Normandy are exhausted.

On the enemy's side, fresh forces and great quantities of war material are flowing into his front every day. His supplies are undisturbed by our air force. Enemy pressure is growing steadily stronger.

In these circumstances we must expect that in the forseeable future the enemy will succeed in breaking through our thin front, above all, Seventh Army's, and thrusting deep into France. Apart from the Panzer Group's sector reserves, which are at present tied down by the fighting on their own front and - due to the enemy's command of the air - can only move by night, we dispose of no mobile reserve for defense against such a break-through. Action by our air force will, as in the past, have little effect.

The troops are everywhere fighting heroically, but the unequal struggle is approaching its end. It is urgently necessary for the proper [POLITICAL][2] conclusion to be drawn from this situation. As C-in-C of the Heeresgruppe I feel myself in duty bound to speak plainly on this point.

(Signed) Rommel[3]

---

[1]This hints that the Germans were still expecting an invasion of the Pas-de-Calais and did not want to pull troops away from the area.

[2]In the first draft of the "ultimatum," the word "political" was too obviously inflamatory; Rommel was pursuaded to omit it.

[3]Hart, Rommel Papers, pp. 486-487.

Appendix VI

Rommel's Record of Service and Promotions Following World War I:

18 Oct 1918	Hauptmann Pat. R 5 r
25 June 1919	Kp. Fhr.
8 Dec 1921	Hptm. b.St. I.Btl. J.R. 13
	RDA. 18.10.18 (34)
1 July 1924	Hptm. b.ST.u.Furs. Offz.
1 Oct 1924	Chef 4. (M.G.)/J.R. 13
1 Oct 1929	Inf. Schule
	MKF. 3b
1 Apr 1932 *	(22) Major
1 July 1933	Kdr. Dresden (Infanterie Schule)
1 Oct 1933	Kdr. III./J.R. 17
1 Oct 1934	Kdr. III./J.R. Gottingen

7 Jan 1935	Verf. Chef H.L.
25 Jan 1935	Kdr. III./K.R. Gottingen
1 Mar 1935 *	(5) Oberstleutnant
15 Oct 1935	Ltr. Lehrg. A. Kr.Sch. Potsdam
25 Feb 1937	zugl. Verb. Offz. z. RJF.
1 Aug 1937 *	(25) Oberst
10 Nov 1938	Kdr. Kr.Sch. Wr. Neustadt
	neues RDA. 1.10.35 (39a)
Mar 1939	Kdt. d. Fhr. H.Qu.
Aug 1939 *	(7) Generalleutnant[1]
23 Aug 1939	Kdt. F.H.Qu.
1 Sep 1939	Kdt. Führ.H.Qu.
15 Feb 1940	Kdr. 7. Pz.Div.
7 Feb 1941 *	Generalmajor[1]
	RDA 1.8.41 (6)
14 Feb 1941	Befh. d.deutschenTruppen in Libyen
9 Feb 1941	Befh. d. deutschen Afrikakorps
1 Jul 1941 *	(5) General der Panzertruppen
1 Sep 1941	Befh. d. Pz.Gruppe Afrika
30 Jan 1942	Befh. d.Panzerarmee Afrika[2]
1 Feb 1942 *	(1) Generaloberst
22 June 1942 *	Generalfeldmarschall
23 Feb 1943	OB. der Heeresgruppe Afrika[3]
15 July 1943	OB. H.Gru. B
17 July 1944	wounded in the strafing incident
4 Sep 1944	FR.OKH. (V)
14 Oct 1944	Death by suicide

---

*Indicates a promotion.
[1]On the original of Rommel's service, the rank of Generalmajor is listed before that of Generalleutnant.
[2]This command was not listed on Rommel's service record.
[3]This command was not listed on Rommel's service record.

BIBLIOGRAPHY

Unpublished Documents

Air Historical Branch Translations of Captured Documents. (New Zealand). Translation No. VII/2, 5, 6, 25, 63, 72, 80-81: High Level Reports and Directives dealing with the North African Campaign 1940-1943. 87 (KTB DAK), 88 (KTB DAK), 101 (KTB DAK), 104, 105 (KTB Pz. Armee Afrika), 106, 111-118 (KTB Pz. Armee Afrika), 128, 129.

Henne, Hans H., "Die tödliche Landschaft. Skizzen von einer Besichtigungsfahrt mit Generalfeldmarschall Rommel." O.U. Den 9.4.44 (personal copy).

Letters to W.M. James, Jr.   F. Ruge, April 1951. Dr. W. Meise, 21 March, 1964. General der Panzertruppen (Ret.) Geyr von Schweppenburg, 11 February 1965. (personal copies).

New Zealand Translations of Captured German Records Pertaining to German Army Units Participating in the North African Campaign from August 1941 to May 1943.
 Section 1: Panzergruppe Afrika
 Section 2: Deutsches Afrikakorps
 Section 3: 10 Panzer Division
 Section 4: 15 Panzer Division
 Section 5: 21 Panzer Division
 Section 6: 90 Leichte Division
 Section 7: 164 Leichte Division

Rommel, Lucie. Statement to Captain Charles Marschall and Tec. 3 Thomas Greiner. [n.d.]

Rommel, Manfred. Statement to Captain Charles Marschall and Tec. 3 Thomas Greiner. 27 April 1945.

_____. Statement, 24 May 1945.

United States National Archives. Miscellaneous German Records Collection: The Rommel Collection. Microcopy T-84. Rolls 273, 274, 276, 277, 296.

_____. Office of Strategic Services. Report Numbers:
2906143
OB-2953
OB-3101
OB-3260
OB-3830
OB-3938
OB-3971
OB-4414
29296
29411
45937
69349: "Secret Inspection Trip of Hitler and Rommel"
122313: "Consolidated Interrogation Report," Section III-E: "Rommel's Death"
128345: "Rommel's Accident"

_____. Record Group 242: EAP-21-X-14/9B.

_____. Records of the German Field Commands, Armies. Microcopy T-312. Roll 114: Armeeoberkommando 4. Rolls 1568 and 1569: Armeeoberkommando 7.

_____. Records of the German Field Commands, Panzer Armies. Microcopy T-313. Rolls 458, 466, 467, 470, 471: Panzer-Armeeoberkommando Afrika. Roll 416: Panzer-Armeeoberkommando 5.

_____. Records of the German Field Commands, Army Corps. Microcopy T-314. Roll 921: 39 Armee-Korps. Rolls 2, 15, 16, 18, 21, 23: Deutsches Afrika Korps.

_____. Records of the German Field Commands, Division. Microcopy T-315. Rolls 400, 401, 405, 409: 7 Panzer Division. Rolls 768 and 769: 21 Panzer Division. Roll 115: 3 Panzer Division.

_____. Report: Trip of the O. B. H. GR. B to 346 Inf. Div., 16.LW F. D. and 21. Pz. Div. 15 July 1944

a. U.S. National Archives:
1. Miscellaneous Records 12. SS Panzer Division. Microcopy T-354. Rolls: 154, 156.
b. Bundesarchiv Militärarchiv (BAMA) Freiburg:
1. III H 410/5 (alt): Gen StdH/Op Abt III. Schematische Kriegsgliederungen. 1944.

2. RH 10.: OKH/Generalinspekteur der Panzertruppen.
   a. 10/312. 1. SS Leibstandarte Panzer Division.
   b. 10/319. 10.SS Frundsberg Panzer Division.
   c. 10/321 12.SS Hitler Jugend Panzer Division.
3. RH 19IV. Records Oberbefehlshaber West (OB West).
   a. 19IV/43/44. Kriegstagebuch, 1a.
   b. 191V/62K/63K/64K. Lagekarten.
   c. 19IV/132/133/134. Records, Meyer-Detring, 1c.
4. RH 19IX. Records Herresgruppe B (Rommel)
   a.19IX/3. Verluste, Ist Stärkemeldungen, Zustandsberichte der Panzerdivisionen.
   b. 19IX/4. Operationalbefehle.
   c. 19IX/7. Führerbefehle.
   d. 19IX/8. Wochenmeldungen.
   e. 19IX/84/85/86. Kriegstagebuch, 1a.
5. AOK 7. Records 7 Army.
   a. AOK 7/57350/2. Anlage zum Kriegstagebuch.
6. Pz AOK 5. Records Panzergruppe West.
   a. Pz AOK 5/63181/1. Kriegstagebuch Panzergruppe West.
   b. Pz AOK 5/63181/4. Miscellaneous Records.
7. RS 3-9 Records 9. SS Hohenstauffen Panzer Division.
   a. RS 3-9/2. Lageberichte, Tagesmeldungen.
8. RS 3-12. Records 12. SS Hitler Jugend Panzer Division.
   a. RS 3-12/1. Tagebuch der Divisions-Begleit-Kompany 1943-1945.

Published Documents:

Greiner, Helmuth and Schramm, Percy, eds. Kriegstagebuch des Oberkommandos der Wehrmacht, 1940-1945. 4 Vols. Frankfurt am Main: Bernard and Graefe Verlag für Wehrwesen 1961-1965.

Handbook on German Military Forces, 1 September 1943. Washington, D.C.: Department of the Army, 1943.

Hitler's Lagebesprechungen. Die Protokollfragmente seiner militärischen Konferenzen 1942-1945. Herausgegeben von Helmut Heiber. Stuttgart: Deutsche Verlags-Anstalt, 1962.

Jacobsen, Hans-Adolf, ed. Dokumente zur Vorgeschichte des Westfeldzuges 1939-1940. Berlin: Musterschmidt-Verlag, 1956.

Lagevorträge des Oberbefehlshabers der Kriegsmarine vor Hitler 1939-1945. Herausgegeben von Gerhard Wagner. München: J.F. Lehmanns Verlag, 1972.

Lowenheim, Francis L.; Langley, Harold D.; and Jones, Manfred, eds. Roosevelt and Churchill: Their Secret Wartime Correspondence. New York: E.P. Dutton, 1975.

Müller-Hillebrand, Burkhart. Das Heer 1933-1945. Entwicklung des organisatorischen Aufbaues. Bd. III. Der Zweifrontenkrieg. Frankfurt am Main: E.S. Mittler und Sohn, 1969.

Trevor-Roper, H.R., ed. Hitler's War Directives. London: Sidqwick and Jackson, 1964.

Diaries, Memoirs, and Reminiscences

Churchill, Winston S., The Grand Alliance. Vol. III of The Second World War. Boston: Houghton Mifflin Co., 1950.

Ciano, Galeazzo. Ciano's Diary, 1933-1943. London: William Heinemann Ltd., 1947.

Goebbels, Joseph. The Goebbels Diaries 1942-1943. Edited by Louis P. Lochner. New York: Doubleday and Company, Inc., 1948.

Halder, Franz. Kriegstagebuch. Edited by HansAdolf Jacobsen. 3 Vols. Stuttgart: W. Kohlhammer Verlag, 1962.

Hart, B.H. Liddell, ed. The Rommel Papers. New York: Harcourt, Brace and Co., 1953.

Hassel, Ulrich von. The von Hassell Diaries, 1938-1944. London: Hamish Hamilton, 1948.

Keitel, Wilhelm. The Memoirs of Field Marshal Keitel. New York: Stein and Day, 1966.

Kesselring, Albert. Soldat Bis Zum Letzten Tag. Bonn: Athenaum-Verlag, 1953.

_____. A Soldier's Record. New York: William Morrow and Company, 1954.

Montgomery, Bernard. The Memoirs of Field Marshal/The Viscount of Alamein. New York: World Publishing Co., 1958.

Ruge, Friedrich. Rommel in Normandy: Reminiscences by Friedrich Ruge. San Rafael, Ca.: Presidio Press, 1979.

Schmidt, Heinz Werner. With Rommel in the Desert. London: George G. Harrap and Co. Ltd., 1951.

Speidel, Hans. Aus unserer Zeit: Erinnerungen. Berlin: Ullstein Verlag, 1977.

_____. Invasion 1944. Chicago: Henry Regnery Co., 1950.

_____. We Defended Normandy. London: Herbert Jenkins, 1951.

Foreign Military Studies

Blumentritt, Günther. "Three Marshals, National Character and the 20 July Complex." B-344.

Buerker, Ulrich, "Commitment of the 10th Panzer Division in Tunisia." D-174.

Christian, Eckhard. "The El Alamein Crisis and Its Aftereffects in the OKW." D-172.

Dihm, Friedrich. "Rommel's Views on Tactical, Technical and Strategic Problems of the Defense." B-259.

Feige, Richard. "The Relationship between Operations and Supply in Africa." D-125.

Feuchtinger, Edgar. "History of the 21st Panzer Division from the Time of Its Formation until the Beginning of the Invasion." B-441

Greiner, Helmuth. "Greiner Diary Notes, (Aug. 12, 1942-Mar. 12, 1943)." C-065A.

_____. "The Greiner Series Africa 1941." C-065F.

Hegenreiner, Heinz. "The Operations of Marshal Graziani Prior to the Arrival of German Troops." O-216.

Kraemer, Fritz. "I SS Panzer Corps in the West in 1944." C-024.

Krause, Fritz. "Studies of the Mareth Position." D-046.

Kriebel, Rainer. "North African Campaign." Vol. I. T-3.

Liebenstein, Kurt von. "The Drive via Gafsa Against Kasserine Pass." D-124.

Meyer, Hubert. "12. SS Panzer Division 'Hitlerjugend,' Juni bis September 1944." P-164.

Nehring, Walther. "The First Phase of the Battle of Tunisia." D-147.

Pemsel, Max. "Die 7. Armee in der Schlacht in der Normandie und in den Kämpfen bis Avranches (6.6-29.7.44)." B-763.

Ruge, Friedrich. "Rommel and the Atlantic Wall." A-982.

Schweppenburg, Freiherr Geyr von. "Die Invasion. Geschichte der Panzergruppe West." B-464.

_____. "Meldung Schweppenburg an Generalinspekteur der Panzertruppen über seine Erfahrungen in den ersten Invasionstagen." B-019.

Speidel, Hans. "Background for 20 July 1944." B-721.

_____. "Die Schlacht in der Normandie 1944. Führung, Gedanken Feldmarschall Rommels." C-017.

_____. "The Battle in Normandy 1944." C-017.

_____. "Ideas and Views of Generalfeldmarschall Rommel on Defense and Operations." B-270.

Staubwasser, Anton. Das Feindbild beim O.dHG B. 6.6-24.7.44. B-782.

_____. Das Feindbild beim O.dHG B. 25.7-16.9.44. B-825.

Toppe, Alfred, "German Experiences in World War II: Desert Warfare." P-129.

Vaerst, Gustav von. "Fifteenth Panzer Division." D-083.

_____. "Vormarsch und Angriff eines Panzer-Regiments in der Wüste, 26/27 Mai 1942." P-149.

Zimmermann, Bodo. "OB West: Atlantic Wall to Siegfried Line, A Study in Command." B-308.

Secondary Sources
Books:

Agar-Hamilton, J.A.I., and Turner, L.C.F. The Sidi Rezegh Battles 1941. Capetown: Oxford University Press, 1957.

Alman, Karl. Panzer Vor: Die dramatische Geschichte der Panzerwaffe und ihrer tapferen Soldaten. Rastatt: Erich Pabel Verlag, 1966.

Bender, Roger J., and Law, Richard D. Uniforms, Organization and History of the Afrikakorps (Mountain View, Ca.: R. James Bender Publishing, 1973.

Braddock, D.W. The Campaign in Egypt and Libya, 1940-1942 (Aldershot: Gale Ploden Ltd., 1964).

Brown, Anthony Cave. Bodyguard of Lies. New York: Harper and Row, 1975.

Burdick, Charles B. Germany's Strategy and Spain in World War Two. New York: Syracuse University Press, 1968.

_____. Unternehmen Sonnenblume: Der Entschluss zum Afrika-Feldzug. Wehrmacht im Kampf Series, Bd. XLVIII. Nekargemünd: Kurt Vowinckel Verlag, 1972.

Büschleb, Hermann. Feldherren und Panzer im Wüstenkrieg: Die Herbstschlacht "Crusader" im Vorfeld von Tobruk, 1941. Die Wehrmacht im Kampf Series, Bd. XL. Neckargemünd: Kurt Vowinckel Verlag, 1966.

Caccia-Dominioni, Paolo. Alamein 1933-1962: An Italian Story. London: Allen and Unwin, 1966.

Carell, Paul. Die Wüstenfuchse. Hamburg: Henri Nannen Verlag, 1958.

_____. Invasion - They're Coming. New York: E.P. Dutton & Co., Inc., 1963.

Carter, Joseph. 1918: Year of Crisis, Year of Change. Englewood Cliffs, New Jersey: Prentice-Hall, 1968.

Connel, John. Auchinleck: A Biography of Field Marshal Sir Claude Auchinleck. London: Cassel and Co. Ltd., 1959.

Deutschland im Ersten Weltkrieg. Berlin: Akademie-Verlag, 1970.

Ellis, L.F. The Battle for Normandy. Vol. I of Victory in the West. London: Her Majesty's Stationery Office, 1962.

Esebeck, Hanns-Gert von. Afrikanische Schicksalsjahre: Das Deutsche Afrika-Korps unter Feldmarschall Rommel. Rastatt in Baden: Erich Pabel Verlag, 1960.

Esposito, Vincent S. A Concise History of World War II. New York: Frederick A. Praeger, 1964.

Goerlitz, Walter. Paulus and Stalingrad. New York: The Citadel Press, 1963.

Guderian, Heinz. Panzer Leader. New York: E.P. Dutton & Co., Inc., 1960.

Harrison, Gordon A. Cross Channel Attack. Washington, D.C.: Office of the Chief of Military History, Dept. of Army, U.S. Government Printing Office, 1951.

Hayn, Friedrich. Die Invasion. Von Cotentin bis Falaise. Wehrmacht im Kampf Series. Bd. II. Heidelberg: Kurt Vowinckel Verlag, 1954.

Heckmann, Wolf. Rommel's Krieg in Afrika: Wüstenfuchs gegen Wüstenratten. Bergisch Gladbach: Gustav Lubbe Verlag, 1976.

Hoffman, Peter. The History of the German Resistance. 1933-1945. Cambridge, Mass.: The MIT Press, 1977.

_____. Hitler's Personal Security. London: Macmillan Press Ltd., 1979.

Howe, George F. Northwest Africa: Seizing the Initiative in the West. Washington, D.C.: Office of the Chief of Military History, Dept. of Army, U.S. Government Printing Office, 1957.

Irving, David. Hitler's War. New York: The Viking Press, 1977.

_____. The Trail of the Fox. New York: E.P. Dutton & Co., 1977.

Jacobsen, Hans Adolf. Dünkirchen: Ein Beitrag zur Geschichte des Westfeldzuges 1940. Die Wehrmacht im Kampf Series, Bd. XIX. Neckargemünd: Scharnhorst Buchkameradschaft, 1958.

Kurowski, Franz. Die Geschichte des Panzerregiments 5. Bochum: Heinrich Poppinghaus Verlag, 1975.

Lewin, Ronald. Rommel as a Military Commander. London: B.T. Batsford Ltd., 1968.

_____. Ultra Goes to War. New York: McGraw-Hill, 1978.

Lichem, Heinz von. Rommel 1917: Der "Wüstenfuchs" als Gebirgssoldat. München: Hornung Verlag, 1975.

Long, Gavin. To Benghazi. Canberra: Australian War Memorial, 1966.

Manteuffel, Hasso von. Die 7 Panzer-Division im Zweiten Weltkrieg: Einsatz und Kampf der "Gespenster Division" 1939-1945. Kameradenhilfe e.V. Kolin, 1965.

Maughan, Barton. Tobruk and El Alamein. Canberra: Australian War Memorial, 1966.

Mellenthin, F.W. von. Panzer Battles: A Study of the Employment of Armor in the Second World War. Ballantine Books. Oklahoma: University of Oklahoma Press, 1956.

Milward, Alan S. "Hitlers Konzept des Blitzkriegs." Probleme des Zweiten Weltkrieges. Edited by Andreas Hillgruber. Berlin: Kiepenheuer and Witsch Verlag, 1967.

Munzel, Oskar. Die deutschen gepanzerten Truppen bis 1945. Herford: Maximilian Verlag, 1965.

Murphy, W.E. The Relief of Tobruk. Wellington: Department of Internal Affairs, 1961.

Payne, Robert. The Life and Death of Adolf Hitler. New York: Praeger Publishers, 1973.

Playfair, C.B. The British Fortunes Reach Their Lowest Ebb. Vol. III of The Mediterranean and the Middle East. London: Her Majesty's Stationery Office, 1960.

_____. The Germans Come to the Aid of Their Ally. Vol. II of The Mediterranean and the Middle East. London: Her Majesty's Stationery Office, 1956.

Richardson, William, and Freidin, Seymour, eds. The Fatal Decisions. London: Michael Joseph Ltd., 1956.

Ritgen, Helmut. Die Geschichte der Panzer Lehr Division im Westen 1944-1945. Stuttgart: Motorbuch Verlag, 1979.

Ryan, Cornelius. The Longest Day. New York: Simon and Schuster Inc., 1959.

Schulman, Milton. Defeat in the West. New York: E.P. Dutton Co., Inc., 1948.

Scoullar, J.L. The Battle for Egypt: The Summer of 1942. Wellington: Department of Internal Affairs, 1962.

Shores, C., and Ring, Hans. Fighters over the Desert. London: Spearman, 1969.

Taysen, Adalbert von. Tobruk 1941: Der Kampf in Nordafrika. Einzelschriften zur militärischen Geschichte des Zweiten Weltkrieges. Freiburg: Rombach Verlag, 1976.

Toland, John. Adolf Hitler, New York: Doubleday, 1976.

Trevor-Roper, H.R., ed. Blitzkrieg to Defeat. Holt, Rinehart and Winston, 1965.

Walker, Ronald. Alam Halfa and El Alamein. Wellington: Department of Internal Affairs, 1962.

Warlimont, Walter. Inside Hitler's Headquarters, 1939-45. New York: Frederick A. Praeger, 1964.

Wheeler-Bennett, J.W. The Nemesis of Power. New York: Harper & Brothers, 1964.

Wilmont, Chester. The Struggle for Europe. New York: Harper and Row, 1952.

Young, Desmond. Rommel the Desert Fox. New York: Harper & Brothers, 1950.

Periodicals

After the Battle Number 8: It Happened Here - Rommel's Accident. [n. d.]

After the Battle Number 19: Hitler's Headquarters. [n. d.]

Gause, Alfred. "Command Techniques Employed by Field Marshal Rommel in Africa." Armor Magazine, (July-August, 1958)

Jaggi, O. "Normandie 1944." Auswirkungen der alliierten Luftüberlegenheit auf die deutsche Abwehr. In: Allgemeine Schweizerische Militärzeitschrift. Jg. 124. H. 5. 1958.

James, W.M. "Invasion 1944: The Controversy over the German Armor Deployment on D-Day." The Irish Defence Journal, (July, 1977)

Kershaw, Andrew, and Close, Ian, eds. "The Desert War." <u>Purnell's History of the World Wars</u>, (Special Issue, 1968)

Ruge, Friedrich. "Rommel und die Invasion." <u>Europäische Wehrkunde</u>, XXVIII Jahrgang. München. Oktober 1979. Heft 1c.

Wehrli, E. "Taktische Bombenteppiche." In: <u>Allgemeine Schweizerische Militärzeitschrift</u>. Jg. 13o. 1964. Nr. 7.

Unpublished Materials:

Burdick, Charles B. "The Ultra Question." Speech presented at San Jose State University, April 1979.

Ehle, Curt., Letter to Craig Luther, dated 21 February 1979.

Ruge, Friedrich. "Rommel as I Saw Him." Address given before the U.S. Officers Club in Stuttgart, 16 March 1980.

Stark, M.W. "The Creation of the Africa Corps." Unpublished Master's Thesis, San Jose State College, August, 1964.